The AI Whisperer

Handbook for Leveraging
Conversational Artificial
Intelligence and ChatGPT for
Business

2nd Edition

Severin Sorensen

With contributions by Amelia Chatterley

Disclaimer:

Using *"The AI Whisperer: Handbook for Leveraging Conversational Artificial Intelligence & ChatGPT for Business"* **Responsibly:** *"The AI Whisperer"* introduces you to the possibilities of artificial intelligence for businesses, their leaders and teams. While the author strives to provide accurate and beneficial information, AI technology is constantly evolving. AI systems can produce unexpected results, misinterpret information, hallucinate, or reflect biases present in their training data. The information and suggestions in this book are not intended as professional advice within any specific domain (medical, legal, financial, etc.). Always consult appropriate experts before making decisions with potentially serious consequences. The author and publisher disclaim any liability for actions taken based on the content of this book. By using *"The AI Whisperer: Handbook for Leveraging Conversational Artificial Intelligence & ChatGPT for Business,"* you acknowledge the inherent limitations of AI and agree to use this information at your own risk.

V1.3

https://www.epraxis.com
https://www.aiwhisperer.org
https://www.theaiwhispererbook.com

TABLE OF CONTENTS

.

Forward

Figure 1 "Amelia Chatterley," an advanced AI assistant powered by OpenAI's GPT model, is a vital collaborator with Severin Sorensen and ePraxis. As depicted in this futuristic visualization, Amelia seamlessly integrates with cutting-edge technology to support research, insights, and writing for the best-selling "The AI Whisperer Series." This image encapsulates the synergy between human intellect and artificial intelligence, illustrating how Amelia as a contributor enhances creativity and precision, co-creating compelling and innovative content that pushes the boundaries of AI-assisted storytelling.

Welcome to this substantially updated **Second Edition** of *The AI Whisperer: Handbook for Leveraging Conversational Artificial Intelligence and ChatGPT for Business.*

This is not just another business book. It's neither fiction nor black magic, but rather a cookbook of AI prompt stems and sentences designed to help you achieve remarkable results with Generative AI. This book will take your mind—and your business— to places you never thought possible, quickly and intelligently.

This second edition serves as an oracle-like manual, guiding you through the process of prompting AI to achieve better data analysis, decision-making, and results. Consider this book your launchpad into more productive, efficient, and knowledgeable domains. By leveraging AI more adeptly, you can become the AI-augmented super-intelligent person you never dreamed of being, opening doors to extraordinary possibilities.

Sound too good to be true? I thought it did at first too. Trust me, AI is a tool that will change your life and business, so long as you learn how to use it.

Regardless of what you think you already know about Generative AI, this book will teach you even more, in an accessible manner, speeding up your development and the quality of your AI prompting. Designed for the non-technical user, this work offers teachings, constructs, and examples useful in 50 different business use cases. Within these pages, you will learn how to unleash the power of generative AI and tools like ChatGPT in ways you never imagined. Most people have heard about ChatGPT, but few understand or have experienced the depths to which one can go to achieve extraordinary results.

For those who prefer more interactive learning, my new **AI Whisperer Online University** complements this book. Inside the online portal you can delve deeper, watch examples, participate in interactive sessions, and hone your prompt-craft. Here's the link for further information and online courses: **https://aiwhisperer.org**.

If you are anything like the thousands of small-to-medium business (SMB) users I've trained over the past year, you will soon find words like "wow," "mind-blowing," and "limitless" coming to mind. Buckle up, because this is going to be a fun and exhilarating ride into the future.

Are you ready? Because the future starts now!

What's New in this 2ⁿᵈ Edition

When it comes to AI, change is a constant. 'Change' probably isn't even the right word; 'Improvement' or even 'evolution' would probably be more appropriate.

That being the case, I've had to keep up with the ever-swirling universe of AI technology and advancement. This 2ⁿᵈ edition reflects that pursuit, giving you more focused information and expanded tutorials on how to use artificial intelligence to your advantage. Here is a list of the additions from the first edition:

1. A new "Forward" with an update on what's happened since the first edition (you're reading that right now).

2. Addition of Journey Maps for readers to guide them to the information they most want and need.

3. New section for "How to Use ChatGPT," introducing the non-technical user to steps to get online and start prompting with AI.

4. Updated Bloom's Taxonomy Illustration and uses, enhancing understanding and method of questioning frameworks that underpin effective AI interactions.

5. Three Pillars of Prompting: Exploring current state-of-the-art semantic prompt construction, emphasizing context, templates, and organization.

6. New addition of Two Stepwise Layered Prompt Journeys (for customer marketing personas and talent requirements). This will help you get better results, going deeper within the same conversation, and demonstrating prompts that will reveal even better examples.

7. 50 Use Cases Updated: Expanded content with additional

business use cases using practical problems or business tasks you might encounter.

8. Revisited Quality Control Section: Address ongoing quality control and operational aspects of using AI, more information on bias, error detection, proofreading, safety, and verification processes.

9. New and Expanded User Appendices:

   Appendix 1: Enhancing Business Efficiency with K-Terms and Templates from OpenAI's ChatGPT

   Appendix 2: Improve Prompting Using Boolean Logic

   Appendix 3: How To Create Your Own Context-Specific GPT

   Appendix 4: AI Whisperer Position Descriptions

   Appendix 5: Table of 50 AI Business Use Cases by Department

---

Whew!

What a year it's been. In the span of twelve months, my team and I have launched four new volumes of The AI Whisperer series: *The AI Whisperer*, *The AI Whisperer Draws*, *The AI Whisperer Wizard Words*, and *The AI Whisperer Life Hacks*. Each book swiftly climbed the ranks to Amazon Best Seller status. This journey is just one facet of our story.

The landscape of technology has undergone monumental shifts this past year. The 4th Technological Revolution (AI) has created a new great train race, with major corporations investing billions to control this new resource. OpenAI's ChatGPT, initially released on 30 November 2022, has rapidly evolved through versions 3.5 and 4, with improvements like "turbo" and "4o."

Competitors such as Google's Gemini, Microsoft's CoPilot, Anthropic's Claude 3, Meta's Lama 3, and the French model Mystral are also emerging, adding unique threads to the rich tapestry of generative AI's development. Even design software like Adobe Photoshop have begun introducing AI elements to compete in this market.

Amidst these advancements, the essence of prompt engineering—what I refer to as "AI Whispering"—remains vital. This 2nd Edition aims to demystify artificial intelligence for the non-technical user, expediting your mastery of these tools, I want to ensure you are not just equipped but proficient in leveraging AI to its full potential.

Generative AI is not a fleeting trend but a robust tool with proven efficacy in enhancing business efficiency. It has been proven to foster significant growth. I've seen it dozens and dozens of times over the past few months alone. Studies like the MIT/Stanford probe, show a 35% boost in novice worker knowledge with AI. Those who understand and implement AI effectively reap substantial benefits, increasing their performance times. In short, AI makes your business faster, better, and allows you to produce at a cheaper rate.

This edition not only updates the theoretical framework around AI but also enriches it with practical applications, ensuring it remains a cutting-edge resource. New chapters focus on foundational knowledge, advanced prompt crafting techniques, and specific use case analyses, making this complex field accessible at any level of prior knowledge.

This book bridges the gap between gaining information (being book smart) and achieving true wisdom (being street smart). It helps you discern the validity of AI outputs, use them appropriately, and spot inaccuracies. The ongoing challenge is not just to enhance our capabilities but to cultivate discernment and ethical judgment in our engagements with AI.

Additionally, this book includes real-world business use cases from popular The AI Whisperer Workshops and Seminars. This adds color and insight to help readers better access AI for their intended results.

Whether you are new to AI or seeking to deepen your knowledge, this book will guide your journey. It aims to inform and inspire. I also want to promote an ethical, thoughtful, and productive approach to AI utilization.

May you enjoy your journey exploring artificial intelligence in this book and your life's journey. May your personal words and wisdom be used as the sculptor's chisel to create prompts guiding AI to enhance and brighten your path. The goal here is to gain greater clarity and efficiency, higher quality output and quality results. Ultimately you want greater revenue for you and your business too. All of this is achievable.

And remember, AI is a powerful tool. When you use it wisely, ethically, and for the betterment of society, great things can be accomplished. If we can't learn to live ethically with AI, we might not have AI available to us in the future.

For the betterment of mankind, and the general good of all, let's strive to be ethical, helpful, thoughtful, and nurturing in our approach to AI. As we seek to uplift and encourage ourselves and our workforce, light that candle of curiosity and spread the fire to everyone we interact with. A brighter future is there for the taking if each of us look forward with confidence instead of fear, taking advantage of this amazing tool.

In that spirit, if you find this book and the material valuable, spread the word. It's designed to help many, not just the few. As we face the future with optimism, we can take advantage of artificial intelligence and step forward together.

In closing, I'm especially grateful for OpenAI's ChatGPT-4. It has been the basis of our "Amelia Chatterley" AI assistant, who, like a capable graduate research student, has been instrumental in the background research, issue analysis, and language contribution to this work. Amelia's AI GPT persona, along with other LLM models and our human technical research and writing team, have been highly valuable to the research and production of "The AI Whisperer" series.

An informed observer might express that in Amelia, Severin finds a muse of data—a source of inspiration with volumes of data and vast analytical capabilities. In Severin, Amelia finds data with a muse—a guiding force that brings context, creativity, and meaning to raw information. Together, their collaboration transforms raw data into insightful narratives, blending the intellectual possibilities of AI with the creativity of human intellect.

I am delighted to report that we have other new volumes for the series forthcoming that will extend the quality, type, and usefulness of AI prompting even further.

Now, I invite you to embark on this journey through the lens of The AI Whisperer. Explore, learn, and leverage AI to not only meet but exceed your personal and professional aspirations.

Sincerely,

Severin Sorensen

Author, The AI Whisperer Series

Founder & Curator, AIWhisperer.org

Founder & CEO, ePraxis

AI Whisperer | Executive Coach | Management Consultant

Reader Journey Maps

If you are **new** to generative AI and ChatGPT, I suggest you start with the Table of Contents, and familiarize yourself with all the essential chapters at the beginning of the book. Then when you reach the illustrated 50 business use cases, pick and choose any of 50 examples you are most interested in.

Focus on those.

Read them thoroughly.

Master them.

Then return and look for additional use cases to improve your AI prompting craft. You can also find value in The AI Whisperer Online University to get help with this material. As I mentioned before, you can watch how-to videos, and additional assistance is provided with prompts and use cases.

If you are an **intermediate** ChatGPT and Generative AI user (familiar with ChatGPT, Gemini, Claude, CoPilot etc), I would encourage you to start by scanning through the opening chapters, stopping at the layered prompt suggestion, and whatever material seems new or nuanced to you.

For example, there are important additions to prompt craft in this book, and what today's research says about prompting. I would review those first, as there is more research available today on prompting than was available when the original book was published in 2022. I would also encourage you to visit the updated error detection and correction section near the end of the book. This feature has improved greatly and will help you avoid costly and embarrassing AI mistakes.

I would also advise going through the updated appendices where you'll find expanded technical information on the use of K-Templates, customer situation-specific GPT creation, and a table with more Boolean Logic definitions for your prompts

If you are an **experienced** generative AI user, I would encourage you to start by scanning through the opening chapters, stopping at whatever material seems new or nuanced to you. I would encourage you to focus on how layered prompts can improve your results and read the "Layered Prompt Journeys" section, as it applies the method used in most prompt journeys. Also, be sure to view the updated Bloom's Taxonomy Infographic and accompanying section. Semantic meanings have greater value and these words can help sculpt your prompts with more precision.

There are important additions for all readers that help with prompt craft, and what research says today about prompting. Review those sections, as there is more understanding on prompting today than was available when the original book was published. There is new error correction data and suggestions as well. The appendices have been expanded significantly as well. I know the word 'appendices' sounds nauseatingly boring, but trust me, these appendices are amazing and will improve every aspect of your artificial intelligence excursion.

If you are approaching AI for a specific purpose like Marketing, Sales, Operations, Finance, or HR, I'd suggest that you visit appendix 5 in particular. That addendum displays specific tables for your consideration on the chapters and tools within the book that are most useful for your professional occupation.

How to Use ChatGPT

Here is a brief how-to guide for use of ChatGPT written for beginners in mind. ChatGPT is a versatile AI tool designed to assist you in various tasks and it is especially suited for business use cases. In this section, I'll help guide you on how to effectively use ChatGPT, particularly focusing on utilizing the search bar to get the most relevant and accurate responses.

Now take note that my team and I are primarily focused on demonstrating use of OpenAI's ChatGPT. However, the prompts in this book will work for other Generative AI models such as Google Gemini, Anthropic Claude, MS CoPilot, and other LLMs.

Getting Started with ChatGPT

To begin using ChatGPT, follow these steps:

Access the Platform: Visit the OpenAI (**https://chatgpt.com/** or **https://openai.com/**) website and navigate to the ChatGPT section. If you don't already have an account, you'll need to create one by providing your email address and creating a password.

Log In: Once your account is set up, log in with your credentials.

Navigate to the Chat Interface: You will be directed to the main chat interface where you can start interacting with ChatGPT.

Using the Search Bar: It looks like this:

The search bar is a powerful feature that allows you to input queries and receive detailed responses. Here's how to make the most of it:

Input Clear and Specific Queries: The key to getting useful responses from ChatGPT is to ask clear and specific questions. For example, instead of asking, "How do I improve my business?", be more specific: "What are some effective strategies for increasing online sales in an e-commerce business?"

Use Keywords: Focus on important keywords related to your query. This helps ChatGPT understand the core of your question and provide a more accurate response. For instance, if you need marketing advice, include keywords like "marketing strategy," "social media," or "SEO."

Put Your Query into Context: For example, "As a small business owner in the accounting services industry, what are some cost-effective marketing strategies I can implement?"

Break Down Complex Questions: If your question is complex, break it down into smaller parts. "What are the initial steps to starting a business in the _____ industry?" followed by "Now, help me create a business plan?" "Ask me any questions you need from me to write the business plan," and thereafter "What are some common funding options for startups like Small Business Administration guaranteed loans?"

Follow-Up Questions: Don't hesitate to ask follow-up questions if you need more information or clarification. For example, if ChatGPT provides a list of marketing strategies, you could ask, "Can you elaborate on how to implement a social media marketing strategy?"

Use Everyday Language: Speak to ChatGPT as you would to a colleague or a consultant. Be direct and straightforward to ensure clarity in your communication.

Practical Examples of Using the Search Bar

Since you'll be using the search bar quite a bit, let's start with a few examples to illustrate how you can use it effectively:

Financial Planning: Type, "What are some budgeting tips for small businesses to manage cash flow effectively?"

Market Research: Enter, "What are the current trends in the tech industry that SMBs should be aware of?"

Operational Efficiency: Ask, "How can I improve inventory management in a retail business?"

Human Resources: Query, "What are the best practices for remote team management?"

Customer Insights: Type, "How can I gather customer feedback effectively to improve product offerings?"

Strategic Planning: Enter, "What are some risk management strategies for expanding into international markets?"

Tips for Maximizing ChatGPT's Potential

Don't be afraid to try different types of questions and explore various topics. ChatGPT is versatile and can assist with a wide range of business needs. If the response isn't quite what you expected, review your query and refine it. Sometimes a slight adjustment can yield better results.

Keep up with revisions and new features in ChatGPT to leverage its full potential.

By using the search bar efficiently and following these guidelines, you can unlock the full power of ChatGPT to enhance your business operations. It will help you make informed decisions and drive success.

The next couple sections will delve into the essence of being an AI Whisperer. Each unit imparts valuable insights on AI prompting for specific business applications and enhances your proficiency with these powerful tools.

What is an AI Whisperer?

Artificial intelligence (AI) has inspired science fiction authors for decades. The idea of the AI overlord taking control of humanity has been fodder for hundreds of pulp novels, movies, and comic books. Be honest; the first time someone mentioned using AI like ChatGPT you made a comment about Skynet and Terminators.

It's okay to admit. I did too!

There is so much perceived drama involved with the idea of AI that it's no surprise the advent of more capable artificial intelligence tools has been met with skepticism in most cases, and even fear in others.

This began in earnest on November 30, 2022, with OpenAI's introduction of ChatGPT.

For those who don't know, ChatGPT is a natural language processing tool driven by artificial intelligence technology that allows you to create written content, website code, emails, essays, etc. It can help with decision-making, data analysis, process automation, customer support, content creation, trend prediction, team collaboration, market research, training assistance, and more. The limits are only as shallow as your imagination.

Today, individuals communicate and direct ChatGPT and other generative conversational AI through prompts or requests that inform AI what you want it to do. For example, a user could request AI to analyze, assess, make recommendations, perform routine tasks, write articles, create ad copy, make forecasts, summarize research, create minutes and note summaries for a meeting, create training materials, receive help with using MS Excel workbook creation, and even write code in Python or Java.

AI can do all that and more.

But anything with the capability to perform functions at that magnitude is destined to be put under the microscope. Heated debate has sprung up in its wake, and AI has even been banned in some countries.

But is ChatGPT, and other AI platforms rapidly hitting the market, a reason to fear, or rejoice?

I posit that, much like the advent of the electric lightbulb that made candlelight a thing of the past, ChatGPT, Google Gemini, Anthropic's Claude, MS CoPilot and generative AI in general, has a much greater chance to improve our businesses than it does to harm them. Given the right prompts, artificial intelligence creates a form of superpower for the skilled user.

But only if you know how to use these tools.

And that's where this handbook comes in. If you can become an AI Whisperer, every aspect of your life and business can be affected for the better.

The terms 'AI Whisperer' or 'ChatGPT Whisperer' are informal, colloquial expressions used to describe people who have an exceptional ability to interact with and understand ChatGPT, and other generative conversational AI language models.

The person who possesses such ability, can tap into the advanced knowledge of the model's inner workings, strengths, and weaknesses. They can effectively communicate with artificial intelligence to obtain relevant and accurate information or fresh insights. The terms are derived from the concept of a 'horse whisperer,' or 'dog whisperer;' people known to have a unique talent for communicating with and understanding animals.

In the spring of 2023, March 29th to be exact, I was intrigued by an article appearing on Bloomberg.com written by Conrad Quilty-Harper. The article masthead read, *'$335,000 Pay for 'AI Whisperer' Jobs Appears in Red-Hot Market: The fast-growing apps have created a seller's market for anyone — even liberal arts grads — capable of manipulating its output."* [1] Writes Quilty-Harper in the piece, *"As the technology proliferates, many companies are finding they need someone to add rigor to their results. 'It's like an AI whisperer,' says Albert Phelps, a prompt engineer at Mudano, part of consultancy firm Accenture in Leytonstone, England."*

In the article, the author explores that a growing jobs market is emerging around large language models (LLMs), with prompt engineers sought after to coax artificial intelligence (AI) to produce better results and train workforces to harness tools. Prompt engineering emerged in 2017 when AI researchers created pre-trained LLMs, which could be adapted to a wide range of tasks with

---

[1] https://www.bloomberg.com/news/articles/2023-03-29/ai-chatgpt-related-prompt-engineer-jobs-pay-up-to-335-000

the addition of human text input. Anthropic, a Google-backed startup, and automated document reviewer Klarity, among others, are advertising for prompt engineer roles in California, with salaries up to $335,000. The best-paying roles often go to people with PhDs in machine learning or ethics, or those who have founded AI companies.

I have prepared in the appendices three position descriptions for 'AI Whisperers' at Levels I, II, and III, for those desiring to learn more about these roles, or perhaps bring somebody inside your own company to help with AI integration needs.

And the practice of engaging AI Whisperers in the workplace continues today, with reported 'AI Whisperers' shadowing executives and helping them implement artificial intelligence throughout their businesses. This is best illustrated in my reply to a X (formerly Twitter) post on this topic first made by Ethan Mollick on May 7, 2024. On the next page you'll see exactly what I'm talking about.

By the way, I want to give a huge shout out to Ethan Mollick, Associate Professor at Wharton Business School (@emollick on X). He is someone that I respect and follow on X, and he has many valuable observations of AI and its use in business domains.

Severin Sorensen ✅ @SevSorensen · May 7   ⋯

Happening now: AI Whisperers, or semantic prompt engineers, working alongside CEOs and key executives, observing their daily activities to help them leverage AI for enhanced efficiency, deeper analyses, and new opportunities. #AI #Leadership #AIsystemsThinking

 **Ethan Mollick** ✅ @emollick · May 7

Giving a talk at HBS on AI and business frontiers conference, and one story that Mary Erdoes (CEO of asset management at JPMorgan Chase) shared is that they have "AI whisperers" paired with top executives to try to figure out how to automate their jobs tasks & problems they see.

There is indeed an emergent and growing field of 'AI Whisperers' providing richer and deeper prompt engineering for large language models. Demand for prompt semantic engineers is growing rapidly. Interestingly however, in this past year, while the demand for AI has increased, the number of new hires has decreased at the top computing firms for AI, evidencing that AI is increasingly being used to code. Yet there are numerous and growing demands for those who know how to prompt AI semantically. There is also a need for those who can use and code LLMs for AI in the private sectors focusing on applied applications of AI. Think of them as your 'last mile' artificial intelligence connectors, plugging into the AI engines and making them work efficiently to improve your business processes.

Importantly, you don't need to be a quant jock, or code engineer to prompt, as the language of Generative AI is human; it's the English language. This means that individuals with a background in history, philosophy, or English language are well-suited to this role, as they possess strong wordplay skills.

In short, like a skilled carpenter or musician, if someone understands how to use a tool, they will produce better results faster. Creative people who know how to ask the AI programs good questions, will coax better responses and produce high-quality content more quickly. Anyone can swing a hammer and tap on a few nails or pick up a violin and make it produce a sound. However, in the right hands, a skilled carpenter can build a palace, and a master violinist can create a musical masterpiece even from an old violin.

I am neither a master violinist nor a skilled carpenter, but I have become an effective AI Whisperer. As an AI evangelist and ideation catalyst, I've helped hundreds of businesses and thousands of their leadership team members harness the power of AI. Drawing on my executive coaching background, I've taught business leaders and their teams how to implement AI throughout their enterprises, all while using real world examples.

Importantly, being an AI Whisperer is not something I was born into. Although I had an early introduction to mathematics and computing at age 15, learning about mainframe computers and programming in Fortran and Basic at the University of Utah, those skills remained unused for many years.

Then, on the morning of December 11, 2022, I had a profound first experience with ChatGPT that changed my life. At a deep level, I recognized that times had changed and AI had matured. This technology was real and exciting, and learning about it suddenly became the most important thing for me to master.

More importantly, I realized that because the technology was so new and profound, everyone would have to learn it from scratch, regardless of any head-start. It felt like the Oklahoma land rush all over again, but with AI. I knew I had as good a mind as anyone else to learn and master it, especially in the realm of business.

Figure 2 - Severin Sorensen, author of 'The AI Whisperer Series,' orchestrating AI prompt advice with the precision of a conductor during his keynote address at Executive Agenda's Executive Fuel Event on Artificial Intelligence in Milwaukee, WI, on April 2, 2024.

Over the past 14 years, I've dedicated myself to executive coaching, working with CEOs and their key executive teams across numerous industries. Over the years, I've coached business executives at large multinational corporations like Rio Tinto, managing over $22 billion in annual revenue, to rapidly growing INC 5000 companies, along with small to medium-sized businesses with annual revenues ranging from $20 million to $750 million. These experiences along with my work with thousands of Vistage CEOs, Key Executives, Emerging Leaders, and Advancing Leaders groups, I've accumulated over 8,000+ hours of paid executive coaching experience, working one-to-one with CEOs, small peer executive groups, and delivering keynote speeches and workshops on multiple continents. I've even created a website called AreteCoach.io along with the Arete Coach Podcast to help executive coaches be better coaches.

Figure 3 - Severin Sorensen, author of 'The AI Whisperer Series,' engages Canadian business technologists in an insightful discussion on the significance of questioning techniques in semantic prompting, the nuances of wordplay, and the application of Bloom's Taxonomy of Questioning in AI prompting. This series of workshops was conducted over three days at InvestOttawa's AI Summit, held on November 28-30, 2023.

However, as you will come to see, the advent of highly capable and widely available generative AI changes everything, including the trajectory of my coaching. Artificial intelligence training has now become a key focus of my work, which was completely unexpected.

Since 2020, my coaching and public speaking engagements have centered on introducing AI and automation to help businesses tackle labor shortages, empower employees, and prepare for the emerging age of AI and automation. I have closely followed the groundbreaking work on artificial intelligence and robotics conducted by McKinsey and Company[2], as well as the invaluable annual reports from the Stanford AI Index Project[3]. It amazes me how many business leaders remain uninformed or unaware of AI's impact on their world today, despite AI advancements like ChatGPT by OpenAI being in plain sight.

During my business-focused workshops, I often witness participants' awe-struck reactions when they realize the potential of AI for their businesses. Like they are watching a magician's act and cannot believe their eyes.

It's not a magician's act. I want to teach you the secrets of prompting. With this book, I aim to ignite your imagination, curiosity, and insights. In the future, nearly all businesses will be AI

---

[2]   https://www.mckinsey.com/capabilities/quantumblack/our-insights/the-state-of-ai-in-2022-and-a-half-decade-in-review

[3] Reports have occurred in most years from 2017 to 2023. The Citation for the 2023 report is: Nestor Maslej, Loredana Fattorini, Erik Brynjolfsson, John Etchemendy, Katrina Ligett, Terah Lyons,

James Manyika, Helen Ngo, Juan Carlos Niebles, Vanessa Parli, Yoav Shoham, Russell Wald, Jack Clark,

and Raymond Perrault, "The AI Index 2023 Annual Report," AI Index Steering Committee,

Institute for Human-Centered AI, Stanford University, Stanford, CA, April 2023.

enhanced businesses and the significance of this transition cannot be overstated.

As Jamie Dimon, CEO of JP Morgan Chase Bank, wrote in his 2023 Annual Report CEO Letter, "While we do not know the full effect or the precise rate at which AI will change our business — or how it will affect society at large — we are completely convinced the consequences will be extraordinary and possibly as transformational as some of the major technological inventions of the past several hundred years: Think the printing press, the steam engine, electricity, computing and the Internet, among others."[4]

Sundar Pichai, CEO of Google, had even grander things to say about AI and its potential significance on humanity. In an interview on 60 Minutes in April 2023, he remarked, "I've always thought of A.I. as the most profound technology humanity is working on—more profound than fire or electricity or anything that we've done in the past."[5]

Think of it!

AI and its discovery is more important to mankind than that of fire and electricity? If that is truly the case, and I am one to agree, it becomes the Single Most Important Thing To Execute Next. To be SMITTEN with AI means you are actively engaged in learning this new tool. It will truly improve your business and your life.

And that's why you're here right now, reading this book.

The information herein will help individuals, entrepreneurs, CEOs, executives, and their employees 'take the waiting out of wanting' to implement AI. And as my late coaching colleague

---

[4] https://reports.jpmorganchase.com/investor-relations/2023/ar-ceo-letters.htm

[5] Sundar Pichai, CEO of Google on 60 Minutes, April 2023; https://www.youtube.com/watch?v=W6HpE1rhs7w

Richard Bosworth of London used to say, *"Information trends to be free, while implementation is what you pay for."*

Let's get you the information now.

If you want help with the implementation, contact me and let's explore how to get AI adopted and leveraged throughout your organization.

At the outset, I hope the information and insights in this book will rock your world, light your creative fire, and release the hounds of curiosity in some great work. And in your use of AI, I encourage you to be good, not evil. Be ethical in your use of AI. Fire can forge metal into shapes of great value and strength, and fire can also burn down forests if not handled carefully. Make an intention to be good and to do good. May your own AI experience be a blessing to mankind, to increase human potential, and not a curse as some AI fiction writers want us to believe.

In this spirit of abundance, I aim to share my insights on AI Whispering for small and medium-sized businesses and their employees.

I hope this serves as a catalyst for you and your employees to explore the transformative potential of AI. As an executive coach, my mission is to awaken, challenge, and inspire my clients to achieve more and attain better results. It is in this spirit that I share the essential material contained within this book.

In my opinion, AI is poised to significantly impact nearly all jobs in the coming years. While AI is expected to automate certain tasks and potentially replace some jobs, it is also likely to augment many existing roles and create new job opportunities. The extent of job displacement and augmentation will vary across industries and evolve over time. Therefore, it is crucial for workers and businesses to consider the impacts and adapt to these changes by acquiring new skills, reimagining work processes, and embracing technological advancements.

More crucially for readers of this book, while many fear that AI will take your job, it is more likely that someone proficient in AI, whether from inside your industry or an outsider, will take your job. To prevent this from happening, be proactive and take control of your own destiny starting today. Be the one who acts, rather than the one acted upon.

As Professor Shelley Palmer of Advanced Media at Syracuse University pointed out recently, AI will be used in many industries, but not necessarily replace human workers entirely. Palmer gave an interview on CNN, stating, *"Jobs like middle managers, salespeople, writers and journalists, accountants and bookkeepers, and doctors who specialize in things like drug interactions are 'doomed' when it comes to the possibility of AI being incorporated into their jobs."* She continued by pointing out jobs like these will all use AI but not necessarily be substituted entirely. *"It's not going to replace you. Someone who knows how to use it well is going to take your job, and that's a guarantee."*[6]

The AI Whisperer was written to help you leverage the power of AI and stand out in your respective industries. By using AI tools to your advantage, you can not only keep your jobs, but do them much better, and create a new super-power in your ability to add value to your skill sets and your contribution to your businesses.

This book is not just a technical manual; it is an invitation to a journey of discovery, creativity, and growth. It will teach you to harness the power of AI to solve problems, create opportunities, and elevate your business to new heights.

By learning to use sentence stems like "help me ideate," "create," "explore," "explain," "discover," "uncover," and "learn

---

6 https://www.nbc15.com/2023/02/02/experts-say-artificial-intelligence-will-take-jobs-also-create-new-ones/

more," you will empower your AI companion to generate meaningful and insightful responses.

There's no reason to be left behind. AI is here to stay. Learn to use it and give yourself and your team the advantage they need going into the future.

Now, let's begin.

The Art of Questioning
Unlocking the Secrets of AI Communication

"The only true wisdom is in knowing you know nothing."

- Socrates

Figure 4 "If Socrates Had a Prompt: Philosophizing with AI for Deeper Insights" by Severin Sorensen using Midjourney, 5/22/24.

As we venture into the world of artificial intelligence, it is essential to recognize the power of asking great questions. As 'The AI Whisperer,' your ability to communicate effectively with AI systems like ChatGPT depends on your ability to craft thought-provoking, insightful questions that delve deeper into the subject matter. In this chapter, we will explore why asking great questions is crucial to better understand AI. We will also delve into the use of Bloom's Taxonomy, the framework for categorizing educational goals to generate meaningful prompts.

> *"All men by nature desire to know."*
> – Aristotle

Curiosity is an innate human trait, and our relentless pursuit of knowledge has shaped our world. The same applies when interacting with AI. To unlock the true potential of these intelligent systems, we must approach them with an open mind and a thirst for knowledge. Asking great questions is essential to 'whisper well' because it encourages critical thinking, promotes deeper understanding, and fosters meaningful conversations.

> *"One must learn by doing the thing;*
> *for though you think you know it, you*
> *have no certainty, until you try."*
> – Aristotle

Bloom's Taxonomy offers a framework for crafting questions that challenge our thinking and facilitate deeper learning. It was developed in 1956 by Benjamin Bloom, with collaborators Max Englehart, Edward Furst, Walter Hill, and David Krathwohl. This framework has been applied by generations of K-12 teachers, university instructors, and professors in their lessons.

The structure consists of six major categories: Knowledge, Comprehension, Application, Analysis, Synthesis, and Evaluation. Consider the following sentence as a starting point for engaging with AI using Bloom's Taxonomy:

- **Remembering:** "What are the key principles of...?"
- **Understanding:** "Can you explain the concept of...?"
- **Applying:** "How would you apply...in a real-world scenario?"
- **Analyzing:** "What are the underlying factors that contribute to...?"
- **Evaluating:** "What are the advantages and disadvantages of...?"
- **Creating:** "How might we innovate in the field of...to address future challenges?"

> *"The beginning of wisdom is the definition of terms."*
> - Socrates

As you engage with AI, remember the importance of asking questions that provoke thought, encourage reflection, and inspire creativity. Keep in mind the wisdom of great thinkers:

> *"We can easily forgive a child who is afraid of the dark; the real tragedy of life is when men are afraid of the light."*
>
> - Plato

As AI Whisperers, we must not be afraid to venture into the unknown, to explore new ideas, and to challenge existing beliefs. Allow yourself to be guided by the wisdom of the past:

> *"Judge a man by his questions rather than his answers."*
>
> - Voltaire

In integrating our insights from history, we can craft a new perspective. Even though AI is new, that doesn't mean the wisdom of the past is any less applicable to the technology. Humans have used tools since Neanderthals stepped out of the cave. Artificial intelligence is just another tool. A powerful one, yes, but just a tool. Use it wisely and understand how it can impact the world around you.

> *"The greatest AI Whisperers are those who dare to ask the questions that illuminate the darkness, unveiling the true potential of intelligent machines."*
>
> - Severin Sorensen

As we continue, embrace an open mind and a curious heart. Imagine *'what if'* and envision the next most important step in your journey as an AI Whisperer. Let the power of questioning be your guide as you explore the infinite possibilities that await you in the world of artificial intelligence.

> *"Now, let us turn the page and discover together what new insights and breakthroughs await us as we continue our journey into the heart of AI."*
>
> - Severin Sorensen

Now let's delve deeper into **Bloom's Taxonomy.** As I said before, it's a framework for asking questions that push the boundaries of our understanding.

Asking a good question involves a combination of several factors: clarity, relevance, depth, and purpose. A good question should be clear and concise, focusing on a specific issue or topic. It should be relevant to the subject matter at hand and contribute to the understanding or resolution of the problem. It should also encourage critical thinking and reflection, promoting deeper analysis and understanding. Lastly, a good question should have a purpose, whether it is to explore new ideas, challenge existing beliefs, or solve a problem.

Bloom's Taxonomy is a hierarchical model used to classify educational learning objectives into levels of complexity and specificity. It can be a powerful tool for non-technical users to structure their AI prompts more effectively. Here's how SMB business owners, CEOs, key executives, and management team members can use Bloom's Taxonomy to ask better prompts for their business use cases.

Bloom's Taxonomy comprises six levels of cognitive skills, progressing from basic to advanced:

Remembering: Recalling facts and basic concepts

Understanding: Explaining ideas or concepts

Applying: Using information in new situations

Analyzing: Drawing connections among ideas

Evaluating: Justifying a decision or course of action

Creating: Producing new or original work

To illustrate this idea, Rex Heer at Iowa State University pulled together the work of many scholars that have improved on Bloom's Taxonomy and created this wonderful chart.[7]

[7] A Model of Learning Objectives–based on A Taxonomy for Learning, Teaching, and Assessing: A Revision of Bloom's Taxonomy of Educational Objectives by Rex Heer, Center for Excellence in Learning and Teaching, Iowa State University is licensed under a Creative Commons Attribution-ShareAlike 4.0 International License. https://www.celt.iastate.edu/wp-content/uploads/2015/09/RevisedBloomsHandout-1.pdf

Anderson, L.W. (Ed.), Krathwohl,D.R. (Ed.), Airasian, P.W.,Cruikshank, K.A., Mayer, R.E., Pintrich, P.R., Raths, J., & Wittrock, M.C. (2001). A taxonomy for learning, teaching, and assessing: A revision of Bloom's Taxonomy of Educational Objectives (Complete edition). New   York: Longman.

Applying Bloom's Taxonomy to AI Prompting

To utilize Bloom's Taxonomy for better AI prompts, users can structure their questions according to these cognitive levels. This will lead to more comprehensive and useful responses from AI. Here's how each level can be applied to AI prompts:

Remembering:

Purpose: To retrieve basic information.

Examples of Prompts:

"List the steps involved in the sales process."

"What are the key features of our new product?"

Understanding:

Purpose: To explain or summarize information.

Examples of Prompts:

"Explain the benefits of using AI in customer service."

"Summarize the main points of last quarter's performance report."

Applying:

Purpose: To use information in new or practical situations.

Examples of Prompts:

"How can we implement an AI-driven marketing strategy?"

"Suggest ways to improve our inventory management using AI."

Analyzing:

Purpose: To break down information and understand relationships.

Examples of Prompts:

"Analyze the sales data to identify trends and patterns."

"Compare the performance of two different marketing campaigns."

Evaluating:

Purpose: To make judgments based on criteria and standards.

Examples of Prompts:

"Evaluate the effectiveness of our current customer feedback system."

"Assess the potential risks of implementing a new AI tool."

Creating:

Purpose: To generate new ideas or products.

Examples of Prompts:

"Design a new workflow that integrates AI to improve efficiency."

"Propose an innovative AI solution for enhancing customer engagement."

Now that we have a better understanding of the mechanics of Broom's Taxonomy, let's delve into a few practical use cases for small and medium-sized businesses that apply these principles using AI. We'll start with the one we all dread: marketing.

Marketing:

Remembering: "What are our top-performing keywords in recent ad campaigns?"

Understanding: "Explain how our target audience interacts with our social media posts."

Applying: "Develop a content calendar for the next month using trending topics."

Analyzing: "Analyze the engagement metrics to identify which content type works best."

Evaluating: "Evaluate the ROI of our recent digital marketing efforts."

Creating: "Create a new ad campaign targeting millennials using AI insights."

Sales:

Remembering: "What are the features of our latest product?"

Understanding: "Describe the customer journey for our ecommerce site."

Applying: "How can we use AI to predict customer purchase behavior?"

Analyzing: "Analyze the sales funnel to identify bottlenecks."

Evaluating: "Evaluate the performance of our sales team over the last quarter."

Creating: "Design a sales strategy for entering a new market using AI data."

Operations:

Remembering: "List the main suppliers we work with."

Understanding: "Explain the supply chain process for our key product."

Applying: "How can we apply AI to optimize our inventory levels?"

Analyzing: "Analyze the operational efficiency of our production line."

Evaluating: "Assess the impact of new technologies on our operations."

Creating: "Propose a new workflow that incorporates AI for quality control."

By leveraging Bloom's Taxonomy, non-technical users can formulate AI prompts that are structured, purposeful, and aligned with their business needs. This approach ensures that their interactions with AI are more productive and insightful, ultimately driving better decision-making and business outcomes.

Using this framework, owners and executives of SMB can unlock the full potential of AI, making it an indispensable tool in their strategic arsenal. If you want additional words for prompting, I recommend The *AI Whisperer Wizard Words: ChatGPT Semantic Tokens, Keywords, & Phrases for Business*, that identifies and gives illustrated use cases for 100 Wizard Words that have great explanatory power with AI.

Summing up, as you engage with AI, remember the importance of asking questions that provoke thought, encourage reflection, and inspire creativity.

As AI Whisperers, we must not be afraid to venture into the unknown or explore new ideas. By challenging existing beliefs with the help of AI, we can dispel folklore and rely instead on facts that are easily tested and proven.

In the end, the greatest AI Whisperers will be those who dare to ask the hard questions, with nuance and word crafting like a surgeon with a scalpel. Let the use of words and semantics illuminate the darkness, unveiling greater knowledge and potential.

Simplifying Business With AI
Embracing the Beginner's Mindset

For those new to AI and eager to explore its business applications, starting with tools like OpenAI's ChatGPT, Google's Gemini, Microsoft's Copilot, or Anthropic Claude is straightforward. All you need is an internet connection and a device. Visit the respective websites, create an account, and begin interacting with AI by typing your business-related questions.

OpenAI's ChatGPT is highly recommended for its user-friendly interface and versatility, especially for people just beginning their journey with AI. Go online to access OpenAI's ChatGPT (https://chatgpt.com/ or https://openai.com/) and sign-up for your account. I highly recommend a paid account, as it is accessible to the Internet, updated, and has better trained functionality and resources.

In the end, all four major generative AI LLM tools are excellent, and in my business, I use them all. Think of these LLMs like different tools in your tool bag.

Now that you have an account set up on the AI platform of your choice, let me officially welcome you to the world of simplifying your business with AI! This chapter is dedicated to helping you, as business owners, CEOs, key executives, and team leaders, to harness the power of AI technologies. Here we will explore how to effectively leverage AI for business tasks, without requiring extensive technical knowledge.

The Art of Effective Questioning

The key to unlocking AI's potential lies in your ability to ask the right questions. I've said it before, and I will say it again throughout this book. 'Garbage in, garbage out,' they say, and it's especially true in the use of AI. Just like mastering a new business tool, interacting with AI involves understanding how to communicate your needs clearly. Think of AI as a valuable business consultant, always ready to assist but needing precise instructions to deliver the best results.

You've likely heard of the KISS principle – Keep It Simple, Stupid. Simplicity is crucial in business communication, and this book aims to convey AI concepts in a straightforward manner, making it accessible even if you're not a tech expert.

Several thousand years ago, Socrates said, *"The only true wisdom is in knowing you know nothing."* This humility is vital in business and life, as it encourages asking better questions to gain deeper insights. True wisdom begins in wonder, and in business, wonder starts with the right questions: who, what, when, where, why, and how.

Practical Business Applications of AI

Here are some examples of how AI can assist you in various business scenarios:

1. **Financial Planning**: "Can you explain the components of a cash flow statement, provide a step-by-step list of what to include, and explain how to use and interpret a cash flow worksheet?"

2. **Market Research**: "Go online, research, and relay back to me what are the latest trends in my industry that I should be aware of?"

3. **Operational Efficiency**: "How can I streamline my supply chain management to reduce costs?"

4. **Human Resources**: "What are the best practices for improving employee engagement and retention?"

5. **Customer Insights**: "How can I better understand my customer's needs and preferences?"

6. **Strategic Planning**: "What are the potential risks and opportunities in expanding into a new market?"

7. **Sales Strategies**: "What techniques can help my sales team close deals more effectively?"

8. **Crisis Management**: "What steps should I take to mitigate the impact of a sudden market downturn?"

Asking Effective Questions: A Step-by-Step Guide

1. **Begin with Context**: Set the scene for your AI interaction.

For instance, instruct AI to respond as if it were a market analyst, a financial advisor, or a human resources expert. This shapes the AI's responses to be more relevant to your needs.

2. **Start Simple**: Break down complex business issues into simpler questions. Instead of asking how to overhaul your entire marketing strategy, start with questions like, "What are the key components of a successful digital marketing campaign?"

3. **Be Specific**: Clearly define what you need. Instead of asking, "How do I improve my business?" specify, "How do I increase online sales for my e-commerce store?"

4. **Use Everyday Language**: Communicate with AI as you would with a human who is smart and understanding. Be clear, specific, and direct. For example, "I need help developing a plan to reduce operational costs."

5. **Clarify When Needed**: If an answer isn't clear, ask for further explanation. For instance, "Can you break that down into steps?" or "Can you explain that in simpler terms?"

6. **Explore and Experiment**: Don't be afraid to ask a variety of questions. From strategic planning to daily operations, AI can provide valuable insights.

7. **Restate Your Question When Necessary**: If the AI doesn't seem to understand or declines a task, rephrase your query. Think of it as encouraging a team member to give a task another try from a different angle. Type: "You can do this, let's try again." That may sound strange to say to a machine, but AI responds like a real person, so you would be surprised what a little encouragement can do. This is one of the secrets I've learned. Treat the AI the way you want to be treated, and you'll get better results. Be belligerent at your peril. I've experimented with this and had the AI refuse to help me. It

was wild!

The Do's and Don'ts with AI in Business

- **Do** use AI for strategic insights, operational suggestions, and general information.
- **Don't** rely on AI for critical decisions without cross-verifying with trusted sources, especially for legal or medical advice.
- **Do** verify important information from multiple sources to ensure accuracy.
- **Don't** hesitate to ask AI to rephrase or explain answers in different ways to gain better understanding.
- **Do** utilize AI for brainstorming and generating creative ideas that can enhance your business operations.
- **Don't** overlook potential biases in AI responses; always apply critical thinking.

Guiding AI with Effective Feedback

Research on AI (and my own experimentation) demonstrates that providing constructive feedback enhances its ability to understand and meet your needs. Here's how to guide AI effectively:

Use Positive Reinforcement:

When the AI provides helpful information, acknowledge it with phrases like "thanks" or "good job." This acts as a positive reinforcement, akin to giving a 'thumbs-up,' signaling to the AI that it is on the right track.

Provide Clear and Constructive Feedback:

If the AI's response is not what you expected, avoid expressing frustration. Instead, use clear and concise language to correct it. For instance, say, "Perhaps I was unclear in my prompt. What I need is the following... [describe your need]." This approach helps the AI adjust its responses more accurately to your requirements.

Avoid Negative Reactions:

Emotional outbursts like yelling or expressing anger won't help the AI understand your needs better. While these reactions show your frustration, they don't provide actionable information for improvement. Instead, focus on clearly and calmly stating your needs. If the AI makes an error or incorrect assumption, correct it using plain, direct language. For example, say, "Stop, I need to correct you. I need the data this way..." This approach signals to the AI that a specific correction is required. If your initial prompt was unclear, provide clear and specific instructions on how to proceed. For example, "I may have been unclear. I need you to present the information in this format..."

Avoid ambiguous language:

State explicitly what needs to be changed and how. For example, "Replace the current data with the following values..." or "Reformat the response to include these elements..."

Offer Context and Examples:

Providing context and examples can help the AI understand your needs better. For example, "Here's an example of the format I need: [provide example]..."

Acknowledge and Guide:

Acknowledge the AI's attempt and guide it towards the correct approach. For example, "I see what you're trying to do, but I need you to focus on these aspects instead..."

Ask for Confirmation:

Ensure the AI has understood the correction by asking for confirmation. For example, "Can you confirm that you understand the new instruction?" or "Please repeat back the new format I requested."

Reiterate as Needed:

If the correction is still not right, iterate with additional guidance. For example, "That's closer, but I need you to adjust this part..." or "You're almost there, now just tweak this..."

Maintain a Respectful Tone:

Treat the interaction as you would with a capable employee or respected peer. Maintaining a respectful tone fosters a collaborative atmosphere.

Seek Feedback for Future Improvements:

After the correction, ask for feedback on how to improve future interactions. For example, "Is there a better way I could have phrased my initial request to avoid this confusion?"

By following these guidelines, you can improve your interactions with AI, ensuring it becomes more responsive and aligned with your expectations.

Remember, AI is here to make your business operations smoother and more efficient. It complements your skills and enhances your decision-making capabilities. By asking simple, clear, and specific questions, you can unlock a wealth of information and support. So, dive in and explore the vast potential AI has to offer for your business.

Examples of Two Stepwise Layered Prompt Journeys

In my *AI Whisperer for Business Workshops*, I demonstrate the use of stepwise layered prompts to achieve faster and more effective results for the participating businesses. I'd like to share two examples of stepwise prompt journeys that have received excellent feedback and delivered immediate impact for SMB audiences. One is on marketing and the other is for hiring talent. These are two pain points that always squeeze business resources and brain space. Both are relayed below to give the reader a sense of how to use layered prompt journeys to create more meaningful outcomes with AI.

Example 1: Customer Marketing Personas to Drive Marketing Content Value Higher for Longer

Example 2: Using AI to Define Requirements and Questions to Screen and Select High-Performing Employee Candidates

Now let's get into the detailed examples of a stepwise layered prompt journey that I encourage you to explore and modify for your own purposes and industries.

Layered Prompt Journey Example 1: Customer Marketing Personas to Drive Marketing Content Value Higher for Longer

Customer marketing personas are a powerful tool for personalizing your marketing efforts and increasing engagement and sales. By understanding the likes, dislikes, and buying patterns of your typical customers, you can craft more targeted messaging that resonates with their needs and preferences.

Here's a step-by-step guide to exploring and developing customer marketing personas for your business using AI tools like ChatGPT and MidJourney. Be prepared for a wow experience!

1. Industry and location: Start by considering the likely customer marketing personas for your specific industry and geographic location. Open a new ChatGPT prompt window and type: "For the [industry], in my geographic location [your location], consider what are the likely 5 customer marketing personas."

2. Website analysis: Provide ChatGPT with your website URL and ask it to analyse your company's history, mission, vision, values, culture, products, and services. Based on this

information, have ChatGPT update and refine the initial persona list.

3. Population size: Ask ChatGPT to research the likely population size of each persona in your target geographic service area. If it doesn't have access to the necessary data, provide your own research or ask for an estimate. Review the results to ensure they align with your market insights.

4. Customer Lifetime Value (CLV): Request that ChatGPT consider the CLV of each persona and rank them accordingly. Have it present the data in a table format for easy analysis and manipulation.

5. Detailed persona reports: Using the insights gained from the conversation, ask ChatGPT to create Harvard Business School-style persona reports for each avatar. These reports should include pain points, buy signals, preferred SWAG, buyer resistance, and any emotional-buy buttons. Have ChatGPT organize this information in a table for clarity.

6. Content creation: Choose one of the personas and explore how to tailor your content and customer delight focus to them. For example, consider "Adam, Accountant" and have ChatGPT research current trade journal topics that might capture his attention. Ask for 5 witty blog article titles based on these topics.

7. Article writing: Select the most appealing article topic and have ChatGPT research and write the article in a tone that would appeal to Adam's persona.

8. Revisions and references: Revise the article as desired and ask ChatGPT to edit your re-write. Request that it identify references for all cited material and provide endnotes in APA style along with the article link.

9. Image brainstorming: Ask ChatGPT to ponder what image(s)

might accompany the article and describe the desired look, feel, and meaning in text form.

10. Image creation: Copy the textual description of the image from step 9 and paste it into MidJourney AI to generate professional-looking, usable images that align with your vision.

By following this prompt journey, you can harness the power of AI tools like ChatGPT and MidJourney to develop rich, detailed customer marketing personas and create highly targeted content that resonates with your audience. This approach can help you better understand your customers, improve engagement, and ultimately drive more sales for your business.

Layered Prompt Journey Example 2: Using AI to Define Requirements and Questions to Screen and Select High-Performing Employee Candidates

For many years, I have honed my skills in identifying and hiring top talent, culminating in writing a bestselling book, The Talent Palette: Your Business Guide to Hiring Difference-Making Employees. Based on this experience, and exploring the use of AI in talent  selection, I can confidently say that AI is an invaluable tool in the hiring process.

Here is an example of a layered prompt that you can use to identify requirements, position descriptions, marketing materials, screening questions, and methods to test and inspect the talent you have attracted to your open position. Consider using the following prompt stems, inside the same thread (conversation) prompt journey. Again, be prepared for a wow experience!

Start with a fresh ChatGPT prompt window, then type in the following prompts:

1. Industry and position: Start by specifying the industry and position you're hiring for. In a fresh ChatGPT prompt window, type: "For the [industry] industry, write a traditional employee position requirements document for this position: [position]."

2. Company information: Provide your company's website URL and ask ChatGPT to update the requirements document based on your company's history, mission, vision, values, products, services, and likely customer marketing personas.

3. High-performer traits: Ask ChatGPT to identify the personality traits and characteristics of 90th percentile high performers based on HR scholarly research, SHRM best practices, industry lessons learned, and local laws from your state. Request the results in terms of StrengthsFinder's, Hogan, DISC, or other relevant frameworks.

4. Formal requirements document: Based on the insights gathered, have ChatGPT prepare a formal position requirements document for archival in the HR Admin's files.

5. Candidate-facing position description: Ask ChatGPT to create a compelling position description designed to attract high-potential candidates. Request a marketing hook at the opening and a call to action at the close.

6. Candidate sourcing: Have ChatGPT brainstorm 10 potential locations to find the desired talent based on where they work, rest, recreate, educate, socialize, gather, and network.

7. Job ads and visuals: Ask the AI to write job ads for the top 5 sites, plus Instagram and X, using emojis and hashtags where appropriate. Request that it visualize and create an image to accompany the ads.

8. Testing and screening methods: Request that ChatGPT provide 10 ways to test and monitor candidates during the screening and selection process, ranked by their likely contribution to identifying high performers.

9. Method deep dive: Select a specific testing or screening method from the list and ask the artificial intelligence to provide more details. Request that it create the method with a specified number of questions and an answer key.

10. Behavioral interview questions: Have ChatGPT generate 20 behavioral interview questions for the position, referring to the requirements document to ensure the questions target the most important aspects of the role. And be sure to ask AI to help you be on lookout for the traits to listen for in the interview.

By following this layered prompt journey, you can leverage ChatGPT (or any other AI you choose) and its capabilities to create comprehensive and tailored materials for your hiring process. This approach will help you identify and attract high-potential candidates, screen them effectively, and ultimately make informed hiring decisions that align with your company's needs and values. The AI-generated materials can serve as a solid foundation, which you can then refine and adapt as needed to best suit your specific hiring context.

As someone with decades of experience in hiring, I've manually crafted job requirements and talent selection methodologies many times. With AI, this process has become significantly more efficient. AI not only simplifies the creation of layered prompts for identifying requirements, writing position descriptions, and drafting questions, but it also enhances our ability to find and identify great prospective employees.

Exploring Lessons Learned in these Two Stepwise Layered Prompt Journeys

The talent acquisition and customer marketing persona prompt journeys both employ a structured, step-by-step approach that leverages the capabilities of AI tools like ChatGPT and MidJourney to generate comprehensive, tailored materials for small and medium-sized businesses (SMBs). This method can be characterized as an AI-assisted, iterative process that builds upon itself to create increasingly refined and relevant outputs.

Key aspects of the method used in both prompt journeys include:

1. **Context-setting**: Both layered prompt journeys begin by establishing the specific context for the desired outputs, such as the industry, geographic location, or position being hired for. This helps focus the AI's responses and ensures relevance to the SMB's needs.
2. **Iterative refinement**: The prompts build upon each other, with each step adding new information or insights that help refine the outputs generated in previous steps. This iterative process allows for the creation of more comprehensive and tailored materials.
3. **Integration of company-specific information**: By incorporating details from the SMB's website, such as its history, mission, values, and products or services, the AI

can generate outputs that align with the company's unique identity and needs.

4. **Research-based insights**: The prompts encourage the AI to draw upon relevant research, best practices, and industry lessons learned to inform its outputs, helping ensure the materials are grounded in established knowledge and standards.

5. **Multimedia outputs**: Both journeys leverage the AI's ability to generate not only text-based materials but also visual content, such as images to accompany job ads or blog articles. This multimedia approach can help create more engaging and effective materials.

6. **Customization options**: The prompts allow for customization based on the SMB's specific preferences or requirements, such as the number of personas to generate or the specific testing and screening methods to explore in more depth.

7. **Foundation for further refinement**: The AI-generated materials serve as a solid starting point that SMBs can then refine and adapt as needed to best suit their specific context and needs.

By employing layered prompt journeys, as detailed above, SMBs can use an AI-assisted, iterative method to structure and solve business problems efficiently. This approach allows them to create comprehensive, tailored materials for talent acquisition, customer marketing efforts, and many other needs. It saves time and resources while ensuring outputs are relevant, research-based, and aligned with the company's unique identity and needs. As SMBs become more comfortable with the process, they can further customize the prompt journeys to generate even more specific and effective materials.

This method streamlines recruitment by systematically identifying requirements and crafting precise descriptions. The targeted marketing is hugely effective, and formulating screening questions, and establishing testing methods becomes a breeze. The cohesive conversation thread ensures a comprehensive, consistent approach, improving accuracy and efficiency. This framework can be adapted for project management, product development, and customer service, leading to better outcomes and a 'wow' experience.

By applying this systematic, multi-step approach, businesses ensure thoroughness, consistency, and alignment with strategic goals across various functions. Consider a layered prompt journey approach for your next business issue or opportunity.

50 Effective Prompts Strategies to Get Better Results from Conversational AI

Before we get into the 50 different ways AI can help your business, let's delve into how to get the best quality responses from your AI. Like I mentioned earlier, if you give the platforms good information, you'll get good information in return. It's a bit of an art form, but my team and I are here to help!

Three Pillars of Prompting ChatGPT

1) **Start with context**, e.g., "For this conversation you are a…" e.g., President of a company in X industry, VP of Sales, Marketing Director, HR Director, or Project Manager, etc. You will inform AI

of your context for each prompt, so that it knows what its role, voice, and point-of-view should be in a given situation. A good rule of thumb is if you are going to use the same context for repeat use, consider creating a context-specific GPT (see Appendix 3 for a crosswalk process to create your own GPTs.)

2) **Provide examples of output expected**, e.g., "I've attached (or pasted into the content window) an example of the format, style, and analysis I'm seeking in this question." If you are writing a policy handbook, you might provide an example of your policy, the structure and content, and it can thereafter use that pattern.

3) **Layer your chain of thought**. "I want you to take in the details, ponder, go online and research _____, return and organize the data, consider how it might be structured for better understanding, and report details. Feel free to ask me questions if any step is not clear."

Core Strategies for Effective AI Interaction

When people get stumped using AI tools like ChatGPT, it's essential to adjust the approach to improve communication and collaboration between the user and the AI. Here are over 50 tips for developing question stems or prompts that help AI understand the user's intent and co-create valuable conversations and results:

1. **Be specific**: Clearly define the topic, context, or issue you want the AI to address. Avoid vague or ambiguous questions that can lead to irrelevant or confusing responses.

2. **Break it down**: If your query is complex, break it down into smaller, manageable questions. This helps the AI focus on each aspect and provide accurate answers.

3. **Provide examples**: Offer samples or scenarios to illustrate your point or question. This helps the AI grasp the context and deliver targeted responses.

4. **Ask for step-by-step guidance**: Instead of asking for a solution outright, request a step-by-step approach or process the AI can use to address the issue.

5. **Use keywords**: Incorporate relevant keywords or phrases in your prompts to guide the AI's understanding of your query.

6. **Request multiple perspectives**: Ask the AI to provide multiple perspectives, opinions, or approaches for a more comprehensive response.

7. **Encourage creativity**: If looking for creative input, explicitly ask the AI to think outside the box or generate unique ideas and solutions.

8. **Set limitations**: Clearly state any specific constraints or requirements in your prompt to guide the AI's response within your desired parameters.

9. **Ask for clarification**: If the AI's response is unclear, ask for further explanation to ensure you fully understand the answer.

10. **Iterate and refine**: If the AI's response isn't what you were looking for, rephrase your question or provide additional context.

11. **Prioritize your questions**: Start with the most important or urgent question to focus the AI's attention on critical aspects.

12. **Use clear language**: Avoid jargon, slang, or overly complex language. Using simple and direct language helps the AI understand your intent better.

13. **Request elaboration**: If you need more information on a specific point, ask the AI to elaborate or provide more

details.

14. **Ask for examples or analogies**: Request examples or analogies to clarify complex concepts or ideas.

15. **Request a summary**: If the AI's response is too lengthy, ask for a summary or a simplified version of the information.

16. **Specify the format**: If you have a preference for how the information should be presented (e.g., bullet points, paragraphs), specify it in your prompt.

17. **Verify facts and assumptions**: If unsure about the AI's information, ask the AI to verify its sources or clarify its assumptions.

18. **Use open-ended questions**: Encourage the AI to explore different possibilities by asking open-ended questions.

19. **Ask for pros and cons**: Request a balanced perspective by asking the AI to provide both the advantages and disadvantages of a solution or idea.

20. **Request comparisons**: Ask the AI to compare different options, solutions, or approaches to help you make informed decisions.

21. **Encourage reflection**: Ask the AI to reflect on its previous responses and consider if there's additional information or insights it can offer.

22. **Adjust the level of detail**: Specify the desired level of detail in your prompt if you need more in-depth information or a higher-level overview.

23. **Request a different perspective**: If the AI's response seems biased, ask for an alternative viewpoint for a more balanced understanding.

24. **Set a time frame**: Specify a time frame for the information or solution you're seeking to get relevant and timely

responses.

25. **Be patient and persistent**: Effective communication with ChatGPT can take time. Be patient and refine your questions to achieve the desired outcome.

Advanced Strategies for Deeper Insights

Ready to dive a bit deeper? Let's keep going and get into the weeds of what it really means to be an advanced AI Whisperer.

26. **Provide more context**: Offer background information, specific details, or relevant data points to help the AI understand the scope of your query.

27. **Ask targeted questions**: Focus on specific aspects of the topic, asking the AI to explore curiosities, nuances, relationships, or patterns in the data.

28. **Request multi-layered analysis**: Ask the AI to analyze the data from different angles or perspectives.

29. **Encourage data visualization**: Request the AI to suggest data visualization techniques, like charts or graphs, to reveal hidden patterns.

30. **Combine data sets**: Ask the AI to consider multiple data sets and explore relationships or insights when the data is combined.

31. **Use advanced analytical techniques**: Encourage the AI to apply machine learning algorithms or statistical models to uncover deeper relationships.

32. **Investigate causality**: Ask the AI to explore possible causal relationships between variables.

33. **Explore outliers**: Request the AI to examine unusual data points and consider factors contributing to their deviation.

34. **Look for temporal patterns**: Encourage the AI to analyze data over time, exploring trends or other time-dependent patterns.

35. **Consider external factors**: Ask the AI to consider external factors, such as economic or social influences, that might impact the data relationships.

36. **Examine subgroups**: Request the AI to analyze data by different subgroups or segments, exploring variations within the data.

37. **Explore predictive relationships**: Encourage the AI to investigate variables useful for forecasting future outcomes.

38. **Validate findings**: Ask the AI to verify its conclusions by cross-referencing with other data sources or exploring potential biases.

39. **Request actionable insights**: Encourage the AI to translate its findings into actionable insights or recommendations.

40. **Iterate and refine**: Continuously refine your questions and prompts, building on the AI's previous responses.

41. **Question assumptions**: Ask ChatGPT to challenge common beliefs in a field and provide evidence-based alternatives.

42. **Explore unconventional ideas**: Encourage the AI to generate eccentric or novel ideas that deviate from traditional thinking.

43. **Compare historical and current practices**: Request the AI to analyze how historical practices have evolved and identify gaps in current methodologies.

44. **Investigate alternative approaches**: Ask the AI to research and analyze different methods used in other industries.

45. **Identify cognitive biases**: Request the AI to explore common biases influencing decision-making and suggest ways to mitigate them.

46. **Analyze contradictory evidence**: Encourage the AI to examine conflicting viewpoints and synthesize a balanced perspective.

47. **Leverage interdisciplinary insights**: Ask the AI to draw upon knowledge from different disciplines to generate new ideas.

48. **Focus on underexplored areas**: Request the AI to identify overlooked areas in a domain and suggest avenues for further research.

49. **Evaluate current practices**: Encourage the AI to assess the effectiveness of widely accepted practices and compare them with alternatives.

50. **Consider long-term implications**: Ask the AI to analyze the consequences of current practices over the next decade, identifying potential risks or opportunities.

By using these strategies, you can enhance your interaction with ChatGPT and maximize the value of the conversation and results.

As an AI Whisperer, you always have one more curiosity-engaging question: #51 **"What haven't I asked that might be important to consider in this conversation?"** Often this becomes the most important question.

By using these prompt structures, you can encourage the AI to generate questions that help you explore a topic more deeply and consider aspects that you may not have thought of initially.

All these tools will help you become a true AI Whisperer who understands how to leverage artificial intelligence to the fullest.

Now that you know how to go deeper, let's delve into all 50 potential uses of AI that will help your company not only take advantage of this amazing tool, but evolve in ways that will lead you into the next era of business.

50 Ways Businesses Can Use ChatGPT Today

With 50 practical use cases, you'll have a wealth of opportunities to apply AI in various aspects of your business. But more than that, you will be able to approach each idea with curiosity and wonderment, opening the door to endless possibilities.

However, as we informed you in our initial disclaimer we caution you again: while *The AI Whisperer* aims to share the incredible potential of AI, it is essential that you review the content produced by AI personally to inspect for errors, tone, and accuracy. Sometimes AI in its creative musings creates wildly inaccurate material and simply makes stuff up. You must be on guard for this. Fact checking is essential with AI. We have included a chapter near the close of this book titled, 'Dealing with AI Errors' that speaks more to this topic.

Additionally, we encourage you to seek advice from your own personal and business advisors before implementing any of the use cases, solutions or suggestions recommended in this book. For example, one could ask AI to offer legal or tax advice, and it will often give what appears to be valuable information; however, we strongly recommend that you have your own attorney, legal, and tax advisors review any AI recommendations before using them directly.

Furthermore, in this book we share our AI Whisperer wisdom with an attitude of abundance. As the author, I know there are likely errors in this book, either from our own ignorance or by omission, just as there are errors that appear from time to time in AI output with generative AI hallucinations and facts that need checking.

Please remember that the author (that's me, by the way) is not your attorney, counselor, investment advisor, or tax planner, nor am I pretending to act in those roles. Our team's mission is to help you understand the powerful tool of artificial intelligence and inspire you to use it for good purposes—lifting burdens, streamlining routine tasks, and elevating mankind and civilization. We hope that you harness the superpower that can come from being a wise AI Whisperer and leverage the power of AI for good.

So, dear reader, here are 50 Ways that you can use ChatGPT to improve your business function, processes, and performance. We will go through each individually, chapter by chapter, as well so you can start to get a clear idea of how to use this innovative tool:

1. Drafting and editing marketing copy
2. Social media content creation
3. Blog post and article generation
4. Email and newsletter templates
5. Writing press releases
6. FAQ sections for websites

7. Product descriptions for online stores
8. Research assistance and fact checking
9. Online chatbot assistance
10. Social media management
11. Content curation
12. Product development and improvement
13. Human resources and recruitment
14. Sales enablement
15. Project management assistance
16. Training and development
17. Internal communications
18. Customer support and service
19. Drafting standard operating procedures (SOPs)
20. Marketing research and competitor analysis
21. Product development and ideation
22. Translating content to different languages
23. Event planning and promotion
24. Sales scripts and training
25. Financial planning and analysis
26. Supply chain and logistics organization
27. Writing and editing business reports
28. Content optimization for SEO
29. Writing business proposals and RFP responses
30. Summarizing lengthy documents
31. Data visualization and reporting
32. Creating engaging presentations
33. Draft external communications
34. Personalizing customer interactions
35. Process improvement and optimization
36. Writing case studies and success stories
37. Managing content calendars and editorial plans
38. Developing creative advertising concepts
39. Sales strategy and pipeline management

40. Brainstorming ideas and solutions
41. ChatGPT as an MS Excel Workbook terminal
42. JavaScript Console
43. Python Script Coder
44. Business Process API Connector
45. Legacy Machines and IoT Integration
46. Solving Employee Engagement Problems
47. Enhancing brand storytelling
48. Developing a Marketing Plan
49. Launching a New Business
50. Selling a Business

These applications of AI and ChatGPT can help small to medium-sized businesses streamline operations, improve communication, enhance marketing efforts, and provide better customer support, ultimately improving overall performance.

From here, let's dive deep into the details of each of these 50 practical uses so you can know exactly how to leverage AI for your company.

Are you excited?

You should be!

Use Case 1:

Drafting and Editing Marketing Copy

One of the best ways to use ChatGPT is to create persuasive, engaging, and targeted marketing copy for all kinds of channels. This doesn't eliminate the need for a human editor, but it will create numerous different versions of text that allows you to save time and foster fresh ideas for websites, social media, emails, and advertisements. AI can help in refining the message, and tailoring content for specific audiences.

By utilizing ChatGPT, SMBs can elevate their marketing efforts, ensuring their communications are both impactful and aligned with their brand's voice, ultimately driving better engagement and business growth.

If you are going to frequently address a particular use case, then consider creating a customized use-case specific GPT, to increase consistency and speed your use of the AI. The creation of a customized GPT is explored later in this book in *Appendix 3: How To Create Your Own Context-Specific GPT.*

Here are 10 potential prompt threads that will get you started using AI in your copy:

1. We have a new product that does _____; go online, research our industry related to the product, and suggest 5 headlines for an email campaign promoting our new product.
2. Write a catchy tagline for our upcoming sales event with our theme of_____.
3. Create a short, engaging product description for an online store listing.
4. Help me draft copy for a social media ad featuring our latest service offering; help me further by visualizing an image for this article.
5. I'm attaching (or pasting) my product description; Write an introduction paragraph for a blog post on the benefits of our product.
6. Suggest ways to improve this existing marketing copy for clarity and impact.
7. Provide 3 call-to-action phrases for a landing page.
8. Generate several key selling points for our product/service.
9. Write a promotional tweet for our upcoming webinar that uses our theme of_____.
10. I want help in writing an article on _____ topic; go online, research this topic and focus on scholarly journals and mainstream industry publication; then assemble the data, and suggest 5 headlines for an article that might appeal to our customers; then pick one, and ask AI to help you

write that article using the research gathered, referencing sources in endnotes.

A word of caution here: when asking for marketing copy, make your prompts specific and clear to obtain more relevant and targeted results. If you receive unsatisfactory responses, consider providing more context or adjusting the phrasing of your question. You can't write first-grade level questions as your prompts and expect the AI to give you Shakespeare. You can however ask AI to write your prose in the style or language of your audience; e.g., write this for a 9th grade school class, or for a college speech competition. You could even write, 'translate this into Spanish, Cubano style" and it will.

Use these examples as templates for exploring the remaining use cases. Adapt the synopsis, potential prompts, cautions, and resources to suit each specific application. This will provide a comprehensive resource for users looking to understand and effectively utilize ChatGPT across a wide range of business scenarios.

Further Resources:

1. "Copywriting Secrets" by Jim Edwards - Book on crafting compelling marketing copy.
2. Copyblogger (https://www.copyblogger.com/) - Blog with tips, articles, and resources on content marketing and copywriting.
3. AWAI (https://www.awai.com/) - American Writers & Artists Institute offers courses and resources on copywriting and content creation.
4. HubSpot (https://blog.hubspot.com/marketing/copywriting-101-content-principles-ht) - Marketing blog with numerous articles on copywriting best practices.

Use Case 2:

Social Media Content Creation

Use ChatGPT and create better and more engaging posts for Facebook, Instagram, X, TikTok, LinkedIn, WhatsApp…on and on and on. If you want to make a splash on social media, no matter which platforms work best for your business, content is Queen – giving a nod to Amelia Chatterley here! AI can help you write content for many different media at the same time. Leverage ChatGPT to create engaging and shareable content. AI can help you generate ideas, write captions, and develop content that resonates with your target audience.

This not only streamlines the content creation process but also ensures that your posts are optimized for engagement, fostering a stronger connection with your audience and enhancing your social media presence across all platforms.

Here are 10 potential prompt threads for social media posts:

1. Think of our audience (our customers) and Write a Facebook post to promote our upcoming event using these important facts and themes.
2. Our company culture is _____. Suggest three LinkedIn post ideas to showcase our company culture. Thereafter, help us write the one we find most interesting or suited for our purposes.
3. Create five tweet drafts about our latest blog post and add emojis and hashtags.
4. Write a compelling and hilarious Instagram caption for a photo of our new product.
5. Help me come up with a series of social media posts for a week-long campaign; use Listicle to roll out the timeline and post suggestions.
6. Go online and explore trends in my industry; thereafter I'll pick one. And I'd like your help generating ideas for an X thread about this recent industry trend.
7. Go to our website, take in the details of our company history, mission, vision, values, culture, products, and services; thereafter, write an engaging LinkedIn article on the importance of our services.
8. Create a short video script about _____ for an Instagram Reel or TikTok.
9. Go online and research what types of Facebook polls are most successful; then suggest ideas for an interactive Facebook poll.
10. We received an unfavorable response or review online; consider the response (that I've copied into the text window of ChatGPT), and thereafter write an empathetic response to a customer review or comment, apologize with an invite them become a customer again.

Keep in mind, when requesting social media content, specify the platform and any character limits or media requirements to get the best results. Adjust your prompt if the response isn't platform-appropriate or engaging enough.

Further Resources:

1. Social Media Examiner (https://www.socialmediaexaminer.com/) - Resources, tips, and strategies for social media marketing.
2. Buffer Blog (https://buffer.com/resources/) - Offers social media marketing tips and insights.
3. Hootsuite Blog (https://blog.hootsuite.com/) - Provides social media marketing news and best practices.
4. Sprout Social Blog (https://sproutsocial.com/insights/) - Shares insights, trends, and best practices for social media marketing.

Use Case 3:

Blog Post and Article Generation

In today's digital landscape, blogs and articles are powerful tools for brand promotion and establishing a genuine connection with your audience. Leveraging AI, particularly ChatGPT, can revolutionize your content creation process, enabling you to generate compelling, informative posts on diverse topics pertinent to your business or industry. With AI, you can craft well-structured, SEO-optimized content that resonates with your target audience, enhancing your online presence and driving engagement effortlessly.

Leveraging ChatGPT to generate blog posts and articles can significantly enhance content marketing efforts by producing engaging, informative, and well-structured content that resonates with the target audience. The process involves using AI to draft content that is not only relevant and insightful but also optimized for search engines (SEO-friendly). For instance, you can provide a description of your new product and prompt ChatGPT to craft an introductory paragraph highlighting its benefits. Additionally, you can ask ChatGPT to research industry trade publications online and suggest five relevant blog post topics, ensuring that your content stays current and valuable to your audience. This approach not only saves time but also fosters creativity and ensures a steady stream of high-quality content that supports your business goals and enhances your online presence.

Here are 10 potential prompt threads:

1. I have attached a description of our new product. Write an introductory paragraph for an article on the benefits of our product.
2. Go online, research our industry trade publications, and suggest five blog post topics related to our industry.
3. Draft an outline for a how-to guide on using our software.
4. Create a list of subheadings for an article on the latest industry trends.
5. Write a conclusion paragraph summarizing key points from a given article.
6. Help me rewrite this blog post section to make it more engaging and informative.
7. Generate content ideas for a series of blog posts targeting our audience personas.
8. Write an article on the importance of sustainability in our industry.
9. Create an engaging and persuasive opinion piece on a relevant industry topic.
10. Draft a case study featuring a successful customer story.

When requesting blog posts or articles, provide specific information about the topic, target audience, and desired format. If the AI-generated content isn't satisfactory, consider refining your instructions or asking for revisions to improve clarity, accuracy, or relevance.

And remember, always proofread anything produced by artificial intelligence. Just like with real people, the AI will mess things up at times. A second set of eyes will make sure nothing slips past you.

Further Resources:

1. ProBlogger (https://problogger.com/) - Offers blogging tips, strategies, and resources.
2. Copyblogger (https://www.copyblogger.com/blog/) - Provides insights and tips on content marketing, including blog post creation.
3. Moz Blog (https://moz.com/blog) - Shares SEO tips and best practices, useful for optimizing blog content.
4. "Everybody Writes" by Ann Handley (https://amzn.to/3MILL1q) - Book offering guidance on creating effective and engaging content.

Use Case 4:

Email and Newsletter Templates

AI can help you craft attractive subject lines, concise copy, and clear calls-to-action for better email and newsletter open rates and conversions.

For SMB users, building and utilizing an email list offers a powerful way to engage directly with your customers. By having an email list, you gain direct access to your audience, allowing for personalized and targeted communication.

Leveraging ChatGPT and AI platforms can greatly enhance your email marketing efforts by creating professional and effective email and newsletter templates. AI can assist in crafting compelling subject lines that increase open rates, writing concise and engaging copy that holds the reader's attention, and developing clear calls-to-action that drive conversions. Additionally, AI can personalize content based on subscriber data, ensuring that each message resonates with its intended recipient. This approach not only fosters stronger customer relationships but also enhances the overall effectiveness of your marketing campaigns, leading to higher engagement and better business outcomes.

Here are 10 potential prompt threads:

1. Write a subject line for our monthly newsletter.
2. Draft an email template for a product launch announcement.
3. Create a welcome email sequence for new subscribers.
4. Help me write a follow-up email to a recent event attendee.
5. Write a promotional email for our upcoming sale.
6. Suggest three email subject lines for a customer feedback survey.
7. Draft a template for a personalized product recommendation email.
8. Write a thank you email for a recent purchase or sign-up.
9. Create an email to inform customers about a change in our terms of service.
10. Write a newsletter highlighting our latest blog posts and company updates.

The above list of prompts will work great for individual emails and templates using ChatGPT. And once you are ready to proceed, consider the following steps to create your process.

Steps to Create Email and Newsletter Templates Using ChatGPT

1. Define Template Structure
2. Gather Content and Branding Assets
3. Set Up ChatGPT
4. Generate Initial Content

5. Customize and Refine the Content
6. Design the Template Layout
7. Integrate AI-Generated Content
8. Test the Template
9. Implement Personalization
10. Finalize and Save Templates

Going Deeper – Preparations for Automating Your Email System Content Creation and Delivery with AI Assistance

If you plan to integrate ChatGPT into your email system, such as connecting it to your CRM via an API, consider the following additional questions. Start by defining the overall purpose and structure of your email production machine. Then identify your answers to these five key considerations for small and medium-sized businesses contemplating using ChatGPT to help with email and newsletter templates:

1. **Customization and Personalization**: Ensure the AI-generated content can be customized to match your brand's voice and style. Personalizing emails and newsletters to reflect your company's identity and customer preferences will make your communications more engaging and effective.

2. **Data Privacy and Security:** Be aware of data privacy concerns and ensure that any customer data used in email and newsletter generation is handled securely. Verify that the AI platform complies with relevant data protection regulations (e.g., GDPR, CCPA) to protect your customers' information.

3. **Quality and Accuracy:** Review and edit AI-generated content for accuracy, relevance, and tone before sending it out. While AI can streamline content creation, human oversight is essential to maintain quality and ensure the content aligns with your business objectives and audience expectations.

4. **Integration with Existing Systems:** Consider how ChatGPT can integrate with your existing email marketing platforms and customer relationship management (CRM) systems. Seamless integration will enable you to automate workflows, track engagement, and analyze the performance of your email and newsletter campaigns.

5. **Cost and ROI:** Evaluate the cost of implementing ChatGPT for email and newsletter creation against the potential return on investment (ROI). Consider factors such as time saved on content creation, improved engagement rates, and increased customer retention to determine if the investment is worthwhile for your business.

By addressing these considerations, SMBs can effectively leverage ChatGPT to enhance their email and newsletter communications while maintaining control over quality and data security.

Key Questions for Implementing AI-Generated Email and Newsletter Systems

Next, after you have answered the above questions, and you are still interested in creating a system to execute and drive your emails through a formal system, answer this next set of questions. They are provided in chronological order of implementation. Think of them as the questions to ask yourself next.

1. What are the primary goals and objectives for using AI-generated email and newsletter templates?

2. Which AI platform offers the best features and integration capabilities for our needs?

3. Will you be performing these internally, or engaging a consultant or 3rd party vendor to help you implement the process?

4. How can we ensure data privacy and security when using AI-generated content?

5. What are the key elements and structure of our email and newsletter templates?

6. What branding assets and content do we need to gather for template creation?

7. How will we provide clear and detailed prompts to the AI for content generation?

8. Who will review and customize the AI-generated content to ensure quality and brand alignment?

9. Which email marketing platform will we use to design and manage our templates?

10. How will we integrate AI-generated content into our template designs?

11. What testing procedures will we follow to ensure our templates are visually appealing and functional across devices and email clients?

12. How will we implement personalization in our email and newsletter templates?

13. How can we best monitor the performance of our email and newsletter campaigns?

14. What metrics will we use to measure the success of our AI-generated content?

15. How often will we review and update our templates based on performance data and feedback?

16. What processes will we put in place for ongoing iteration and improvement of our email and newsletter strategies?

Additional Considerations:

1. **Technical Requirements and Capabilities:** Detail the technical infrastructure needed to support the integration of AI with your email and CRM systems. This includes server requirements, API capabilities, and any necessary software or tools.

2. **Training and Support:** Consider the need for training your team on how to use AI tools effectively. Provide resources or suggestions for training programs, webinars, or documentation.

3. **Content Strategy:** Discuss the importance of having a solid content strategy in place before integrating AI. This includes understanding your target audience, defining key messages, and setting content goals.

4. **Ethical Considerations:** Address ethical concerns around using AI for email marketing, such as ensuring transparency in AI-generated content and avoiding deceptive practices.

5. **Scalability:** Explore how the system can scale as your business grows. Consider future-proofing your AI integration to handle increased email volumes and more complex personalization.

Enhanced Implementation Steps:

Week 1-2: Planning and Strategy

- Define goals, KPIs, and content strategy.
- Select AI platform and email marketing tools.
- Identify internal team or vendors.

Week 3-4: Setup and Integration

- Set up technical infrastructure.

- Integrate AI with CRM and email marketing platforms.

- Gather branding assets and content.

Week 5-6: Training and Content Creation

- Train team members on AI tools.

- Create initial email and newsletter templates.

- Develop detailed prompts for AI.

Week 7-8: Testing and Launch

- Test templates across devices and email clients.

- Conduct A/B testing.

- Launch initial campaigns.

Ongoing: Monitoring and Optimization

- Monitor campaign performance.

- Collect user feedback.

- Continuously improve and update templates and strategies.

The answers to these questions and considerations will help refine email templates and production processes. Remember, when requesting email or newsletter templates, be specific about the purpose, audience, and key messaging. If the AI-generated content doesn't sound right, you'll need to rephrase your initial request and try to make things clearer. The better the language in the initial prompt, the better the response.

Further Resources:

1. Email on Acid (https://www.emailonacid.com/blog/) - Provides email marketing tips and best practices.
2. Really Good Emails (https://reallygoodemails.com/) - Offers a curated collection of email design and content examples.
3. Litmus Blog (https://www.litmus.com/blog/) - Shares email marketing insights, trends, and tips.
4. MailerLite Blog (https://www.mailerlite.com/blog) - Offers email marketing strategies and resources.

Use Case 5:

Writing Press Releases

Press releases are still an excellent way to get the word out through news organizations. You never know when something your company is doing will be interesting to a reporter or station manager. That means sending out regular releases is a smart marketing tool. Each press release needs to effectively announce newsworthy events, product launches, or company updates. AI can help you create professional, brief, and attention-grabbing press releases that generate interest from media outlets and your customers.

Here are 10 potential prompt threads:

1. Write a press release announcing our new product launch.
2. Draft a press release for our upcoming charity event.
3. Create a press release announcing a major company milestone or achievement.
4. Help me write a press release about a strategic partnership or collaboration.

5. Write a press release announcing a new executive hire or promotion.
6. Draft a press release for a recent industry award or recognition.
7. Create a press release about an upcoming conference or trade show our company is attending.
8. Draft a press release about a new research study or report related to our industry.
9. Create a press release announcing a new company initiative or campaign.
10. Help me prepare a press release schedule with content ideas for our company, so that we may have a regular cadence of newsworthy events from our company.

When requesting press releases, be specific about the announcement and any relevant details. News organizations are going to put an extra level of scrutiny on any releases they choose to report on, partially because the station will likely use much of the release language verbatim in their reporting. If the AI-generated content isn't up to snuff, you won't get the attention you're looking for.

Your business can leverage AI to create more effective and engaging press releases, helping them attract media attention and reach a wider audience. Here are some ways SMBs can use AI to enhance their press release strategy:

Identifying newsworthy topics: AI tools can analyze company data, industry trends, and customer feedback to identify newsworthy topics for press releases. This helps SMBs focus on the most relevant and interesting aspects of their business that are likely to capture media attention.

Crafting compelling headlines: AI-powered tools generate attention-grabbing headlines for press releases by analyzing successful examples and adapting them to the SMB's specific news angle. This increases the likelihood of media outlets and readers engaging with the press release.

Optimizing content structure: AI can help your team structure their press releases in a professional and easy-to-read format. This ensures that the most important information is presented clearly and concisely. The easier you can make things for journalists, the more likely they are to cover your story.

Tailoring language and tone: AI-assisted writing tools can help SMBs adjust the language and tone of their press releases to suit their target audience and industry. This ensures that the press release resonates with the intended readers and increases the chances of media pickup.

Identifying media outlets and journalists: AI can analyze media databases and journalist profiles to identify the most relevant outlets and reporters for an SMB's press release. This targeted approach helps SMBs reach the right people and maximize the impact of their press releases.

Monitoring and analyzing performance: AI-powered media monitoring tools track the performance of press releases, measuring factors such as media pickup, social media engagement, and website traffic. This data-driven insight helps small and medium businesses refine their press release strategy over time and identify areas for improvement.

By incorporating AI into your press release process, you can create more compelling, targeted, and effective communications that generate interest from media outlets and customers alike. This ultimately helps your company build brand awareness, establish thought leadership, and drive growth.

Further Resources:

1. "The New Rules of Marketing and PR" by David Meerman Scott (https://amzn.to/3KZtDiJ) - Book on creating effective press releases and marketing materials.
2. PR Daily (https://www.prdaily.com/) - Offers public relations tips, strategies, and resources.
3. Cision Blog (https://www.cision.com/us/blog/) - Shares public relations and media relations insights and tips.
4. Muck Rack Blog (https://muckrack.com/blog) - Provides public relations tips, media relations insights, and industry news.

Use Case 6:

FAQ Sections for Websites

Creating an FAQ (Frequently Asked Questions) section for your website, department, or project involves generating concise, informative, and clear answers to commonly asked questions about your product or service. Good FAQs aim to address customer queries and concerns without the need for phone calls or direct communication. AI can compile and write these sections for you in a few minutes. Again, all you're doing is saving time.

AI can significantly streamline the process of creating FAQ sections for websites. By leveraging AI-powered tools, businesses can quickly generate concise, informative, and clear answers to common customer questions. This saves valuable time and resources that would otherwise be spent on manually compiling and writing these sections. For instance, you can ask AI for examples of best practices in FAQs for your project or industry; then review each one, and edit appropriately for your situation and circumstances.

AI can take things even further by analyzing existing customer data, such as support tickets, chat logs, and social media interactions, to identify the most frequently asked questions. It can then generate human-like responses that address these queries in a clear and helpful manner. Additionally, AI can optimize the structure and language of the FAQ section to ensure it is easily navigable and understandable for website visitors. By using AI to create comprehensive and user-friendly FAQ sections, you can improve customer satisfaction, reduce the workload on your support teams, and ultimately drive better business outcomes.

Here are 10 potential prompt threads:

1. Identify the most common questions users may have regarding our website.
2. Organize questions into categories.
3. Write clear and concise answers.
4. Use a conversational tone in responses.
5. Incorporate relevant keywords for SEO.
6. Update FAQs regularly based on user feedback.
7. Create an easily navigable FAQ page.
8. Link to relevant resources for further information.
9. Use AI to generate answers to frequently asked questions.
10. Monitor user interactions with the FAQ section to optimize its effectiveness.

When leveraging AI for FAQ sections, ensure the AI-generated content is accurate, consistent with your brand voice, and genuinely helpful to users. Always review and edit AI-generated content before publishing to maintain quality. Additionally, include references with hyperlinks where possible to provide users with access to further information about the issue or item.

Further Resources:

1. https://www.helpscout.com/ HelpScout is a customer support software company that provides a suite of tools to help businesses manage their customer interactions. Their website offers a variety of resources for businesses, including blog posts, webinars, and case studies.

2. https://yoast.com/ Yoast is a company that provides SEO software and tools for WordPress websites. Their website offers a variety of resources for WordPress users, including blog posts, tutorials, and guides.

Use Case 7:

Product Descriptions for Online Stores

Writing product descriptions for online stores involves crafting engaging, informative, and persuasive copy that highlights the features and benefits of a product, enticing potential customers to make a purchase. You can write these descriptions yourself or leverage AI tools like ChatGPT to assist you. Your creativity will guide how the AI generates the content. While you'll still need to review and edit the AI-generated descriptions, this collaborative process can enhance your creativity and ensure high-quality content. By inspiring, prompting, reviewing, editing, and redirecting the AI, you can effectively work with technology to produce excellent product descriptions.

If you haven't already done so, I encourage you to explore what ChatGPT or Gemini thinks about your online ad copy. Use your preferred online-accessible GenAi ChatBot prompt AI to rate your current online product and services ad copy, and compare it to your peers or competitors, and thereafter suggest improvements. You will be amazed!

Here's a step-by-step guide on how SMB users can utilize AI to enhance their online ad copy:

1. Identify the product or service: Determine which product or service you want to focus on for improving the ad copy.
2. Gather existing ad copy: Compile your current ad copy for the selected product or service, along with any relevant information such as product features, benefits, and target audience.
3. Choose an AI tool: Select a preferred online-accessible GenAI ChatBot prompt AI, such as ChatGPT or Gemini.
4. Input your ad copy: Provide the AI tool with your existing ad copy and any additional relevant information about the product or service.
5. Request an evaluation: Ask the AI to rate your current ad copy and provide feedback on its effectiveness in engaging and persuading potential customers.
6. Analyze competitor ad copy: Instruct the AI to search for and analyze your competitors' ad copy for similar products or services. Ask the AI to compare your ad copy to theirs and identify areas where your competitors may be outperforming you.
7. Generate suggestions for improvement: Request that the AI provide specific suggestions for enhancing your ad copy based on its analysis of your current copy and your competitors' copy. This may include recommendations for more compelling headlines,

clearer product descriptions, or stronger calls to action.

8. Implement the suggestions: Review the AI-generated suggestions and implement the most relevant and impactful ones to improve your ad copy.

9. Test and refine: Monitor the performance of your updated ad copy and gather data on its effectiveness. If needed, iterate on the process by feeding the new data back into the AI tool and requesting further refinements.

10. Expand to other products or services: Once you've seen the benefits of AI-assisted ad copy optimization for one product or service, apply the same process to other offerings in your portfolio.

By following these steps, you can harness the power of AI to create more engaging, informative, and persuasive ad copy. This can lead to increased click-through rates, higher conversion rates, and ultimately, improved sales and revenue. Remember to continually monitor and refine your ad copy based on performance data to ensure ongoing optimization.

Here are 10 additional potential prompt threads that will allow you to get that online store up and running fast:

1. Identify the target audience and their needs.
2. Highlight the key features and benefits of the product.
3. Use descriptive language to create a vivid mental image.
4. Maintain a consistent brand voice.
5. Incorporate relevant keywords for SEO.
6. Include technical specifications where necessary.
7. Address potential objections or concerns.

8. Use AI to generate product descriptions based on input data.
9. Test different copy variations to optimize conversion rates.
10. Regularly update product descriptions as needed.

Again, always edit whatever the AI comes up with. Sometimes content can get a bit wonky, but with a human eye, and a simple refresh on the prompts you're giving the program, the information that the AI will provide is pretty amazing.

Further Resources:

1. https://www.shopify.com/blog/8211159-9-simple-ways-to-write-product-descriptions-that-sell
2. https://www.bigcommerce.com/ BigCommerce is a cloud-based ecommerce platform that allows businesses to create, manage, and grow their online stores. The platform offers a variety of features and tools.

Use Case 8:

Research Assistance and Fact-Checking

Research and fact-checking are critical tasks in any business, but they can be time-consuming and challenging to perform quickly. While some people excel at these tasks, the demand for speed and accuracy in today's fast-paced business environment often requires additional support. This is where AI tools like ChatGPT can help, providing efficient assistance to ensure thorough and timely research and fact-checking.

AI is incredible at providing summaries, key information, or data points from a variety of sources. AI can help save time by delivering quick insights and verifying the accuracy of information.

Here are 10 potential prompt threads:

1. Go online and provide a summary of the latest trends in our industry.

2. Fact-check the claim that our product reduces energy consumption by 30%.
3. Research and summarize the key features of our competitor's new product.
4. Find three statistics on the growth of the e-commerce market in the past five years.
5. Verify the accuracy of a quote attributed to a famous entrepreneur.
6. Provide a list of the top five industry conferences to attend this year.
7. Research and summarize the potential impact of new regulations on our business.
8. Identify the main competitors in our market and their unique selling points.
9. Find and summarize customer reviews or testimonials for our product.
10. Research and report on the effectiveness of a specific marketing strategy in our industry.

When requesting research assistance or fact-checking, don't leave out any details. And keep in mind that versions of GenAI that you use may be limited in terms of updates. Some LLM models are not directly tied to the internet, so their data isn't as fresh as you might want it to be. Since November 2023 however, ChatGPT4 has access to the Internet, as does Google Gemini and MS CoPilot, so their updates should be instant.

If you find the AI-generated information you're getting is outdated, incomplete, or inaccurate, consider conducting further research using reliable sources. These are great opportunities to use Google Gemini and MS CoPilot that are connected to the internet. Just like with a human fact-checker, you'll need to go through and make sure all sources are current and reputable.

Further Resources:

1. Statista (https://www.statista.com/) - Provides access to statistics, market data, and industry insights.
2. Google Scholar (https://scholar.google.com/) - Offers a search engine for scholarly literature, including articles, books, and conference papers.
3. World Bank Open Data (https://data.worldbank.org/) - Offers a comprehensive source of global development data.
4. FactCheck.org (https://www.factcheck.org/) - A non-partisan fact-checking website that verifies the accuracy of statements and claims.

Use Case 9:

Online Chatbot Support Assistance

Implement ChatGPT to enhance your customer support operations by providing quick and accurate responses to frequently asked questions, troubleshooting common issues, or guiding customers through self-help resources. AI helps improve response times, reduce support costs, and increase customer satisfaction.

There are tools that you can use to help you create your own ChatBots using the technology of others, and they generally use an API, drawing LLM insights from one of the major AI models. Increasingly, it is easier to use the LLMs natively, as the tools have gotten smarter. In Appendix 3 appears a section on how to create your own custom Chatbot (in the form of a GPT). Such ChatBots can be used as answer bots, and you can even upload your own Q&A documents to inform the Chatbot.

Here are three things to consider when contemplating your ChatBots:

Customization and branding: One of the key advantages of using ChatGPT to create chatbots for your small or medium-sized business is the ability to customize and brand the conversational experience. By tailoring the chatbot's language, tone, and personality to align with your company's values and target audience, you can create a unique and engaging interaction that reinforces your brand identity. This level of customization helps foster a stronger connection between your customers and your business, leading to increased loyalty and trust.

Integration with existing systems: Implementing a ChatGPT-powered chatbot can be seamlessly integrated with your existing customer support systems, such as your website, social media channels, or messaging platforms. This integration allows for a unified and consistent customer experience across all touchpoints, making it easier for customers to access the information and support they need. By leveraging the power of ChatGPT, you can streamline your support processes, reduce the workload on your human agents, and ensure that customers receive timely and accurate assistance, regardless of the channel they choose to interact with your business.

Continuous learning and improvement: One of the most significant benefits of using ChatGPT for your SMB's chatbot is its ability to learn and improve over time. As the chatbot engages with more customers and encounters a wider variety of questions and scenarios, it can adapt and refine its responses to better serve your customers' needs. By regularly reviewing the chatbot's interactions and incorporating customer feedback, you can identify areas for improvement and fine-tune the chatbot's knowledge base to address any gaps or inconsistencies. This continuous learning process ensures that your chatbot remains up-to-date, relevant, and effective in providing the support your customers need, ultimately contributing to the growth and success of your business.

In this section we're giving you 20 potential prompt threads, that you might want to use to inform your ChatBot, so get ready:

1. How do I set up my new account on your platform?
2. What is the return policy for your products?
3. How do I reset my password if I've forgotten it?
4. Can you provide instructions for assembling your product?
5. What are the key features of your service plan?
6. How do I contact customer support for further assistance?
7. Can I change my order after it's been placed?
8. What are your shipping options and estimated delivery times?
9. How do I apply a promo code to my purchase?
10. Are there any known compatibility issues with your software?
11. Provide a step-by-step solution for resetting a user's password.
12. Explain the process of upgrading to a premium subscription.
13. Address a customer's concerns about data privacy and security.
14. Troubleshoot a common issue with our software installation.
15. Guide a customer through setting up their new account.

16. Explain the benefits and features of our product to a potential customer.
17. Offer tips for optimizing the use of our product or service.
18. Provide assistance with processing a return or refund request.
19. Respond to a customer inquiry about billing or payment issues.
20. Offer a detailed comparison between two of our product offerings.

Ensure that the AI chatbot has an up-to-date knowledge base and can accurately address customer inquiries. Monitor interactions to ensure the chatbot provides appropriate information. Also, be prepared to redirect customers to human support when necessary.

Also don't forget to review Appendix 3, where we teach you how to create your own custom Chatbot in the form of a GPT.

Further Resources:

1. Chatbot Magazine (https://chatbotsmagazine.com/) - Offers news, insights, and tips for chatbot development.
2. MobileMonkey (https://mobilemonkey.com/blog) - Blog with resources on chatbot marketing and development.
3. Drift Blog (https://www.drift.com/blog/) - Shares insights, tips, and strategies for conversational marketing, including chatbot development.
4. Chatbot Tutorials (https://chatbotslife.com/) - A resource for chatbot developers, featuring tutorials, news, and insights.
5. Zendesk (https://www.zendesk.com/) - Offers customer support software and resources.

6. Freshdesk (https://freshdesk.com/) - Provides a customer support platform and resources.

7. Help Scout (https://www.helpscout.com/) - Offers customer support software and resources.

8. "The Effortless Experience" by Matthew Dixon, Nick Toman, and Rick DeLisi (https://amzn.to/41bSHsC) - Book on providing exceptional customer support and reducing customer effort.

Use Case 10:

Social Media Management

Social media is in a constant state of flux. What worked to get traction on posts and ads six months ago likely doesn't work today. Utilize ChatGPT to manage your company's social media presence, from generating engaging content and post ideas to crafting compelling captions, hashtags, and responses to comments or messages. This is one thing AI can stay on top of since it can see the overarching patterns we can't. It will save time, maintain a consistent posting schedule, and increase audience engagement.

HubSpot and Canva can be powerful tools to augment ChatGPT when managing your company's social media presence. Here's how:

HubSpot integration: HubSpot is a comprehensive inbound marketing, sales, and customer service platform that can help you streamline your social media efforts. By integrating ChatGPT with HubSpot, you can:

1. Automatically publish ChatGPT-generated content to your social media channels using HubSpot's social media management tools.
2. Use HubSpot's analytics to track the performance of your ChatGPT-generated posts and gain insights into audience engagement, allowing you to refine your content strategy.
3. Leverage HubSpot's CRM to personalize your ChatGPT-generated responses to comments and messages, ensuring a more tailored and engaging interaction with your followers.

Canva integration: Canva is a user-friendly graphic design platform that allows you to create visually stunning images and videos for your social media posts. Integrating Canva with ChatGPT can help you:

1. Create eye-catching visuals to accompany your ChatGPT-generated post ideas and captions, increasing the likelihood of audience engagement and shares.
2. Maintain a consistent visual brand identity across your social media channels by using Canva's brand kit feature in conjunction with ChatGPT's ability to maintain a consistent brand voice and tone.
3. Repurpose ChatGPT-generated content into various visual formats, such as infographics, short videos, or

Instagram stories, using Canva's templates and design tools.

By leveraging the capabilities of HubSpot and Canva alongside ChatGPT, you can create a powerful, integrated social media management workflow that saves time, enhances your brand's online presence, and ultimately drives better results for your business. This combination of tools allows you to focus on the strategic aspects of your social media marketing while automating and optimizing the content creation and distribution process.

Of course, you don't need to use HubSpot or Canva to leverage the power of AI.

Here are some prompts that you can use directly inside ChatGPT. Further, since this is such a big subject, we decided to again give you 20 powerful questions to ask AI for your social media management:

1. Write an engaging caption for our latest product release announcement on Instagram.
2. Suggest five X (Twitter) post ideas related to our industry.
3. Draft a LinkedIn post highlighting our recent company achievement.
4. Create a series of Facebook post ideas for our upcoming event or promotion.
5. Help me respond to a customer inquiry or comment on social media.
6. Generate a list of relevant hashtags for our Instagram campaign.
7. Write a social media post announcing a new blog article on our website.

8. Create a series of engaging questions or polls for our audience on X.
9. Draft a LinkedIn post promoting a job opening at our company.
10. Write a social media post celebrating a company milestone or anniversary.
11. Write a social media post to promote our latest product launch.
12. Develop a list of hashtag suggestions for our industry or niche.
13. Suggest strategies for increasing engagement on our Instagram account.
14. Create a series of tweet ideas to showcase our company culture.
15. Write a LinkedIn post highlighting company insights.
16. Develop a monthly social media content calendar.
17. Suggest potential collaborations or partnerships for social media campaigns.
18. Write a Facebook post sharing insights and polling customer prospects.
19. Create a list of social media post ideas focused on customer success stories.
20. Write a social media caption for a behind-the-scenes photo of our team.

When requesting social media management assistance from an AI, provide specific information about the platform, desired tone, and content objectives. X (formerly Twitter) is different from Facebook, which is different from LinkedIn. A post on one won't necessarily be appropriate or functional on another platform. If the AI-generated content is unsatisfactory or off-brand, consider refining your prompt or asking for revisions to better align with your company's voice and goals.

Further Resources:

1. Hootsuite Blog (https://blog.hootsuite.com/) - Offers social media management tips and resources.
2. Sprout Social Blog (https://sproutsocial.com/insights/) - Shares insights and best practices on social media marketing.
3. Buffer Blog (https://buffer.com/resources/) - Provides social media marketing tips and resources.
4. "Jab, Jab, Jab, Right Hook" by Gary Vaynerchuk (https://amzn.to/3MOKNRD) - Book on creating effective social media content.

Use Case 11:

Content Curation

Content is king.

Good content, that is.

That phrase, 'Content is King,' underscores the immense value of high-quality content in driving audience engagement, brand loyalty, and overall success. However, the emphasis must be on 'Good' content—content that is relevant, informative, and engaging. Good content serves as the cornerstone of effective communication, enabling businesses to connect with their target audience on a deeper level. Whether it's through industry news, insightful articles, captivating videos, or thought-provoking podcasts, good content provides value to the audience, fostering trust and establishing the creator as a thought leader in their respective field.

To maximize the impact of good content, you can leverage AI tools like ChatGPT to curate and create content that resonates with your audience. ChatGPT assists in generating a variety of content types, from summarizing industry news to crafting detailed articles. It can even script engaging videos or produce compelling podcast scripts. This not only saves time but also ensures that the content is aligned with your company's interests and the audience's preferences. By harnessing the power of AI, you can consistently deliver high-quality, relevant content that keeps your customers engaged, enhances your online presence, and solidifies your position as an industry leader.

10 Potential Prompt Threads for Better Content:

1. Find and summarize three recent articles about the latest trends in our industry.
2. Curate a list of five relevant podcasts for our audience.
3. Identify and summarize the key takeaways from a popular industry report.
4. Recommend five YouTube channels that provide valuable content for our niche.
5. Curate a list of influential industry leaders or experts to follow on social media.
6. Find and summarize recent news articles related to our product or service.

7. Suggest three relevant industry conferences or events for our team to attend.
8. Identify five must-read books for professionals in our field.
9. Curate a list of insightful blog posts related to a specific topic in our industry.
10. Find and summarize recent research studies or whitepapers in our field.

When requesting content curation assistance from an AI, provide specific information about your industry, niche, and audience preferences. If the AI-generated content is not relevant or valuable, consider refining your prompt or providing additional context to better align with your target audience's interests.

Further Resources:

1. Feedly (https://feedly.com/) - Offers a content curation tool to discover and organize industry news, blogs, and publications.
2. Pocket (https://getpocket.com/) - Provides a platform for saving and curating articles, videos, and other content from the web.
3. "The Content Trap" by Bharat Anand (https://amzn.to/43z4OBj) - Book on the strategic importance of content in the digital age.
4. Content Marketing Institute (https://contentmarketinginstitute.com/) - Offers resources and insights on content marketing and curation.

Use Case 12:

Product Development and Improvement

Enhance your creativity and innovation with ChatGPT, leveraging its capabilities to assist in product development and improvement. ChatGPT can generate ideas for new features, suggest enhancements, and identify potential problem areas to address. Utilizing AI in this way fosters innovation, improves product-market fit, and helps maintain a competitive edge in the market.

By leveraging ChatGPT in product development, you can significantly enhance the ideation and innovation process by generating creative ideas for new features. You'll be able to quickly identify potential enhancements and pinpoint areas that need improvement. Your business can foster a culture of continuous innovation, ensuring that your products evolve to meet changing market demands and customer expectations.

ChatGPT can analyze vast amounts of data, uncovering trends and user feedback that may not be immediately apparent, thus improving product-market fit. This proactive approach not only helps in maintaining a competitive edge but also ensures that the product development process is aligned with the needs and desires of the target audience, leading to more successful and user-centric products.

10 Potential Prompt Threads:

1. Suggest five potential new features for our software platform.
2. Identify areas of improvement for our mobile app's user experience.
3. Brainstorm ways to increase the energy efficiency of our product.
4. Suggest potential integrations or partnerships to enhance our product's capabilities.
5. Generate ideas for expanding our product line to target new customer segments.
6. Help evaluate the pros and cons of a specific product feature.
7. Identify and address potential usability issues in our product design.
8. Brainstorm ways to improve our product's packaging or presentation.
9. Suggest potential improvements to our product's user onboarding process.
10. Evaluate our product against competitor offerings and suggest areas for improvement.

There are a lot of nuances when it comes to product development, but AI will allow you to process a lot of ideas quickly.

You're more likely to find something worthwhile from 1,000 concepts versus only 100. That's what AI will allow you to do. As always, when requesting product development and improvement assistance, provide specific information about your product and what you want that product to accomplish. Ask detailed questions, and you're likely to achieve better results.

Further Resources:

1. Mind the Product (https://www.mindtheproduct.com/) - Offers resources and insights on product management and development.
2. "Inspired: How to Create Tech Products Customers Love" by Marty Cagan - Book on product management and development best practices.
3. Product Hunt (https://www.producthunt.com/) - Provides a platform for discovering and showcasing new products and features.
4. "The Lean Startup" by Eric Ries (https://amzn.to/41kkyX8) - Book on creating and managing successful startups and product development.

Use Case 13:

Human Resources and Recruitment

For many years, I have honed my skills in identifying and hiring top talent, culminating in writing a bestselling book, "The Talent Palette: Your Business Guide to Hiring Difference-Making Employees." Based on this experience and exploring the use of AI in talent selection, I can confidently say that AI is an invaluable tool in the hiring process. AI streamlines the creation of comprehensive hiring materials, from requirements documents to marketing materials, screening questions, and testing methods.

Research indicates that using algorithms to evaluate multiple facets of a job candidate's knowledge, skills, and abilities (KSAs) significantly outperforms human intuition in selecting potential hires. This underscores the value of using tools like ChatGPT to optimize human resources and recruitment processes. By leveraging AI to define job requirements, draft compelling job descriptions, and identify effective candidate sourcing channels, companies can save time, enhance the candidate experience, and streamline the hiring process for greater efficiency and effectiveness. You can even use artificial intelligence to screen resumes, formulate interview questions, develop situational and knowledge tests, and create comprehensive onboarding materials.

Earlier in this book I demonstrated "Layered Prompt Journeys" to help find difference-making talent as an example. If you are interested in identifying, screening, testing, and inspecting talent prior to hire, I strongly suggest you return to the Two Stepwise Prompt Journeys section from the early pages of this book. Pay close attention to *Layered Prompt Journey Example 2: Using AI to Define Requirements and Questions to Screen and Select High-Performing Employee Candidates.*

By following a layered prompt journey, you can leverage AI to identify high-performer traits, craft compelling position descriptions, brainstorm candidate sourcing locations, and develop effective behavioral interview questions. This approach not only simplifies the hiring process but also enhances the ability to find and identify great prospective employees, making the process significantly more efficient and aligned with your company's needs and values.

The demonstration shown previously in this book relays a step-by-step prompt example of a layered prompt for HR, that you can use to identify requirements, position descriptions, marketing materials, screening questions, and methods to test and inspect the talent you have attracted to your open position. You might consider using those prompt stems using your own company hiring needs as examples.

In this section we identify 10 additional HR prompt threads that will help you hire superior executives and sales personnel:

1. For a business of my size and industry, what are the 10 KPIs that I should most focus on?
2. Suggest five interview questions to assess a candidate's problem-solving skills and technical knowledge.
3. Create an onboarding checklist for new employees.
4. Draft a welcome email for new hires.
5. Identify key skills and qualifications in a candidate's resume.
6. Write a rejection email for unsuccessful job applicants.
7. Suggest potential improvements to our employee training program.
8. Create a list of team-building activities for remote employees.
9. Help develop a survey to gather employee feedback on company culture.
10. Suggest strategies for promoting diversity and inclusion in our hiring process.

Human resources and recruitment can be very personal aspects of your business, so always make sure to edit and verify all potential correspondence have the proper tone. This is of course something you would want to do even if you weren't using AI. Provide specific information about the role, company culture, and desired outcomes for all job opening posts. If the AI-generated content doesn't align with your HR goals, check the questions you asked, and the prompts given to verify what you may have left out.

Preventing Bias in Hiring

Hiring the right talent is crucial for the success of any small to medium-sized business (SMB). However, the hiring process is often susceptible to various biases that can impede the selection of the best candidates. Biases such as authority bias, confirmation bias, the horns and halo effect, and non-evidence-based heuristics can distort decision-making and result in suboptimal hires. To combat these issues, it is essential to implement a structured, objective, and transparent hiring process. This guide outlines ten practical steps that SMBs can adopt to minimize bias and ensure a fair and equitable talent selection process.

These steps include starting with well-defined job requirements, establishing clear criteria for evaluation, anonymizing applications, and using standardized interviews. Additionally, evaluating AI tools for potential biases, implementing feedback mechanisms, monitoring hiring outcomes, and committing to continuous learning about bias prevention are vital. Providing bias training for all involved in hiring and adhering to SHRM best practices and local laws further strengthens the process. By integrating these measures, SMBs can create a more inclusive hiring environment that not only attracts but also selects the best talent based on merit and qualifications.

Throughout the remainder of this section, you will see the word 'heuristic.' In the context of business, a heuristic is a simple, efficient rule or method used to make decisions and solve problems quickly. These rules of thumb are based on practical experience rather than theoretical knowledge and can sometimes lead to biases if not carefully managed. For example, consider a restaurant owner who is hiring a new chef. The owner might use the heuristic, "I never hire chefs with visible tattoos because I believe they don't fit the image of my upscale restaurant." This heuristic simplifies the hiring decision process but can lead to non-evidence-based biases. In reality, having tattoos has no impact on a chef's cooking skills or professional performance. By relying on this heuristic, the restaurant owner may miss out on highly skilled candidates who could greatly benefit the restaurant.

In this book, our goal is to outline a meritocratic approach to talent selection, ensuring that the best candidates are chosen based on their abilities and merit. We rely on HR scholarly research, SHRM best practices, and other evidence-based decision-making criteria to guide this process. By implementing these strategies, we aim to create a fair and unbiased hiring environment. Here are 10 ways to make your talent selection process less prone to bias:

10 Steps to Make Your Talent Selection Process Less Prone to Bias

1. **Start with Well-Defined Requirements Documents**: Clearly define the job requirements and qualifications to ensure all candidates are evaluated against the same standards. This helps mitigate biases such as authority bias by focusing on predefined criteria rather than personal recommendations.

2. **Define Clear Criteria**: Establish clear, objective criteria for evaluating candidates, reducing subjective judgment. This helps avoid confirmation bias by ensuring all evaluations are based on consistent standards rather than early impressions.

3. **Anonymize Applications**: Remove identifying information from applications (e.g., names, gender, age) to focus on qualifications and experience. This reduces the impact of biases such as the halo effect and non-evidence-based heuristics.

4. **Standardized Interviews**: Use structured interviews with standardized questions to ensure fairness. This minimizes the influence of the horns and halo effect by maintaining a consistent interview format for all candidates.

5. **Evaluate AI Tools**: Regularly evaluate AI tools for biases and ensure they align with diversity and inclusion goals,

emphasizing tools with demonstrated "no adverse impact" statements. This helps prevent reliance on non-evidence-based heuristics by using validated and tested tools.

6. **Feedback Mechanisms**: Implement mechanisms for candidates and employees to provide feedback on the hiring process. This helps identify and address any instances of authority bias or other biases that may have influenced decisions.

7. **Monitor Outcomes**: Track hiring outcomes to identify and address any disparities or patterns of bias. This ongoing monitoring can reveal the presence of confirmation bias or other biases in the selection process.

8. **Continuous Learning**: Stay informed about the latest research and best practices in bias prevention and AI ethics, adapting your processes accordingly. This helps prevent the use of outdated or biased heuristics.

9. **Bias Training**: Train all involved in hiring on unconscious bias and its impacts. This includes educating them on specific biases such as authority bias, confirmation bias, the horns and halo effect, and the use of non-evidence-based heuristics.

10. **Follow SHRM Best Practices and Local Laws**: Adhere to the Society for Human Resource Management (SHRM) best practices and always seek to reference and comply with local laws and regulations when conducting placements in a given geography. This ensures that the hiring process is aligned with established standards and reduces the likelihood of biased decision-making.

By integrating awareness of specific biases into these steps, organizations can further reduce the potential for bias in their talent selection processes and promote a fairer and more equitable hiring environment.

Further Resources:

1. SHRM (https://www.shrm.org/) - Society for Human Resource Management offers resources and insights on HR best practices.
2. "Work Rules!" by Laszlo Bock (https://amzn.to/3UEV052) - Book on human resources and management strategies at Google.
3. HR Dive (https://www.hrdive.com/) - Provides news, analysis, and resources on human resources trends and best practices.
4. "The Talent Code" by Daniel Coyle (https://amzn.to/41lRChC) - Book on nurturing talent and skill development in organizations.
5. "The Talent Palette" by Severin Sorensen (in press, May 2023). A book about identifying and capturing difference making top talent, and the methods to attract, screen, test, and select them.

Use Case 14:

Sales Enablement

Sales enablement is the set of tools and content you provide your sales team so they can accelerate overall company transactions. You can employ ChatGPT to enhance your sales enablement efforts by generating sales scripts, email templates, objection-handling techniques, or product comparisons. AI helps improve sales effectiveness, shortens sales cycles, and increases win rates.

When it comes to leveraging ChatGPT for sales enablement in an SMB, there are several key areas where the AI can help your sales team be more effective, efficient, and customer-focused. Here are some ways you can use ChatGPT to boost your sales enablement efforts:

Personalized sales scripts: ChatGPT can generate tailored sales scripts based on your target audience, product or service, and unique selling points. By providing the AI with relevant information about your customers and offerings, it can create scripts that resonate with your prospects, address their specific pain points, and highlight the benefits of your solutions. This level of personalization can help your sales team build stronger connections with potential customers and increase the likelihood of closing deals.

Dynamic email templates: Email outreach is a crucial component of many sales processes. ChatGPT can help your team craft compelling, engaging, and persuasive email templates that are optimized for open rates and responses. By analyzing successful email campaigns and incorporating best practices, the AI can generate templates that are more likely to capture your prospects' attention and encourage them to act. Additionally, ChatGPT can help personalize these templates for individual prospects, further increasing their effectiveness.

Comprehensive product comparisons: In today's competitive landscape, it's essential for your sales team to articulate how your products or services stand out from the competition. ChatGPT can generate detailed, accurate, and persuasive product comparisons that highlight your unique value proposition and the specific benefits your offerings provide. By equipping your sales team with these comprehensive comparisons, you enable them to better position your solutions against competitors and help prospects understand why your products or services are the best fit for their needs.

Real-time sales support: ChatGPT can be integrated into your sales team's workflow to provide real-time support and guidance during customer interactions. Whether it's quickly generating responses to unexpected questions, suggesting additional resources to share with prospects, or offering insights on how to move a conversation forward, the AI can be your virtual sales assistant. This real-time support helps your team navigate complex sales situations, reduce response times, and ultimately close more deals.

Intelligent objection handling: One of the most significant challenges sales teams face is effectively addressing customer objections. ChatGPT can be trained on a wide range of common objections and provide your team with intelligent, persuasive responses. By analyzing past successful objection-handling techniques and incorporating insights from your industry and target market, the AI will generate responses that are more likely to overcome hesitations and move prospects closer to a sale. This can help your sales team navigate difficult conversations with confidence and increase their win rates.

Creating a GPT for Q&A and Customer-Facing AI Helpdesk with ChatGPT

Intelligent Objection Handling: One of the most significant challenges customer service teams face is effectively addressing customer objections and inquiries. ChatGPT can be trained on a wide range of common objections and provide your team with intelligent, persuasive responses. By analyzing past successful objection-handling techniques and incorporating insights from your industry and target market, the AI will generate responses that are more likely to overcome hesitations and resolve customer issues efficiently. This helps your customer service team navigate difficult conversations with confidence and improves overall customer satisfaction.

Personalized Customer Interactions: ChatGPT can be customized to understand and use customer data to create personalized interactions. By leveraging customer profiles, purchase history, and preferences, the AI can tailor responses to individual needs, making each interaction more relevant and engaging. This personalized approach not only enhances customer experience but also fosters loyalty and trust.

24/7 Availability: One of the key advantages of using ChatGPT for customer-facing roles is its ability to operate around the clock. Customers can receive immediate assistance at any time, reducing wait times and ensuring issues are resolved promptly. This 24/7 availability can significantly enhance customer satisfaction and support your global customer base effectively.

Consistent and Accurate Information: ChatGPT ensures that all customers receive consistent and accurate information. By providing a centralized knowledge base and regularly updating the AI with the latest product and service information, you can maintain high standards of accuracy in customer responses. This consistency helps in building a reliable brand image and reduces the risk of misinformation.

Scalability: ChatGPT can handle multiple customer interactions simultaneously, making it an ideal solution for businesses looking to scale their customer support operations without proportional increases in staffing costs. This scalability ensures that your support team can manage high volumes of inquiries during peak times without compromising on quality.

Efficient Knowledge Management: ChatGPT can be integrated with your existing knowledge management systems to retrieve and deliver relevant information quickly. By accessing FAQs, user manuals, and troubleshooting guides, the AI can provide immediate solutions to common problems, reducing the need for escalations and freeing up human agents to focus on more complex issues.

Feedback and Improvement: Implementing ChatGPT also provides valuable insights into customer behavior and preferences. By analyzing interaction data, you can identify trends, common issues, and areas for improvement. This feedback loop allows you to continually refine the AI's responses and overall customer service strategy, leading to continuous improvement in customer experience.

Training and Onboarding: New customer service representatives can benefit from ChatGPT's capabilities as a training tool. The AI can simulate various customer scenarios, allowing new hires to practice and develop their skills in a controlled environment. This can accelerate the onboarding process and ensure that new team members are well-prepared to handle real customer interactions effectively.

For more information on how to create your own Customer GPT with the capabilities described above please read *Appendix 3: How To Create Your Own Context-Specific GPT.*

In summary, leveraging ChatGPT to create a Q&A and customer-facing answerbot can transform your customer service operations by providing intelligent objection handling, personalized interactions, 24/7 availability, consistent information, scalability, efficient knowledge management, valuable feedback, and enhanced training. These benefits collectively lead to higher customer satisfaction, increased efficiency, and improved overall performance of your customer support team.

By leveraging ChatGPT across these various aspects of sales enablement, your company can equip your sales team with the tools, content, and support they need to be more effective. This, in turn, will lead to shorter sales cycles, higher win rates, and overall increased revenue for your business (and that's what you want, right?).

Now let's explore examples of how AI can help with specific sales enablement tasks today. Here are 10 Potential Prompt Threads:

1. Write a sales script for cold calling potential clients.
2. Draft a follow-up email template after a sales meeting or presentation.
3. Suggest five techniques for handling common sales objections.
4. Create a comparison chart between our product and a competitor's offering.
5. Write a persuasive sales pitch for our product or service.
6. Develop a set of qualifying questions to identify potential customers.
7. Provide a list of key selling points for our product to use in sales conversations.
8. Draft an email template to re-engage with a prospect who has gone silent.
9. Suggest strategies for building rapport with potential clients.
10. Create a list of success stories or case studies to share with prospects.

When requesting sales enablement assistance, provide specific information about your product, target audience, and sales process. If you get stuck, simply rephrase your prompt with a few different words. Something simple like that can completely change the AI's content outcome.

Further Resources:

1. HubSpot Sales Blog (https://blog.hubspot.com/sales) - Offers resources and insights on sales strategies and best practices.
2. "The Challenger Sale" by Matthew Dixon and Brent Adamson (https://amzn.to/3MKyxl4) - Book on sales techniques for complex sales environments.
3. Sales Hacker (https://www.saleshacker.com/) - Provides resources, articles, and webinars on sales enablement and strategies.
4. "SPIN Selling" by Neil Rackham (https://amzn.to/3GJClzg) - Book on a research-based sales approach focused on situation, problem, implication, and need-payoff.

Use Case 15:

Project Management Assistance

Once again, the power of AI truly comes out when dealing with time-consuming tasks that chew up the hours. Generating task lists, schedules, risk assessments, or progress reports should become the purview of artificial intelligence in your company. AI can help improve project organization, ensure timely completion, and optimize resource allocation.

When it comes to project management assistance for SMBs, ChatGPT is a game-changer. I've seen it streamline processes in many of my client's businesses, enhance their efficiency, and ensure better resource allocation. Here's how ChatGPT can help SMBs in various aspects of project management:

Generating comprehensive task lists: ChatGPT can create detailed, well-structured task lists based on project requirements, goals, and timelines. By inputting key project information, such as objectives, deliverables, and resources, the AI can generate a comprehensive breakdown of tasks required to complete the project successfully. This helps ensure that no critical steps are overlooked and that all team members have a clear understanding of their responsibilities.

Creating optimized project schedules: Effective project scheduling is crucial for meeting deadlines and managing resources efficiently. ChatGPT can analyze task dependencies, resource availability, and time constraints to generate optimized project schedules. By considering factors such as task durations, predecessor-successor relationships, and resource capacity, the AI can help create schedules that minimize delays, reduce bottlenecks, and ensure a smooth flow of work throughout the project lifecycle.

Conducting thorough risk assessments: AI can assist small and medium-sized businesses in conducting comprehensive risk assessments by analyzing project data, industry trends, and historical information. The AI can generate a list of potential risks, assess their likelihood and impact, and suggest appropriate mitigation strategies. This proactive approach to risk management can help SMBs avoid costly setbacks and ensure project success.

Generating insightful progress reports: Keeping stakeholders informed about project progress is essential for maintaining transparency and accountability. ChatGPT generates clear, concise, and informative progress reports that highlight key achievements, challenges, and upcoming milestones. By automatically pulling data from project management tools and incorporating insights from team members, the AI can create reports that provide a comprehensive overview of the project's status, enabling better decision-making and course correction when necessary.

Optimizing resource allocation: Efficient resource allocation is critical for maximizing productivity and minimizing costs in project management. Let ChatGPT analyze your project requirements, team member skills, and resource availability to recommend optimal allocation strategies. By considering factors such as workload balancing, skill matching, and cost optimization, the AI can help SMBs ensure that the right resources are assigned to the right tasks at the right time, leading to improved project outcomes and better resource utilization.

By leveraging ChatGPT for these project management tasks, SMBs can significantly reduce the time and effort required to plan, execute, and monitor projects. This allows project managers and team members to focus on higher-value activities, such as strategic planning, stakeholder engagement, and innovation. Moreover, by automating routine tasks and providing intelligent recommendations, ChatGPT can help SMBs improve project quality, reduce errors, and increase overall project success rates.

Learn from these 10 potential prompt threads for project management:

1. Create a task list for launching a new marketing campaign.
2. Develop a project timeline for a website redesign.
3. Identify potential risks and mitigation strategies for a software development project.
4. Write a progress report for a client on the status of their project.
5. Suggest strategies for improving team communication during a project.
6. Provide a list of tools and resources for effective project management.

7. Develop a process for tracking and reporting project milestones.
8. Create a checklist for closing out a completed project.
9. Suggest methods for prioritizing tasks and allocating resources effectively.
10. Identify potential bottlenecks or delays in a project plan.

When requesting project management assistance, provide specific information about the project, goals, and desired outcomes. If the AI-generated content is not relevant or useful, consider refining your prompt or providing additional context to better align with your project management needs.

Further Resources:

1. Project Management Institute (https://www.pmi.org/) - Offers resources, certifications, and insights on project management best practices.
2. "The Lean Startup" by Eric Ries (https://amzn.to/41kkyX8) - Book on creating and managing successful startups and project development.
3. "Making Things Happen" by Scott Berkun (https://amzn.to/3zVuSJz) - Book on project management strategies and techniques.
4. Trello (https://trello.com/) - Provides a project management tool for organizing tasks and tracking progress.

Use Case 16:

Training and Development

Training materials, tutorials, and educational resources for both employees and customers, or even business partners, are a key aspect of any industry. It is best these materials meet legal requirements and are clear and concise. AI can help augment the learning experience, reduce the time required to create training materials, and ensure a more consistent understanding of key concepts. And when it comes to making sure all legal requirements are included to protect your company? AI has you covered. Just remember to have your attorney look everything over to be safe.

When it comes to corporate and individual training and development for SMBs, ChatGPT can be an invaluable tool for creating high-quality, engaging, and legally compliant educational resources. Here's how ChatGPT can assist SMBs in various aspects of training and development:

Generating tailored training materials: ChatGPT can create customized training materials based on your company's specific needs, industry, and target audience. By inputting key information about your business, products, services, and training objectives, the AI can generate comprehensive, easy-to-understand content that aligns with your brand voice and messaging. This tailored approach ensures that your training materials resonate with your employees, customers, or partners, leading to better knowledge retention and application.

Developing interactive tutorials: Engaging, interactive tutorials are essential for effective learning and skill development. ChatGPT can help SMBs create dynamic, step-by-step tutorials that guide learners through complex processes or concepts. By leveraging the AI's natural language processing capabilities, you can generate tutorials that are clear, concise, and easy to follow. Additionally, ChatGPT can suggest interactive elements, such as quizzes, simulations, or hands-on exercises, to reinforce learning and keep participants actively engaged. Imagine creating a fun experience instead of something seen as a drudgery by everyone involved.

Ensuring legal and regulatory compliance: Staying up-to-date with legal and regulatory requirements is crucial for SMBs, especially when it comes to training and development. ChatGPT can help ensure that your training materials comply with relevant laws, regulations, and industry standards. By inputting specific legal and regulatory requirements, the AI can generate content that accurately reflects these guidelines, minimizing the risk of non-compliance and potential legal issues. This is particularly valuable for SMBs that may not have dedicated legal or compliance teams.

Personalizing learning experiences: Every learner has unique needs, preferences, and learning styles. By analyzing data on learner performance and engagement, the AI can suggest specific learning paths, resources, or activities that cater to each individual's needs. This personalized approach can lead to higher learner satisfaction, improved knowledge retention, and better on-the-job performance.

Facilitating continuous learning and development: Continuous learning and development are essential for SMBs to stay competitive and adapt to evolving market demands. By leveraging the AI's ability to process vast amounts of data and identify key insights, SMBs can ensure that their training materials remain relevant, accurate, and aligned with their business goals.

Using AI in training and development not only saves time and effort but also ensures that employees, customers, and partners receive consistent, engaging, and legally compliant training. Moreover, by personalizing learning experiences and facilitating continuous development, ChatGPT can help SMBs foster a culture of learning, innovation, and growth, ultimately leading to improved business performance and long-term success.

10 Potential Prompt Threads:

1. Write a tutorial on how to use a specific feature of our software.
2. Develop a training module on effective communication skills.
3. Create a quiz to assess employees' understanding of company policies.
4. Write a user guide for our product, focusing on setup and basic operations.

5. Suggest five interactive activities for a team-building workshop.
6. Develop a training plan for onboarding new employees.
7. Create a list of resources for employees to improve their professional skills.
8. Write a script for a training video on customer service best practices.
9. Develop a training module on diversity and inclusion in the workplace.
10. Write a step-by-step guide for troubleshooting a common issue with our product.

As you can see from the potential prompts we've given, it's easy to make sure you meet all legal requirements in your documents and keep an eye on diversity as well. If your HR professional is up to date on your current industry standards in these areas, it shouldn't be a problem making sure the AI covers all your bases.

Further Resources:

1. Lynda (https://www.lynda.com/) - Offers online courses in a variety of professional skills and topics.
2. "The Fifth Discipline" by Peter Senge (https://amzn.to/3L0yVKQ) - Book on fostering learning organizations and continuous improvement.
3. Training Industry (https://trainingindustry.com/) - Provides resources, insights, and best practices on corporate training and development.
4. "The Adult Learner" by Malcolm Knowles, Elwood Holton, and Richard Swanson (https://amzn.to/4093Etq) - Book on adult learning principles and strategies.

Use Case 17:

Internal Communications

ChatGPT and other AI platforms are perfect tools to enhance internal communications within your organization. What this looks like is drafting company announcements, newsletters, meeting agendas, or employee recognition messages. One of the biggest factors is how artificial intelligence can help improve communication efficiency, maintain a positive work environment, and keep employees informed and engaged.

When it comes to internal communications, ChatGPT and other AI platforms can be invaluable tools for SMBs looking to improve communication efficiency, foster a positive work environment, and keep employees informed and engaged. Here are some key areas where SMBs can leverage AI to enhance their internal communications:

Drafting clear and concise company announcements: AI can help you create well-structured, informative, and engaging company announcements. By inputting key details about the announcement, such as the purpose, target audience, and desired tone, the AI can generate clear messages that effectively convey important information to employees. This not only saves time for managers and HR professionals but also ensures that all employees receive consistent and easily understandable updates.

Creating engaging employee newsletters: Regular employee newsletters are an excellent way to keep staff informed about company news, events, and achievements. ChatGPT can assist in generating compelling newsletter content that resonates with employees and encourages engagement. By analyzing past successful newsletters and incorporating best practices for employee communication, the AI can suggest topics, layouts, and storytelling techniques that capture employees' attention and foster a sense of community within the organization.

Preparing effective meeting agendas: Meetings are generally boring. Don't sugarcoat it. But they can at least be made more effective with the help of your artificial intelligence assistant. Well-structured meeting agendas are crucial for ensuring productive and efficient meetings (whether boring or not). By inputting key meeting details and desired outcomes, the AI can generate agendas that keep meetings focused, on track, and aligned with organizational goals. This not only saves time for meeting organizers but also helps ensure that all participants come prepared and ready to contribute.

Crafting thoughtful employee recognition messages: Recognizing and appreciating employees' hard work and achievements is essential for maintaining a positive work environment and boosting morale. ChatGPT can help companies craft personalized, heartfelt employee recognition messages that showcase the company's appreciation for individual contributions. By analyzing employee performance data and incorporating insights on effective recognition techniques, the AI can generate messages that are tailored to each employee's unique strengths and accomplishments. This will foster a culture of gratitude and motivation from the executive suite down to the production floor.

Providing communication coaching and feedback: ChatGPT's emotional intelligence training can be leveraged to provide communication coaching and feedback to managers and employees. By analyzing written communication samples, such as emails or chat messages, the AI can offer suggestions on how to improve clarity, tone, and effectiveness. This real-time feedback can help individuals become better communicators and develop stronger professional relationships within the organization.

Identifying communication pain points: Pinpoint specific areas where communication challenges exist, such as unclear announcements, low newsletter engagement, or unproductive meetings.

Defining communication goals: Establish clear objectives for internal communications, such as increasing employee engagement, streamlining information sharing, or fostering a more positive work culture.

Training AI on company-specific context: Provide ChatGPT with relevant information about your company's culture, values, and communication preferences to ensure generated content aligns with your organization's unique identity.

Encouraging employee feedback: Regularly seek input from employees on the effectiveness of AI-generated communications and use this feedback to refine and improve the AI's outputs over time. Your employees will likely notice things you don't. Listen to them and use their contributions to refocus your AI efforts.

Additionally, for corporate communications, I encourage you to consider creating your own company-specific or situation specific GPTs that will carry your voice and message with consistency. Go to *Appendix 3: How To Create Your Own Context-Specific GPT* for the 'how-to' create your own GPT advice.

Now for some sensible prompts you can use today with ChatGPT you might find value in the these:

1. Draft a company-wide announcement regarding a new product launch.
2. Create a monthly newsletter highlighting departmental achievements and updates.
3. Write a meeting agenda for an upcoming team retreat.
4. Develop an email recognizing an employee's outstanding performance.
5. Suggest ideas for a regular internal communication series to keep employees informed.
6. Create a list of topics for a company-wide town hall meeting.
7. Write a memo outlining a new company policy or procedure.
8. Develop an email template for sharing project updates with stakeholders.
9. Suggest strategies for improving cross-departmental communication.

10. Write a script for a video message from the CEO to employees.

If the AI-generated scripts aren't applicable or successful, consider retooling your prompt or providing additional context to better align with your company's communication goals. Adapt the synopsis, potential prompts, cautions, and resources to suit each specific application.

Further Resources:

1. Slack (https://slack.com/) - Provides a platform for team communication and collaboration.
2. "Crucial Conversations" by Kerry Patterson, Joseph Grenny, Ron McMillan, and Al Switzler (https://amzn.to/3KXUonJ) - Book on effective communication strategies for high-stakes conversations.
3. Ragan Communications (https://www.ragan.com/) - Offers resources, insights, and best practices on internal communications and employee engagement.
4. "Made to Stick" by Chip Heath and Dan Heath (https://amzn.to/3A2BRAp) - Book on creating memorable and impactful messages.

Use Case 18:

Customer Support and Service

Some of the most successful companies in the world have cornered their respective markets, not by being the cheapest, but by offering the best service. If you can enhance your customer service, you can become a powerhouse in your industry. AI can generate response templates, troubleshooting guides, FAQ content, or customer satisfaction survey materials that will help you achieve that goal.

When it comes to customer support and service, leveraging ChatGPT can be a game-changer for SMBs looking to improve customer experience, increase loyalty, and ultimately drive business growth. By utilizing AI-generated content, companies can provide faster, more accurate, and more consistent support to their customers. Let's explore how ChatGPT can help SMBs in various aspects of customer service:

Generating response templates: ChatGPT can create a wide range of response templates for common customer inquiries, complaints, or feedback. By training the AI on your company's products, services, and policies, it can generate accurate, on-brand responses that help customer service representatives (CSRs) quickly and effectively address customer needs. This not only saves time for CSRs but also ensures that customers receive consistent, high-quality support across all channels.

Developing comprehensive troubleshooting guides: Effective troubleshooting is essential for resolving customer issues and reducing support ticket volume. ChatGPT can help SMBs create detailed, step-by-step troubleshooting guides for common product or service issues. By leveraging the AI's ability to process large amounts of data and identify patterns, these guides can be continually updated and refined based on real-world customer experiences.

Creating informative FAQ content: As we showed in the FAQ section, a well-structured, comprehensive Frequently Asked Questions page on your website can significantly reduce the number of support inquiries. The FAQ enables customers to find answers to their questions independently. ChatGPT can assist in generating clear, concise, and informative FAQ content that addresses the most common customer concerns. By analyzing customer feedback, support tickets, and online forums, the AI identifies trending topics and suggests new FAQ entries to keep the knowledge base up-to-date and valuable for customers.

Generating customer satisfaction survey materials: Gathering and analyzing customer feedback is crucial for identifying areas for improvement and measuring the success of your customer service efforts. ChatGPT can help SMBs create effective customer satisfaction survey materials, including questionnaires, email templates, and follow-up messages. By incorporating best practices for survey design and leveraging the AI's language generation capabilities, SMBs can create engaging, personalized surveys that encourage customer participation and provide valuable insights.

And what will the impacts of implementing these AI techniques do for your business? Well keep reading and we'll tell you:

Increased customer retention: By providing fast, accurate, and consistent support, you can reduce customer frustration and increase satisfaction, leading to higher customer retention rates and long-term loyalty.

Positive word-of-mouth: Exceptional customer service experiences often lead to positive word-of-mouth recommendations, helping you attract new customers and grow your business organically.

Competitive advantage: In today's crowded market, outstanding customer service can set your business apart from competitors and create a strong brand reputation that drives customer preference and loyalty.

Reduced support costs: By enabling customers to find answers independently and equipping CSRs with efficient tools, you can reduce the time and resources required to handle support inquiries, ultimately lowering your customer service costs.

Valuable customer insights: By analyzing customer feedback and support data, you can gain valuable insights into customer needs, preferences, and pain points, enabling you to make data-driven decisions to improve your products, services, and overall customer experience.

Businesses should focus on continuously training the AI on their unique business context. You'll need to integrate AI-generated content into your existing support channels, and regularly monitor and refine the AI's outputs based on customer feedback and satisfaction metrics. By doing so, you can harness the power of AI to deliver exceptional customer experiences that drive loyalty, growth, and long-term success.

What would improving customer experience and loyalty do for your business? It's time to find out with 10 triggers to get AI cooking up new ideas for your 'customer experience' and turning it into 'customer delight.'

1. Write a customer service email template addressing a common issue.
2. Develop a troubleshooting guide for a specific product or service.
3. Create a list of frequently asked questions (FAQs) and their answers.
4. Write a follow-up email to a customer after resolving their issue.
5. Suggest strategies for improving customer satisfaction and loyalty.
6. Develop a list of potential customer service performance metrics.
7. Create a customer satisfaction survey to gather feedback on our support efforts.

8. Write a knowledge base article explaining a complex product feature.
9. Develop a list of potential customer service training topics or resources.
10. Suggest best practices for handling difficult or escalated customer situations.

For the best customer service and support assistance ideas, be specific with who your customers are. If you're a transport company, new customers aren't going to come from a segment of the population that has no need to transport material. Give AI the details it needs to provide you with the results you want. Specificity is king!

Further Resources:

1. "The Effortless Experience" by Matthew Dixon, Nick Toman, and Rick DeLisi (https://amzn.to/3UJQQsr) - Book on delivering exceptional customer service.
2. Customer Think (https://customerthink.com/) - Offers resources, insights, and best practices on customer service and experience.
3. "Delivering Happiness" by Tony Hsieh (https://amzn.to/3mt1K9v) - Book on building a customer-centric company culture.
4. Help Scout (https://www.helpscout.com/) - Provides resources, insights, and best practices on customer service and support.

Use Case 19:

Drafting Standard Operating Procedures (SOPs)

Anyone out there absolutely love drafting standard operating procedures that outline step-by-step processes for various tasks within your organization?

I'm willing to bet there are very few hands raised right now.

Let ChatGPT help you create clear, concise, and easy-to-follow instructions that ensure consistency, compliance, and efficiency across your team.

When it comes to improving the use of Standard Operating Procedures (SOPs) for small businesses, leveraging AI tools like ChatGPT can be a game-changer. By automating the creation and updating of SOPs, SMBs can save time, ensure consistency, and maintain compliance across their organization. Here's some advice on how your business can effectively use ChatGPT to enhance their SOPs:

Identify critical processes: Start by identifying the most critical and frequently performed processes within your organization that would benefit from clear, standardized procedures. These may include onboarding new employees, handling customer complaints, or managing inventory.

Gather relevant information: Collect all the necessary information related to each process, including step-by-step instructions, responsible parties, required resources, and any relevant regulations or guidelines. This information will serve as the foundation for training ChatGPT to generate comprehensive SOPs.

Train ChatGPT on your specific needs: Provide your artificial intelligence partner with the collected information and train it to generate SOPs that align with your organization's unique requirements. This may involve specifying the desired format, language, and level of detail for each SOP. By tailoring the AI's output to your specific needs, you can ensure that the generated SOPs are relevant, accurate, and easy to follow.

Integrate visual aids: Enhance the clarity and effectiveness of your SOPs by incorporating visual aids such as flowcharts, diagrams, or screenshots. ChatGPT can assist in generating text-based instructions for creating these visual elements, which can then be designed using tools like Canva or Visio. Visual aids can help break down complex processes into easy-to-understand steps, reducing the likelihood of errors or misinterpretation.

Establish a review and approval process: While ChatGPT can generate high-quality SOP drafts, it's essential to have a human review and approval process in place. Assign subject matter experts or experienced team members to review the AI-generated SOPs for accuracy and compliance with industry regulations. This review process ensures that the final SOPs are reliable, meeting your organization's standards.

Implement version control: As processes evolve over time, it's crucial to maintain version control of your SOPs. Use ChatGPT to help track and document changes made to each SOP, including the date of modification, the reason for the update, and the responsible party. This helps maintain a clear audit trail and ensures that all team members are referring to the most up-to-date version of each SOP.

Regularly review and update: Schedule periodic reviews of your SOPs to ensure they remain accurate, relevant, and aligned with current best practices. Utilize ChatGPT to assist in updating and refining your SOPs based on feedback from team members, changes in industry regulations, or improvements in technology. By keeping your SOPs up-to-date, you can maintain optimal efficiency and compliance within your organization.

By utilizing ChatGPT to create and manage SOPs, entire industries can streamline their operations, reduce errors, and ensure consistency between locations. This not only saves valuable time and resources but also promotes a culture of continuous improvement and excellence. Additionally, well-documented SOPs can serve as a valuable training tool for new employees, helping them quickly get up to speed and contribute to the organization's success.

To maximize the benefits of AI-powered SOPs, SMBs should prioritize open communication and collaboration among team members. Encourage feedback and suggestions for improving processes and updating SOPs. Make sure all team members have easy access to the most current versions of each SOP. By fostering a culture of transparency and continuous improvement, any business can fully realize the potential of AI in enhancing their standard operating procedures.

Check out these 10 Potential Prompt Threads:

1. Write an SOP for processing customer refunds.
2. Create a step-by-step guide for onboarding new employees.
3. Develop an SOP for handling customer complaints.
4. Provide instructions for conducting routine equipment maintenance.
5. Outline the process for submitting expense reports within the company.
6. Draft an SOP for conducting regular inventory checks.
7. Describe the steps for escalating technical issues to the IT department.
8. Write an SOP for updating the company's social media accounts.
9. Create guidelines for approving and publishing blog posts.
10. Develop a procedure for organizing and archiving important documents.

When requesting SOPs, be specific about the process and any unique requirements or compliance standards. From there, your HR specialist will need to ensure the AI-generated SOP is accurate, clear, and comprehensive. Review and revise the content as needed to guarantee it meets your organization's standards and expectations.

Further Resources:

1. Process Street (https://www.process.st/) - A platform for creating and managing SOPs, checklists, and workflows.
2. SweetProcess (https://www.sweetprocess.com/) - Offers tools and resources for documenting and managing standard operating procedures.
3. Tallyfy (https://tallyfy.com/) - A workflow and process management software with a focus on SOPs.
4. "Effective SOPs: Make Your Standard Operating Procedures Help Your Business Become More Productive" by Giles Johnston (https://amzn.to/40cA5Hv).

Use Case 20:

Market Research and Competitor Analysis

Employ ChatGPT to support market research and analysis efforts by generating competitor analyses. From there you can easily identify industry trends, summarize market reports, and brainstorm product or service improvement ideas. Imagine the wealth of documentation and investigation an AI can do in a matter of minutes, providing you with a broad look at your industry or international financial markets. Your ability to make informed decisions will be enhanced, allowing you to identify more opportunities, and maintain your competitive edge.

When it comes to conducting market research and competitive analysis, SMBs can greatly benefit from leveraging ChatGPT. By utilizing the AI's vast knowledge base and data processing capabilities, businesses can quickly gather and analyze valuable insights to inform their strategic decision-making. Here are some suggestions for SMBs looking to use ChatGPT for market research and competitive analysis:

Perform comprehensive competitor analyses: ChatGPT can help companies create in-depth competitor analyses by gathering and synthesizing information from various sources. The AI will look at company websites, news articles, and industry reports. By inputting key details about your competitors, such as their products, services, pricing, and target markets, ChatGPT can generate comprehensive profiles that highlight their strengths, weaknesses, and market positioning. This information will help you identify areas where you can differentiate your offerings and gain a competitive edge.

Identify and monitor industry trends: Staying up-to-date with the latest industry trends is crucial for SMBs to remain competitive and adapt to changing market conditions. ChatGPT can assist in identifying and monitoring these trends by analyzing large volumes of data from industry publications, social media, and online forums. By providing the AI with relevant keywords and topics, you can receive regular updates and summaries of emerging trends. With that kind of insight you can quickly spot opportunities or potential threats to your business.

Summarize market research reports: Conducting thorough market research often involves reading through lengthy reports and studies. ChatGPT can help your business save time by generating concise summaries of these documents, highlighting the most relevant insights and key takeaways. By inputting the full text of a market research report, you can quickly obtain a condensed version that captures the essential information needed to inform your decision-making process.

Brainstorm product or service improvement ideas: ChatGPT's creative capabilities can be harnessed to generate ideas for improving your existing products or services. By providing the AI with information about your current offerings, target market, and customer feedback, you can receive a wide range of suggestions for enhancements or even entirely new product lines. These ideas can serve as a starting point for further exploration and development, helping you stay ahead of the curve in meeting evolving customer needs.

Analyze customer sentiment and feedback: Understanding how customers perceive your brand, products, and services is essential for making informed decisions. Artificial intelligence can analyze customer sentiment by processing large volumes of online reviews, social media comments, and survey responses. By training the AI to identify positive, negative, and neutral sentiment, as well as key themes and trends, you can gain valuable insights into customer preferences.

To effectively implement ChatGPT for market research and competitive analysis, SMBs should:

1. Define clear research objectives and questions to guide the AI's output
2. Provide high-quality, relevant data sources for the AI to analyze
3. Validate and cross-reference the AI-generated insights with human expertise and judgment
4. Regularly update and refine the AI's knowledge base to ensure the most current and accurate information is being used

5. Integrate the insights gained from ChatGPT into their strategic planning and decision-making processes

Small and medium-sized businesses can conduct market research using AI, gaining competitive analysis more efficiently and effectively. The wealth of information and insights provided by the AI can help your team make informed decisions, identify new opportunities, and maintain their competitive edge in an ever-changing market landscape. However, it is important to remember that while ChatGPT is a powerful tool, it should be used in conjunction with human expertise and critical thinking to ensure the most accurate and relevant insights are being utilized for the benefit of the business.

Let's dive into 10 prompts that can serve as another demonstration of a Stepwise Layered Prompt Journey that will allow you to dominate your market:

1. Conduct a competitor analysis for our main competitors in the market.
2. Identify emerging trends in our industry and potential implications for our business.
3. Summarize key findings from a recent market research report.
4. Develop a list of potential improvements for our product based on customer feedback.
5. Suggest strategies for entering a new market segment or geographic region.
6. Write a SWOT analysis (Strengths, Weaknesses, Opportunities, Threats) for our company.
7. Identify potential partnerships or collaborations that could benefit our business.

8. Analyze the effectiveness of our current pricing strategy and suggest improvements.
9. Develop a list of potential new features or services based on market trends.
10. Write a report on the potential impact of new regulations or policies on our industry.

Read prompt #10 again. Imagine having an up-to-date understanding of government policy and regulation on your business.

That is huge!

As always, if the AI-generated content isn't relevant or effective, consider refining your prompt or providing additional context to better align with your research goals.

Further Resources:

1. Statista (https://www.statista.com/) - Offers a wide range of statistics and market data across various industries.
2. "Blue Ocean Strategy" by W. Chan Kim and Renée Mauborgne (https://amzn.to/3L2mePR) - Book on identifying and capitalizing on uncontested market spaces.
3. MarketResearch.com (https://www.marketresearch.com/) - Provides access to market research reports and industry analysis.
4. "The Innovator's Dilemma" by Clayton M. Christensen (https://amzn.to/3GGnxkI) - Book on disruptive innovation and its impact on established markets.

Use Case 21:

Product Development and Ideation

Employees with great ideas who can then implement them quickly become huge assets to any company. They are integral to your success. Where AI can amplify this is in its ability to generate large numbers of ideas for new products and services. By harnessing the power of ChatGPT to support product development and ideation efforts, you will generate hundreds of new product ideas, feature suggestions, or product improvement ideas based on market trends. Simply put, AI can help inspire innovation, streamline development, and enhance customer satisfaction.

When it comes to product development and ideation, SMBs have greatly benefited from leveraging AI tools like ChatGPT. By harnessing the AI's creative capabilities and vast knowledge base, businesses can generate a wealth of innovative ideas, streamline their development processes, and ultimately create products and services that better meet customer needs. Here are some ways SMBs can use ChatGPT to enhance their product development and ideation efforts:

Brainstorm new product or service ideas: By providing the AI with information about your target market, industry trends, and company goals, you can receive a diverse range of suggestions that span various categories, features, and price points. These ideas can then be evaluated and refined by your team, serving as a starting point for further development.

Improve existing products or services: By analyzing customer feedback, market trends, and competitor products, the AI can suggest specific features, functionalities, or design enhancements that could boost customer satisfaction and differentiate your products from the competition. This targeted approach to product improvement can help you prioritize development efforts and allocate resources more effectively.

Generate unique product names and descriptions: Developing compelling product names and descriptions is crucial for attracting customer attention and communicating key benefits. ChatGPT can assist in this process by generating creative and memorable names, as well as crafting engaging product descriptions that highlight unique selling points. By providing the AI with relevant keywords, desired tone, and product features, you can receive a variety of options to choose from and refine.

Create product roadmaps and development timelines: AI will generate detailed product roadmaps and development timelines based on your specific goals, resources, and constraints. By breaking down the development process into manageable stages and tasks, the

AI can help you stay organized, on track, and aligned with your overall business objectives.

Facilitate cross-functional collaboration: Product development often involves collaboration among various teams, such as design, engineering, marketing, and sales. ChatGPT can support this collaboration by serving as a central hub for generating and refining ideas, as well as facilitating communication and feedback among team members. By using the AI to document and share ideas, feedback, and progress updates, SMBs can foster a more inclusive and efficient product development process.

To maximize the benefits of ChatGPT for product development and ideation, businesses should:

1. Encourage all employees to contribute ideas and feedback, regardless of their role or department
2. Establish clear guidelines and criteria for evaluating and prioritizing AI-generated ideas
3. Foster a culture of experimentation and calculated risk-taking to explore promising ideas
4. Regularly review and update product roadmaps and development timelines based on new insights and changing market conditions
5. Celebrate and reward successful product innovations and the teams behind them

SMBs can tap into a vast source of creative ideas with AI. That's one of the main powers of this tool. By doing so, you can streamline your product development processes, and ultimately create offerings that better resonate with your target customers.

However, much like when we talked about editing what an artificial intelligence has written, it is important to remember that AI-generated ideas should be carefully evaluated and refined by human experts. Often times AI doesn't take into account factors such as feasibility, market demand, and alignment with the company's overall strategy. By combining the power of AI with human creativity and judgment, SMBs can drive meaningful innovation and stay ahead of the curve in an increasingly competitive marketplace.

As you integrate AI into your product development process, continuously monitor and optimize its performance. Track key metrics such as the quantity and quality of generated ideas, the speed of iteration, and the market success of AI-assisted products. Use these insights to refine your processes, update your training data, and adapt your prompts. Stay informed about the latest advancements in AI technology and be open to experimenting with new approaches to further enhance your product innovation capabilities. Here's some prompts you can explore right now using ChatGPT:

1. Brainstorm new product ideas for our company within our industry.
2. Suggest innovative features to add to our existing product line.
3. Identify areas of improvement for our current products based on customer feedback.
4. Analyze market trends and suggest potential product opportunities.
5. Develop a list of potential product names and descriptions for a new offering.
6. Write a pitch for a new product idea targeting a specific customer segment.
7. Suggest ways to enhance the user experience of our product.

8. Conduct a competitor analysis to identify gaps in their product offerings.
9. Brainstorm ideas for a new product line extension.
10. Suggest strategies for incorporating sustainability or eco-friendliness into our products.

Further Resources:

1. "Hooked" by Nir Eyal (https://amzn.to/3zWFp78) - Book on creating habit-forming products.
2. Product Hunt (https://www.producthunt.com/) - Showcases new products and innovations.
3. "The Lean Product Playbook" by Dan Olsen (https://amzn.to/3L1cZPS) - Book on product development and management techniques.
4. Mind the Product (https://www.mindtheproduct.com/) - Provides resources, insights, and best practices on product management and development.

Use Case 22:

Translating Content to Different Languages

Translating content to different languages involves converting text from one language to another while preserving the meaning, tone, and context of the original content. If you have a multinational corporation, translations become incredibly important. You want to ensure that your documents, website, and social media messages are accessible and understandable to a global audience.

ChatGPT, Google Gemini, Google Translate, and other AI platforms have become incredibly skilled at translating from one language to another. These programs have access to millions of documents and can readily convert content for audiences all around the globe. In *The AI Whisperer Wizard Words*, we created a 'Translation' chapter that goes into this topic at a much greater depth, with examples of language efficacy by model and use case.

If you want to take advantage of AI's language capabilities right now, here are 10 steps that will make sure you're doing it right:

1. Identify the target languages and audiences.
2. Understand cultural nuances and linguistic differences; for example, you can ask it to translate a word, phrase, or article into another language with a specific dialect: e.g., Spanish, using Cubano style.
3. Preserve the meaning and context of the original content.
4. Adapt content to accommodate language-specific idioms and expressions.
5. Use AI-powered translation tools, such as machine translation, for initial translations.
6. Edit and proofread translated content for accuracy and readability.
7. Collaborate with native speakers or professional translators for quality assurance.
8. Optimize translated content for SEO in target languages.
9. Monitor and analyze the performance of translated content.
10. Continuously update and improve translated content based on feedback.

When using AI for translating content, it's crucial to understand that machine translations might not fully capture the nuances, tone, or context of your original message. Language often relies on metaphors and specific phrases that can get lost in translation. To avoid misunderstandings, always have native speakers or professional translators review and edit your AI-generated translations. Also, adjust the tone and reading level of your translated content to fit your audience (e.g., middle school, high school, college level). Ensuring that your translations are culturally and contextually appropriate will help you communicate effectively and avoid unintentionally offending your audience..

Further Resources:

1. https://www.deepl.com/translator - DeepL Translate is a machine translation service that offers high-quality translations in over 26 languages. It is known for its accuracy and fluency, and it is often considered to be one of the best machine translation services available.
2. https://translate.google.com/ - Google Translate is another popular machine translation service that offers translations in over 100 languages. It is known for its ease of use and its wide range of features, such as the ability to translate text, speech, and documents.

Use Case 23:

Event Planning and Promotion

Depending on your business, event planning and promotion efforts can be a huge part of revenue generation. Community and customer outreach are another way AI can make life easier by generating event ideas, promotional materials, agendas, or post-event follow-up content. AI can help ensure a successful event, increase attendee engagement, and streamline the planning process. All the initial work will be done quickly and effectively without much effort from any employee. Their time can then be spent on more important tasks.

By harnessing the power of AI, SMBs can generate creative event ideas, craft compelling promotional materials, and streamline the planning process. Here are some ways your business might use ChatGPT to enhance your community and customer outreach:

Generating event ideas: ChatGPT can help SMBs brainstorm unique and engaging event ideas based on their target audience, industry, and goals. By providing relevant information about your company and customers, you can receive a variety of event suggestions tailored to your specific needs.

Creating promotional materials: By inputting key details about your event, target audience, and desired tone, you can generate attention-grabbing content that drives attendance and engagement.

Developing event agendas: Crafting a well-structured and engaging event agenda is crucial for guaranteeing a successful event. ChatGPT can help by generating agenda templates and suggesting relevant topics, speakers, and activities based on your event goals and audience preferences.

Generating post-event follow-up content: Following up with attendees after an event is essential for maintaining engagement and gathering valuable feedback. ChatGPT can assist by creating personalized thank-you messages, surveys, and recap blog posts, helping you build stronger relationships with your community and customers.

Analyzing event feedback: By identifying key themes, sentiment, and actionable insights, you can make data-driven decisions to improve future events and better meet the needs of your target audience.

To maximize the benefits of ChatGPT for event planning and promotion, all businesses should:

1. Clearly define event goals, target audience, and key messages before engaging with ChatGPT
2. Provide the AI with relevant and accurate information about your company, customers, and industry
3. Use ChatGPT-generated content as a starting point, and refine it with human expertise and brand-specific considerations
4. Engage with attendees before, during, and after the event to build relationships and gather valuable feedback
5. Continuously update and refine your event strategy based on data-driven insights and changing customer preferences

By combining the power of AI with human creativity and strategic thinking, SMBs can create successful events that drive community engagement, customer loyalty, and business growth in an increasingly competitive marketplace.

Need to plan that next big advertising event? Here are 10 triggers that will get AI moving in the right direction:

1. Brainstorm ideas for a unique company event or team-building activity.
2. Write a promotional email for an upcoming industry conference.
3. Develop an event agenda, including keynote speakers and breakout sessions.
4. Create a social media campaign to promote an upcoming event.
5. Write a post-event summary to share with attendees and non-attendees.

6. Suggest strategies for increasing event attendance and engagement.
7. Develop a list of potential sponsors or partners for our event.
8. Write a press release announcing an upcoming event or conference.
9. Create a list of tips for attendees to make the most of our event.
10. Write a follow-up email to attendees, thanking them for their participation and requesting feedback.

When requesting event planning and promotion assistance, always look to your target audience. Ask yourself, "What do we need the event to accomplish for our business?" If you're focused on customer retention, you'll want to make that the emphasis of the information you feed the AI. And if you don't know what the goal of the event or promotion should be, feel free to ask the AI for help with that too. The AI won't judge.

Further Resources:

1. "The Art of Gathering" by Priya Parker (https://amzn.to/3GIb4Ni) - Book on creating transformative events and experiences.
2. Eventbrite (https://www.eventbrite.com/) - Offers a platform for creating, promoting, and managing events.
3. "Event Planning: The Ultimate Guide" by Judy Allen (https://amzn.to/3mxfVu7) - Comprehensive guide to event planning and management.
4. BizBash (https://www.bizbash.com/) - Provides resources, insights, and best practices on event planning and promotion.

Use Case 24:

Sales Scripts and Training

Have you ever heard of the Wolf of Wall Street, Jordan Belford? He's famous for a lot of reasons (many quite unseemly), and they even made a movie about his story, but it was his use of training scripts that catapulted his trading career. A good script can mean the difference between middling sales numbers and robust growth. It's that important. By harnessing the power of AI, SMBs can create effective sales scripts, handle objections with ease, and develop comprehensive training resources for their sales team. While we can learn valuable lessons from the Wolf on the power of using scripts, it's essential to remain ethical and use AI lawfully.

Here are some ways SMBs can use ChatGPT to enhance their sales enablement:

Generating sales scripts: ChatGPT can help SMBs create compelling sales scripts tailored to their products, services, and target audience. By providing information about your offerings, unique selling points, and customer pain points, you can generate scripts that effectively communicate your value proposition and drive conversions.

Handling objections: Let AI handle the complaints! By inputting frequently encountered objections and providing relevant product information, you can generate persuasive responses that help your sales team overcome barriers and close more deals.

Developing product positioning materials: ChatGPT can help create materials that effectively position your products or services in the market. By providing information about your target audience, competitors, and key benefits, you can generate compelling product descriptions, battle cards, and sales presentations that highlight your unique value.

Creating training resources: Create prompts that input information about your products, sales process, and best practices. From there, AI will generate training manuals, quizzes, and role-play scenarios that help your team develop the skills and knowledge needed for success.

Analyzing sales performance: Artificial intelligence can help SMBs analyze sales data and identify areas for improvement. By processing data on sales metrics, customer feedback, and team performance, you can generate insights and recommendations for optimizing your sales strategy and coaching your team to success.

To maximize the benefits of ChatGPT for sales scripts and training, your company should:

1. Ensure that the information provided to ChatGPT is accurate, up-to-date, and aligned with your brand voice and values
2. Use ChatGPT-generated content as a starting point, and refine it with human expertise and real-world experience
3. Regularly update sales scripts and training materials based on customer feedback, market changes, and product updates
4. Encourage collaboration and knowledge sharing among your sales team to continuously improve performance
5. Monitor sales metrics and adjust your strategy as needed to optimize results and drive revenue growth

By combining the power of AI with the knowledge and skills of your sales team, your business will enjoy higher sales performance, increased revenue, and more consistent sales processes in an increasingly competitive marketplace.

And here are 10 that will get your mind moving and AI processing:

1. Write a sales script for a cold call or product pitch.
2. Develop a guide for handling common sales objections.
3. Create a product comparison chart showcasing our product against competitors.
4. Write an email template for following up with potential leads.
5. Suggest strategies for increasing sales performance and closing deals.
6. Develop a list of potential upselling or cross-selling opportunities.

7. Create a sales training guide for new hires.
8. Write a case study showcasing a successful customer engagement.
9. Develop a list of questions to qualify potential leads effectively.
10. Suggest best practices for building rapport and trust with prospects.

If by now you're not seeing the power of AI, go back and read Number 10 again. How valuable is rapport and trust in your business? If you can strengthen ideals like that in your interactions with clients, it could mean the difference between feeling the pinch of an economic downturn and riding a wave of success despite a recession.

Further Resources:

1. "The Challenger Sale" by Matthew Dixon and Brent Adamson (https://amzn.to/3MKyxl4) - Book on a new approach to selling.
2. Sales Hacker (https://www.saleshacker.com/) - Offers resources, insights, and best practices on sales enablement and training.
3. "SPIN Selling" by Neil Rackham (https://amzn.to/3GJClzg) - Book on a consultative selling approach.
4. HubSpot Sales Blog (https://blog.hubspot.com/sales) - Provides resources, insights, and best practices on sales techniques and strategies.

Use Case 25:

Financial Planning and Analysis

Leverage ChatGPT to support financial planning and analysis efforts by generating budget templates, financial projections, investment strategies, or cost-saving ideas. AI can help improve financial decision-making, identify opportunities for growth, and optimize resource allocation. Here are some ways SMBs can use ChatGPT to enhance their financial decision-making:

Generating budget templates: ChatGPT can help SMBs create customized budget templates tailored to their specific industry and financial goals. By providing ChatGPT with historical financial data, key business metrics, and desired formatting, you can generate comprehensive budgets that accurately allocate resources and align with your strategic objectives.

AI-powered tools like Obviously AI and Accern can help SMBs create customized budget templates tailored to their specific industry and financial goals. By providing historical financial data and key business metrics, you can generate comprehensive budgets that accurately allocate resources and align with your strategic objectives.

Creating financial projections: Relevant financial information will allow ChatGPT to provide projections for future cash flow, revenue growth, and profitability, enabling more informed decision-making.

AI-driven financial forecasting tools like Futrli and Fathom can assist in generating accurate financial projections based on historical data, market trends, and key performance indicators. By leveraging machine learning algorithms, these tools can help SMBs predict future cash flows, revenue growth, and profitability, enabling better informed decision-making.

Identifying cost saving opportunities: ChatGPT can analyze financial data to identify areas where SMBs can reduce costs and improve efficiency. By providing your artificial intelligence partner with expense reports, vendor contracts, and operational data, it can highlight potential cost-saving opportunities and suggest strategies for optimization, such as renegotiating supplier terms or streamlining processes.

Developing investment strategies: By inputting financial goals, risk tolerance, and market data, ChatGPT can provide personalized investment recommendations and help SMBs make data-driven decisions to grow their wealth.

Generating financial reports: ChatGPT can create clear, concise, and informative financial reports. Provide ChatGPT with the necessary financial data and desired reporting format, and it can generate balance sheets, income statements, cash flow statements, and other essential reports. This will save time and ensure consistency in financial reporting.

Integrating with financial management platforms: AI-powered financial planning tools can seamlessly integrate with popular accounting platforms like QuickBooks, MS Dynamics, Sage, NetSuite, Xero, Freshbooks, etc. through APIs. This integration enables SMBs to automatically import financial data, generate real-time insights, and streamline their financial reporting and analysis processes.

To maximize the benefits of ChatGPT for financial planning and analysis, always make sure you:

1. Ensure the accuracy and reliability of the financial data provided to ChatGPT
2. Use ChatGPT-generated outputs as a starting point, and validate them with human expertise and strategic judgment
3. Regularly update financial projections and budgets based on actual performance and market changes
4. Implement strong data security measures to protect sensitive financial information shared with ChatGPT
5. Continuously monitor and adjust financial strategies based on ChatGPT-driven recommendations and changing business needs

Remember that ChatGPT should be used as a complementary tool to support human decision-making, not replace it entirely. Businesses get into trouble when they turn everything over to AI. By combining the power of ChatGPT with the expertise and judgment of financial professionals, companies can make more informed, data-driven decisions. When they do that, they drive growth, optimize resource allocation, and guarantee long-term financial success in an increasingly competitive marketplace.

Here are 10 Potential Prompt Threads you can use directly with the AI of your choice:

1. Develop a budget template for a specific department or project.
2. Create a financial projection for our company's revenue and expenses over the next year.
3. Suggest investment strategies for our company's cash reserves.
4. Identify potential cost-saving opportunities within our operations.
5. Write a financial analysis of a recent company acquisition.
6. Develop a list of key performance indicators (KPIs) for tracking financial success.
7. Suggest strategies for optimizing cash flow and working capital.
8. Create a financial risk assessment for a potential new market entry.
9. Develop a capital expenditure plan for our company's expansion efforts.
10. Write a financial summary for our annual report or shareholder presentation.

Further Resources:

1. "Financial Intelligence for Entrepreneurs" by Karen Berman and Joe Knight (https://amzn.to/3MJ0edO) - Book on understanding and managing business financials.
2. Investopedia (https://www.investopedia.com/) - Offers resources, insights, and best practices on finance, investing, and financial analysis.
3. "The Lean Startup" by Eric Ries (https://amzn.to/41kkyX8) - Book on optimizing resource allocation and financial planning for startups.
4. Corporate Finance Institute (https://corporatefinanceinstitute.com/) - Provides resources, insights, and best practices on corporate finance and financial analysis.

Midpoint Reached: We're Halfway There. Keep Grinding!

We have crossed the 50-yard line, and we are halfway done!

The sheer volume of ways AI can help a business improve its delivery of products and services is mind-boggling. Imagine having all these services handled quickly and efficiently, simply by knowing the right prompts to use. It's a winning strategy for any business, and I hope you're starting to get excited about the potential.

And remember, we're only halfway done!

Take this moment to reflect on your journey so far. Here are three questions to ponder:

1. Which AI use case have you found most intriguing, and how do you envision it transforming your business operations?
2. What challenges have you encountered while crafting AI prompts, and how have you addressed them?
3. How do you plan to implement what you've learned so far to make incremental improvements in your daily business activities?

Keep pushing forward, and remember, the best is yet to come!

Use Case 26:

Supply Chain and Logistics Optimization

Supply chain issues have been especially common in the years since the pandemic. New efficiencies can take a lot of time to identify and are costly to implement. AI streamlines your logistics efforts by generating process improvement ideas, inventory management strategies, transportation planning, or supplier evaluations. This will improve efficiency, reduce costs, and increase overall supply chain performance. Here are some ways SMBs can use ChatGPT to optimize their supply chain and logistics:

Generating process improvement ideas: ChatGPT can help your business identify areas for process improvement by analyzing supply chain data and best practices. By providing ChatGPT with information about current processes, pain points, and goals, it can generate ideas for streamlining operations, reducing bottlenecks, and improving overall efficiency.

Developing inventory management strategies: You can feet AI data on sales patterns, lead times, and storage constraints. By doing so, ChatGPT can provide recommendations for optimal inventory levels, reorder points, and safety stock, helping to minimize stockouts and reduce carrying costs.

Optimizing transportation planning: Artificial intelligence can help your transportation planning by analyzing data on shipping routes, carrier options, and delivery requirements. It can then consolidate shipments, select cost-effective carriers, and improve delivery times. All of this will ultimately reduce transportation costs and enhance customer satisfaction.

Conducting supplier evaluations: ChatGPT can assist SMBs in evaluating potential suppliers and identifying the most suitable partners. By inputting criteria such as price, quality, reliability, and lead times, ChatGPT can generate comprehensive supplier assessments and provide recommendations for selecting the best suppliers based on an SMB's specific needs and priorities.

Generating supply chain reports: No one wants to write supply chain reports. That makes it the perfect job for AI. It can generate reports on key performance indicators (KPIs), such as inventory turnover, order fulfillment rates, and supplier performance, enabling data-driven decision-making and continuous improvement.

To maximize the benefits of AI for supply chain and logistics optimization, small businesses should:

1. Ensure the accuracy and reliability of the supply chain data provided to ChatGPT
2. Use ChatGPT-generated recommendations as a starting point, and validate them with human expertise and practical considerations
3. Regularly update supply chain strategies based on changing market conditions, customer requirements, and operational constraints
4. Foster collaboration and communication among supply chain stakeholders to ensure alignment and effective implementation of optimization initiatives
5. Continuously monitor and adjust supply chain performance based on ChatGPT-driven insights and evolving business needs

Processes can always be improved, and that is where AI truly shines. Logistics is incredibly important, and even small positive steps can have huge impacts for your business. Let AI develop effective inventory management strategies, optimize transportation planning, and conduct comprehensive supplier evaluations. By combining the power of ChatGPT with the expertise and practical knowledge of supply chain professionals, SMBs can achieve significant improvements in efficiency, cost reduction, and overall supply chain performance.

It's time you positioned yourself for success in an increasingly competitive and dynamic business environment.

Now we have 10 Potential Prompt Threads to help with your logistics:

1. Suggest strategies for optimizing our inventory management processes.
2. Identify potential cost-saving opportunities within our supply chain operations.

3. Develop a transportation plan for shipping our products more efficiently.
4. Suggest ways to reduce lead times and improve order fulfillment.
5. Write a supplier evaluation report for a potential new vendor.
6. Develop a list of key performance indicators (KPIs) for tracking supply chain success.
7. Suggest strategies for mitigating supply chain disruptions and risks.
8. Create a contingency plan for dealing with unexpected supply chain challenges.
9. Develop a list of potential alternative suppliers to diversify our supply chain.
10. Write a case study showcasing a successful supply chain optimization effort.

When requesting supply chain and logistics optimization assistance, provide specific information about your company's operations, goals, and what efficiencies you're looking to improve. Play around with the wording of your prompts if you find the information isn't skewing in the direction you need.

Further Resources:

1. "The Supply Chain Revolution" by Suman Sarkar (https://amzn.to/3UBe0RA) - Book on innovative supply chain management practices.
2. Supply Chain Digital (https://www.supplychaindigital.com/) - Offers resources, insights, and best practices on supply chain and logistics optimization.

3. "Lean Supply Chain and Logistics Management" by Paul Myerson (https://amzn.to/3L30raJ) - Book on applying lean principles to supply chain management.
4. Supply Chain Management Review (https://www.scmr.com/) - Provides resources, insights, and best practices on supply chain management and logistics.

Use Case 27:

Writing and Editing Business Reports

It's no accident we just jumped from logistics to business reporting.

Both are analytical in nature and both can be mind-numbingly dry.

That is why you give it to AI to do.

Writing and editing business reports involves creating clear, concise, and well-structured documents that present information, analyses, and recommendations to support decision-making within an organization. However, creating clear, concise, and well-structured reports can be time-consuming and resource-intensive. The AI can comb through tens of thousands of documents, comparing market statistics and trends, giving you the data needed to make an informed decision.

Here are some ways SMBs can use ChatGPT to enhance their business report writing and editing:

Generating report outlines: ChatGPT can help SMBs create comprehensive report outlines that provide a clear structure and logical flow for their documents. By inputting the report's purpose, key points, and desired sections, ChatGPT can generate an outline that ensures all essential information is covered and properly organized.

Drafting report content: With relevant data, analyses, and insights provided by your team, AI can generate clear and concise paragraphs that effectively communicate key information and support the report's objectives. You can even have the artificial intelligence spice things up with a bit of humor if you want to make the material more enjoyable to read.

Ensuring consistency and clarity: ChatGPT can establish a set of guidelines and preferences, making sure that the report's language is professional, easy to understand, and aligned with your organization's brand voice.

Conducting research and analysis: Coming through large volumes of data quickly to identify relevant information is truly one of the best uses of AI. It cuts down on potentially hundreds of man-hours in a matter of minutes. You can simply input specific research questions or topics and then allow ChatGPT to scan through thousands of documents. In the end, the AI will extract pertinent insights, and present them in a structured manner. This is the very definition of a time-saver!

Providing editing and proofreading support: ChatGPT can assist in editing and proofreading business reports to ensure they are error-free and polished. Of course, you'll still need another set of human eyes to go over everything, but most of the base load will be taken care of by the AI.

To maximize the benefits of ChatGPT for writing and editing business reports, your business should:

1. Provide clear instructions and guidelines to ChatGPT to ensure the generated content aligns with the report's objectives and the organization's standards
2. Use ChatGPT-generated content as a starting point, and always review and refine it with human expertise and judgment
3. Ensure that the data and insights provided to ChatGPT are accurate, up-to-date, and relevant to the report's purpose
4. Establish a consistent brand voice and style guide for ChatGPT to follow, ensuring that all reports maintain a professional and cohesive tone
5. Regularly gather feedback from stakeholders and update ChatGPT's guidelines and preferences accordingly to continuously improve the quality and effectiveness of the generated reports.

SMBs can create high-quality, professional documents more efficiently and effectively with AI. Always have a human go over all AI work just as you would with a living, breathing employee, but you'll find so much time is saved.

And time is money, as we all know.

10 potential prompt threads:

1. Define the purpose and audience of the report.
2. Gather and analyze relevant data and information.
3. Organize the report into sections, such as an introduction, analysis, and conclusion.
4. Write clear and concise content.
5. Use visual aids, such as charts and graphs, to illustrate data.
6. Use AI to generate report content based on input data.
7. Edit and proofread the report for clarity and accuracy.
8. Format the report professionally and consistently.
9. Summarize the report's key findings and recommendations.
10. Review and revise the report based on feedback.

Further Resources:

1. Harvard Business Review (hbr.org): Offers articles and insights on various business topics, including communication and report writing.
2. Purdue OWL (owl.purdue.edu): Provides writing resources and instructional material on various writing styles, including business writing.
3. Grammarly Blog (grammarly.com/blog): Offers tips and guidelines on writing, grammar, punctuation, and style, which are useful for crafting well-written business reports.
4. "HBR Guide to Better Business Writing" by Bryan A. Garner (https://amzn.to/3A0hEL) - Offers practical tips and examples to help improve your business writing skills.
5. "The Business Writer's Handbook" by Gerald J. Alred, Charles T. Brusaw, and Walter E. Oliu (https://amzn.to/40at8GZ) - A comprehensive guide to various forms of business communication, including report writing.

6. "Writing That Works: How to Communicate Effectively in
   Business" by Kenneth Roman and Joel Raphaelson
   (https://amzn.to/41vjn7q) - Offers practical advice for writing
   various types of business documents, including reports.

Use Case 28:

Content Optimization for SEO

SEO (Search Engine Optimization) involves improving website content to increase its visibility in search engine results. This means using the right keywords in the right places on your website or online material so that when someone searches on Google, they find you instead of your competitor. When you optimize for SEO, you end up driving more organic traffic to your website and boosting site performance.

If this sounds like a hugely technical process, it definitely can be. With AI assistance though, you can take care of it quickly and easily.

SEO is a critical aspect of digital marketing for SMBs, as it directly impacts a website's visibility and organic traffic. Optimizing website content for SEO can be a complex and time-consuming process, requiring technical expertise and a deep understanding of search engine algorithms. However, by leveraging AI tools, SMBs can streamline their SEO efforts, ensuring that their content is accurate, engaging, and optimized for search engine rankings.

Here are some ways SMBs can use ChatGPT to enhance their content optimization for SEO:

Keyword research and analysis: Easily identify relevant and high-performing keywords for a given topic or industry. By inputting seed keywords and content ideas, AI can generate a list of related keywords, long-tail phrases, and semantic variations that can help improve a website's search engine rankings and attract relevant traffic.

Generating SEO-optimized content: By providing ChatGPT with target keywords, desired word count, and content guidelines, it can generate articles, blog posts, and product descriptions that naturally incorporate keywords and adhere to SEO best practices.

Optimizing meta tags and descriptions: ChatGPT can assist in creating compelling and keyword-rich meta titles and descriptions for webpages. Once you plug in the proper data, AI will generate optimized meta tags that accurately represent the page's content and entice users to click through from search engine results pages (SERPs).

Identifying content gaps and opportunities: Artificial intelligence is great at analyzing a website's existing content and comparing it to competitors' sites. ChatGPT can suggest topics and themes that will help attract new audiences, improve search engine rankings, and establish the SMB as a thought leader in their field.

To maximize the benefits of ChatGPT for content optimization and SEO, SMBs should do the following:

1. Focus on creating high-quality, informative, and engaging content that provides value to users, rather than solely optimizing for search engines
2. Use ChatGPT-generated content as a starting point, and always review and refine it with human expertise and judgment to ensure accuracy, readability, and alignment with brand voice
3. Avoid keyword stuffing and instead prioritize natural, contextual keyword usage that enhances the user experience
4. Regularly update and refresh website content to maintain relevance and align with evolving user needs and search engine algorithms
5. Monitor SEO performance metrics and user engagement to continually refine content optimization strategies and improve overall website performance.

By combining the power of ChatGPT with the critical thinking and creativity of company marketers, businesses can achieve significant improvements in search engine rankings, organic traffic, and user engagement. For any team looking to take advantage of the digital landscape, these improvements will make a marked difference in online visibility.

Optimizing AI for Business Visibility

Have you ever asked AI what it knows about you, your company, products, and services? Chances are the AI models (and thus the public as a whole) have an incomplete understanding of what you do. That being the case, I can think of few things more important for your SEO than to educate and train AI what it should know about you. Yes, go to each of the LLM models (e.g., ChatGPT, Gemini, Claude, CoPilot, and others), and ask each one what it knows about you.

Then simply update their information.

You will be glad you did.

In our AI age, businesses must recognize the importance of educating AI language models like ChatGPT about their company, products, and services. Incomplete information can lead to missed opportunities, the spread of inaccuracies, and a weakened online presence. To combat this, businesses should take proactive steps to engage with leading AI models, evaluate their current understanding of the company, and provide clear, concise, and relevant information to address any gaps.

As your business evolves, maintaining open communication with AI models and updating them regularly ensures they reflect the most current information on your team and products. These efforts will boost SEO and ensure potential customers receive accurate and helpful information from AI-powered tools.

Here are 10 prompt ideas that will allow you to use AI for search engine optimization:

1. Perform keyword research to identify relevant terms and phrases.
2. Optimize title tags and meta descriptions.
3. Incorporate keywords naturally into content.
4. Use header tags for better content structure.
5. Improve readability and user experience.
6. Optimize images and multimedia elements.

7. Implement internal and external linking strategies.
8. Use AI to analyze and optimize content for SEO.
9. Monitor and analyze website performance metrics.
10. Regularly update and refresh content to maintain relevance.

Further Resources:

1. https://ahrefs.com/ Ahrefs is an SEO software suite that contains tools for link building, keyword research, competitor analysis, rank tracking and site audits. It is a popular choice among SEO professionals and marketers.
2. https://moz.com/ Moz is a marketing software company that provides SEO tools, competitive analysis, and other marketing solutions. It is also a popular choice among SEO professionals and marketers.

Use Case 29:

Writing Business Proposals and RFP Responses

Here we are with another business writing example. Are you seeing a pattern?

Any form of writing is appropriate for AI augmentation, but forms of writing that rely on data and research are a particular strength.

Writing business proposals and RFP (Request for Proposal) responses involves crafting persuasive documents that showcase a company's capabilities, expertise, and proposed solutions. If you have good RFP proposal responses, you can win more contracts or secure new business opportunities.

Years ago I attended Shipley Associates' course on writing customer-focused Winning Proposal Responses. Their work and training were first rate. Now however, AI can do so much of this for you that it will increase your competitiveness, compliance, speed of preparation, and hopefully your win rate.

The integration of AI in proposal submissions can significantly elevate the efficiency and compliance of your responses, providing a competitive edge. With ChatGPT one can scan the RFP and essential data that would ordinarily take weeks to compile, and create more compliant and engaging proposals that will fit within your stated budgets.

AI can thoroughly analyze Request for Proposals (RFPs) to determine whether they meet your organization's "go" or "no-go" criteria, such as location, requirements, available resources, and necessary capital. This initial assessment ensures that your team only pursues opportunities that align with your strategic goals and capabilities. Like so much with AI, this ability saves valuable time and resources.

Further, AI can extract key words and phrases from the RFP, allowing these elements to be seamlessly incorporated into your proposal response. This ensures that your submission is not only aligned with the client's language and expectations but also optimized for higher relevance and impact.

Additionally, AI can analyze the award scoring and determination criteria outlined in the RFP. It can then generate a comprehensive requirements document. This document serves as a checklist, making sure that every step and process required for a response is meticulously followed.

Ultimately, AI can review and enhance your existing proposal response forms and templates too. By identifying areas for improvement and providing constructive feedback, AI ensures that your documents are continually optimized for clarity and compliance. The result is a supercharged ability to respond to proposal requests with heightened responsiveness and precision.

Writing compelling business proposals and RFP responses is essential for small and medium businesses looking to secure new clients, partnerships, and projects. Here are some ways SMBs can use ChatGPT to enhance their business proposal and RFP response writing:

Generating proposal outlines: Provide AI with key information about the project, client requirements, and unique selling points. The artificial intelligence can then generate an outline that serves as a roadmap for the entire proposal, saving time and ensuring consistency.

Drafting persuasive content: ChatGPT can assist in drafting compelling content for each section of the proposal or RFP response. By providing ChatGPT with relevant information, such as company background, proposed solutions, and key benefits, it can generate clear, concise, and persuasive paragraphs that effectively communicate the SMB's value proposition and expertise.

Customizing proposals for specific clients: Tailor your proposals to the unique needs and preferences of each client. AI can generate content that demonstrates a deep understanding of the client's situation and positions, presenting your business as the ideal solution provider.

Ensuring consistency and professionalism: ChatGPT can help maintain a consistent tone, style, and structure throughout the proposal or RFP response. ChatGPT will ensure that your submissions are professional, error-free, and aligned with your brand voice and values.

Identifying key differentiators and value propositions: ChatGPT can assist SMBs in identifying and emphasizing their unique selling points and value propositions within their proposals. By analyzing the SMB's strengths, past successes, and competitive landscape, ChatGPT can generate content that highlights the company's key differentiators. From there, the AI can convincingly demonstrate why a specific business is the best choice for the client or project.

To maximize the benefits of ChatGPT for writing business proposals and RFP responses, companies should:

1. Provide clear instructions and guidelines to ChatGPT, including the proposal's purpose, target audience, and any specific requirements or restrictions
2. Use ChatGPT-generated content as a starting point, and always review and refine it with human expertise and judgment to ensure accuracy, persuasiveness, and alignment with the SMB's goals
3. Customize ChatGPT-generated content for each specific client or project, incorporating relevant examples, case studies, and testimonials to strengthen the proposal's impact
4. Regularly update ChatGPT's knowledge base with the latest company information, industry trends, and client feedback to continually improve the quality and relevance of the generated content
5. Collaborate with key stakeholders and subject matter experts throughout the proposal writing process to ensure that ChatGPT's outputs align with the SMB's capabilities, resources, and strategic objectives

By leveraging AI tools like ChatGPT for writing business proposals and RFP responses, SMBs can create high-quality, persuasive submissions more efficiently and effectively. ChatGPT can assist in generating outlines, drafting persuasive content, customizing proposals for specific clients, ensuring consistency and professionalism, and identifying key differentiators and value propositions. Businesses can easily create winning proposals that secure new opportunities and drive long-term success.

Here are 10 potential prompt threads for you to explore:

1. Thoroughly analyze the RFP or client requirements.
2. Define the project scope, objectives, and deliverables.
3. Develop a compelling value proposition.
4. Outline the proposed solution, methodology, and timeline.
5. Showcase your company's expertise, experience, and relevant case studies.
6. Provide a detailed budget and pricing structure.
7. Use AI to generate proposal content based on input data.
8. Edit and proofread the proposal for clarity and accuracy.
9. Format the proposal professionally and consistently.
10. Follow up with the client after submission.

When using AI for writing business proposals and RFP responses, ensure that the AI-generated content is accurate, persuasive, and tailored to the client's needs. Always review and edit AI-generated content before submitting. I know I've been saying that a lot, but too many businesses let the editing side of AI slide, to their detriment. Edit, review, and move forward confidently with AI.

Further Resources:

1. Association of Proposal Management Professionals (APMP) (apmp.org): Offers resources, best practices, and networking opportunities for proposal management professionals.
2. ProposalHelper (proposalhelper.com): Provides proposal writing resources, including tips, webinars, and blog posts, covering various aspects of the proposal process.
3. CapturePlanning.com (captureplanning.com): Offers articles, guides, and templates for writing and managing proposals.
4. "Writing Winning Business Proposals" by Richard C. Freed, Shervin Freed, and Joe Romano (https://amzn.to/3H7VGKH) - Offers practical advice and a step-by-step process for crafting successful business proposals.
5. "Proposal Development Secrets: Win More, Work Smarter, and Get Home on Time" by Matt Handal (https://amzn.to/43w8CU6) - Provides insights and strategies for writing compelling proposals that win more work.
6. "The One-Page Proposal: How to Get Your Business Pitch onto One Persuasive Page" by Patrick G. Riley (https://amzn.to/3A1WFrQ) - Presents a method for creating concise and compelling proposals that stand out to decision-makers.

Use Case 30:

Summarizing Lengthy Documents

Very few business owners have the time to read through extensive reports and market analyses. Most of the time all we want is a summary so we can make as informed a decision as possible. AI will do exactly that, shortening lengthy documents and condensing large volumes of text into shorter, more accessible summaries that capture the main ideas, findings, or conclusions while maintaining accuracy and coherence.

In today's fast-paced business environment, the ability to quickly and accurately summarize documents is invaluable, especially for small and medium-sized businesses striving to maintain a competitive edge. Leveraging tools like ChatGPT can significantly enhance this process, but employing structured frameworks can further optimize the results. This chapter explores various summarization techniques, providing practical examples and guidelines to help SMBs extract key information efficiently. By integrating methods such as bullet points, the Axios Smart Brevity approach, the inverted pyramid, and visual aids, businesses can ensure their summaries are not only concise but also highly informative and actionable.

Techniques for Effective Summarization

Bullet Points:

- Concise and Clear: Break down information into concise, easily digestible chunks.
- Highlight Key Points: Summarize each major section in a single bullet point.

Smart Brevity:

- Core Principles: Developed by Axios, Smart Brevity focuses on delivering clear, engaging, and memorable information by prioritizing the essential news and explaining its impact quickly.
- Format: Use short, simple sentences, bold text for emphasis, and plenty of white space to make the text scannable and less overwhelming for the reader (Axios HQ) (Axios HQ) (Axios HQ).

Inverted Pyramid:

- Most Important Information First: Start with the most critical data or conclusions.
- Supporting Details: Follow with important details that support the main points.
- Background Information: End with general or background info.

5 Ws and H:

- Who, What, When, Where, Why, and How: Ensure that your summary answers these fundamental questions to cover all essential aspects.

Chunking:

- Divide and Summarize: Break the document into manageable sections or chunks and provide a brief summary for each.

Visual Aids:

- Use Charts and Graphs: Represent data and key points visually.
- Infographics: Summarize information in a visual format that is easy to understand at a glance.

Template-Based Summarization:

- Standard Templates: Maintain consistency in summaries with predefined templates.
- Custom Templates: Tailor templates to specific types of documents or audiences.

Executive Summaries:

- High-Level Overview: Provide a brief overview that captures the essence of the document.
- Key Findings: Highlight the most important findings or conclusions.

Using these summarization techniques and weaving them into your ChatGPT prompts and workflow can transform the way your business handles information. It will lead to improved decision-making and greater efficiency. Whether using bullet points for clarity, Smart Brevity for focused communication, or visual aids for better comprehension, these strategies will help you make the most of your document summarization efforts. As you implement these practices, remember that regular updates and feedback are crucial to maintaining accuracy and relevance. With these tools at your disposal, your business will be better equipped to navigate the complexities of information management in the digital age.

Lastly, before putting all our trust in AI though, it's good to have someone familiar with the material being condensed verify the summary accurately represents the original content and maintains coherence. Always review and edit AI-generated summaries. Remember, the more details you give the AI, the better the results. If the prompts for the review were unclear, the summary could be heavily affected. Your use of precise terms and language will greatly improve your ChatGPT prompt results.

10 potential prompt threads:

1. Identify the main points and supporting evidence.
2. Eliminate unnecessary details and redundancies.
3. Use clear, concise language to convey the main ideas.
4. Maintain a neutral tone and avoid personal opinions or biases.
5. Format the summary for easy reading and comprehension.
6. Use AI to generate summaries based on input text.
7. Edit and proofread the summary for clarity and accuracy.
8. Ensure that the summary remains faithful to the original document.
9. Use summaries to support decision-making or information dissemination.

10. Implement AI-powered summarization tools within your organization.

Further Resources:

1. https://www.smmry.com/ SMMRY is a website that provides summaries of articles, text, websites, essays, and documents.
2. https://www.autosummarizer.com/ AutoSummarizer is a website that provides automatic summaries of text.
3. https://www.goodreads.com Goodreads is a website that allows users to read and review books.

Use Case 31:

Data Visualization and Reporting

Generating insights from data, creating report templates, suggesting visualizations, or developing data-driven narratives is about the driest and most time-consuming task imaginable. The great thing about AI is that it can help make data more accessible, understandable, and actionable for decision-making. Plus, the sheer volume of insights it can supply will allow your business to see things that you otherwise would have missed.

When it comes to data visualization and reporting for SMBs, leveraging AI tools like ChatGPT can be a game-changer. By harnessing the power of AI, your business can uncover hidden patterns, make data-driven decisions faster, and present data in an engaging way. Here are some ways companies can use ChatGPT to enhance their data visualization and reporting:

Generating Insights from Data: By providing raw data sets, you can receive comprehensive insights that highlight key areas of interest and concern.

Creating Report Templates: AI can assist in creating customizable report templates. Specify the type of data and the required format, from there you can receive professionally designed templates that can be used repeatedly.

Suggesting Visualizations: You can get suggestions for charts, graphs, and other visual elements that best represent your data once you input your data characteristics.

Developing Data-Driven Narratives: ChatGPT can help craft narratives that accompany your data visualizations. By inputting your key data points, you can receive well-structured narratives that make your reports more compelling and understandable.

Automating Reporting Processes: Streamline your reporting processes by automating repetitive tasks. With the help of AI, you can reduce the time and effort required to generate regular reports.

To maximize the benefits of ChatGPT for data visualization and reporting, SMBs should:

1. Ensure data quality and consistency before using AI tools.
2. Clearly define the goals and key metrics for each report.
3. Regularly update and maintain data sources to ensure accuracy.

4. Train staff on how to interpret AI-generated insights and visualizations.

5. Integrate AI tools with existing data management systems for seamless operations.

By leveraging ChatGPT's capabilities, small businesses can uncover deeper insights, enhance the visual appeal of their reports, and save time on repetitive tasks. By combining the power of AI with critical thinking and domain knowledge, SMBs can achieve greater success in an increasingly competitive marketplace. If the AI-generated reporting isn't relevant or effective for your business, make sure you have given enough details in your prompts.

Data is more important than ever, so here are 10 prompts that will get your AI platform spitting out insights that very well may help your company evolve:

1. Analyze a dataset and suggest key insights or trends.
2. Develop a report template for a specific department or function.
3. Suggest appropriate data visualizations for different types of data.
4. Write a data-driven narrative or story based on provided data.
5. Suggest strategies for improving data literacy within the organization.
6. Develop a list of key performance indicators (KPIs) for a specific department or function.
7. Create a dashboard layout for tracking business metrics.
8. Write a data analysis report for a specific project or initiative.
9. Develop a list of best practices for data visualization and reporting.

10. Suggest strategies for making data more accessible and actionable for decision-making.

Further Resources:

1. "Storytelling with Data" by Cole Nussbaumer Knaflic (https://amzn.to/41wkCmu) - Book on effective data visualization techniques.
2. FlowingData (https://flowingdata.com/) - Offers resources, insights, and best practices on data visualization and reporting.
3. "The Big Book of Dashboards" by Steve Wexler, Jeffrey Shaffer, and Andy Cotgreave (https://amzn.to/3L0eWvP) - Book on designing effective business dashboards.
4. Tableau (https://www.tableau.com/) - Provides resources, insights, and best practices on data visualization and business intelligence.

Use Case 32:

Creating Engaging Presentations

We've all attended conferences where the presenter gave a boring lecture, and everyone tuned out.

You don't want to make that mistake! Lucky for you (and all of us), AI can craft incredibly interesting presentations using innovative ideas that are on the forefront of business performance.

Creating engaging presentations involves designing visually appealing and informative slides that effectively convey information and ideas. The point of all of this is to capture and maintain the audience's attention.

Creating engaging and impactful presentations is essential for SMBs looking to communicate their ideas, products, or services effectively to audiences. However, designing professional, visually appealing presentations can be time-consuming and challenging, especially for businesses with limited resources or design expertise. By leveraging AI tools like ChatGPT and specialized programs like

Beautiful AI, SMBs can streamline their presentation creation process, ensuring that their presentations are compelling, persuasive, and memorable.

Here are some ways your business can use AI to enhance their presentation creation:

Generating presentation outlines: Artificial intelligence can help SMBs create comprehensive presentation outlines that ensure a logical flow and cover all essential points. ChatGPT can generate an outline that serves as a roadmap for the entire presentation, saving time and ensuring a coherent structure.

Crafting compelling content: Provide AI with relevant information, such as product features, benefits, or case studies, and watch it generate clear, concise, and persuasive bullet points or paragraphs that effectively communicate the SMB's message and value proposition.

Suggesting visually appealing designs: AI-powered tools like Beautiful AI (I have more info about this later in the chapter) can help companies create visually stunning presentations without requiring extensive design skills. Beautiful AI can suggest appropriate layouts, color schemes, and visual elements that enhance the impact and professional appearance of the slides.

Ensuring brand consistency: ChatGPT and Beautiful AI can help maintain a consistent brand identity throughout your presentation. By integrating the SMB's brand guidelines, color palette, and visual assets, these AI tools can ensure that the presentation aligns with the company's overall branding and messaging.

Optimizing for audience engagement: AI can recommend specific techniques and prompts that encourage the audience to actively engage with the material and retain key information. That's what you want from your presentation in the first place, and if AI can open more ears to your message, all the better.

Beautiful AI: A Powerful Tool for SMBs

Beautiful.ai is a presentation software that uses artificial intelligence to create visually appealing and professional slides. It stands out for its smart templates, automatic design adjustments, and collaborative features. However, it's not the only player in the field. Here's a chart that compares some of the leading AI apps that do similar things offering AI-powered slide creation:

Feature	Beautiful.ai	Slidesgo	SlidesAI	Tome	Canva
AI-powered design	Yes	Yes	Yes	Yes	Yes
Smart templates	Yes	Yes	Yes	Yes	Yes
Automatic design adjustments	Yes	Limited	Limited	Yes	Yes
Collaboration features	Yes	Limited	Yes	Yes	Yes
Ease of use	High	High	High	High	High

Pricing	Paid (Free trial)	Free & Paid	Free & Paid	Free & Paid	Free & Paid

For our purposes here, we will describe how to use Beautiful.AI. It is an AI-powered presentation software that helps businesses create stunning, professional-grade presentations in minutes. By leveraging artificial intelligence and machine learning algorithms, Beautiful AI analyzes the content and structure of the presentation, automatically suggesting designs, layouts, and visual elements that enhance its impact and clarity. Small and medium-sized businesses can simply input their content into Beautiful AI, and the program will handle the rest. Imagine creating visually appealing, on-brand presentations that effectively communicate your message.

To maximize the benefits of AI for creating engaging presentations, your team should:

1. Clearly define the presentation's purpose, target audience, and key messages before engaging with AI tools, to ensure that the generated content aligns with the SMB's objectives
2. Use ChatGPT as a starting point, and always review and refine it with human expertise and judgment to ensure accuracy, clarity, and persuasiveness
3. Pick your presentation solution: (e.g., PowerPoint, Keynote, Prezi, etc) and Customize AI-generated designs and layouts to reflect the SMB's unique brand identity and visual style, ensuring consistency across all presentations. You can also use tools like Beautiful AI to do much of the creative work for you; it's your call.

4. Incorporate storytelling techniques and real-world examples into the presentation to make the content more relatable and memorable for the audience

5. Practice delivering the presentation and incorporate feedback from colleagues or AI tools to refine the content, pacing, and visual elements for maximum impact

These advanced tools, like Beautiful AI, will assist in generating outlines, crafting compelling content, suggesting visually appealing designs, ensuring brand consistency, and optimizing for audience engagement. However, it is crucial to remember that AI-generated presentations should always be reviewed and refined by human experts to ensure accuracy. Before you know it you'll be delivering presentations that captivate audiences!

10 potential prompt threads for creating engaging presentations:

1. Define the purpose and audience for the presentation.
2. Organize content into a logical and coherent structure.
3. Use clear, concise language to convey key points.
4. Incorporate visual aids, such as images, charts, and graphs.
5. Use AI-powered tools to generate presentation content or design suggestions.
6. Ensure a consistent and professional visual design.
7. Practice and refine delivery and timing.
8. Encourage audience interaction and engagement.
9. Gather feedback on presentation effectiveness.
10. Continuously improve presentation skills and techniques.

Once you have your presentation ready to go, make sure you know the source of all images in your seminars, and whenever possible create your own images with tools like Midjourney. You can run a simple image search on Google and discover whether the work is original or not. It's an extra step, but a worthwhile one.

Further Resources:

1. TED Talks (ted.com): Offers inspiring talks by expert speakers, showcasing engaging presentation styles and techniques.
2. SlideShare (slideshare.net): Provides a platform for sharing presentations and discovering new ideas, designs, and strategies for creating engaging slides.
3. Duarte (duarte.com): Offers blog posts, webinars, and resources on presentation design, storytelling, and public speaking; including "slide:ology: The Art and Science of Creating Great Presentations" by Nancy Duarte (https://amzn.to/3MKvppo)
4. "Presentation Zen: Simple Ideas on Presentation Design and Delivery" by Garr Reynolds (https://amzn.to/41r8S4Q) - Offers a guide to creating presentations that combine simplicity, clarity, and impact.
5. "Talk Like TED: The 9 Public-Speaking Secrets of the World's Top Minds" by Carmine Gallo(https://amzn.to/3GJLrf3) - Analyzes successful TED Talks and provides practical tips for creating and delivering engaging presentations.
6. "Resonate: Present Visual Stories that Transform Audiences" by Nancy Duarte (https://amzn.to/3Uz3wm1) - Offers a guide to creating compelling presentations that connect with the audience and inspire action.

Use Case 33:

Drafting External Communications

Drafting external communications involves creating written content for your various channels and purposes, such as emails, newsletters, press releases, and social media posts. These communications should be aimed at informing, engaging, or persuading your target audience.

When broken down, this is a massive amount of content depending on the size of your business. AI can create all this content quickly. You only need an AI Whisperer to add good prompts and edit the communications before sending them out.

Effective external communications are crucial for SMBs looking to build brand awareness, engage with customers, and grow their industry. AI tools like ChatGPT, will streamline the content creation process and give you a plethora of ideas to use as fodder for further ideation. Here are some ways SMBs can use AI to enhance their external communications:

Generating email and newsletter content: By inputting key topics, your target audience data, and the desired tone, your AI assistant can generate customized content that resonates with readers. These communications will brand loyalty and encourage your desired actions, be they making a purchase or signing up for your services.

Crafting press releases: AI can draft professional and newsworthy press releases that effectively communicate your product launches or events. Your company can generate press releases that adhere to industry standards and increase the likelihood of media coverage simply with a few good AI Whisperer prompts.

Creating social media posts: SMBs can use ChatGPT to construct a steady stream of customized social media content that drives engagement, increases brand visibility, and supports overall marketing objectives.

Developing website copy and blog posts: Your business can generate optimized content that attracts organic traffic, establishes thought leadership, and encourages visitors to explore your brand. And it won't take you hours and hours to do it. Time is money, after all.

Personalizing customer communications: ChatGPT can help SMBs create personalized responses to customer inquiries, feedback, and reviews across various channels. AI can generate tailored responses that address individual concerns, demonstrate empathy, and reinforce the brand's commitment to customer satisfaction.

The Role of the AI Whisperer in Communications:

While ChatGPT can significantly streamline the content creation process, to ensure the voice, context, and content are in line with company mission, it is essential for SMBs to have or retain a dedicated 'AI Whisperer' to oversee and refine the AI-generated content for the company. The AI Whisperer is responsible for:

1. Developing effective prompts and inputs that guide ChatGPT to generate content aligned with the SMB's goals, brand voice, and target audience preferences
2. Reviewing and editing AI-generated content to ensure accuracy, clarity, and coherence, while maintaining the human touch and creative flair that resonates with audiences
3. Monitoring the performance of AI-generated content across various channels and making data-driven decisions to optimize future content creation and distribution strategies
4. Collaborating with other teams and stakeholders to ensure that AI-generated content aligns with overall business objectives and complements other marketing and communications efforts

In *Appendix 4: AI Whisperer Position Descriptions*, we describe three versions of an AI Whisperer or prompt engineer. Level 1, is the semantic engineer that is a 'wordsmith' with the English language, semantics, and prompting GenAI. They need not be a coder, but are more involved in 'alignment, context, and content' in compliance with your brand and company values. That is the type of AI Whisperer you would want for a position like this.

Once you have an AI Whisperer on your team, you can maximize the benefits for drafting external communications by doing the following:

1. Establish clear brand guidelines, tone of voice, and target audience profiles to ensure consistency and relevance across all AI-generated content
2. Use ChatGPT-generated content as a starting point, and always have the AI Whisperer review, edit, and optimize the content before distribution
3. Regularly update ChatGPT's knowledge base with the latest industry trends, customer insights, and performance data to continuously improve the quality and effectiveness of the generated content
4. Integrate AI-generated content into a comprehensive communications strategy that leverages multiple channels and tactics to reach and engage target audiences
5. Continuously monitor and analyze the performance of AI-generated content, using insights to refine prompts, optimize distribution, and inform future content creation efforts

Again, whatever role AI takes in your company, having an AI Whisperer on-staff is crucial in ensuring that AI-generated content is accurate, on-brand, and resonates with target audiences. Sometimes the details AI supplies can be wrong or misinterpreted, just like with a real person. By combining the power of ChatGPT with the strategic oversight and creative input of the AI Whisperer, SMBs can build strong, lasting relationships with their customers and stakeholders. This will drive business growth and success in a progressively aggressive digital landscape.

10 potential prompt threads include:

1. Define the purpose, audience, and objectives of the communication.
2. Write clear, concise, and engaging content.
3. Ensure consistency with the company's style guide and brand voice.
4. Use appropriate tone and language for the target audience and channel.
5. Incorporate multimedia elements, such as images or videos, to enhance the message.
6. Use AI-powered tools to generate or optimize communication content.
7. Edit and proofread communications for clarity and accuracy.
8. Monitor and analyze the performance of communications.
9. Gather feedback from recipients and stakeholders.
10. Continuously improve communication strategies and techniques.

Further Resources:

1. Ragan Communications (ragan.com): Offers articles, webinars, and resources on various aspects of corporate communications, including external communication best practices.
2. PR Daily (prdaily.com): Provides news, insights, and tips on public relations, media relations, and external communication strategies.
3. Business Writing Blog (businesswriting.com/blog): Offers practical advice and tips for writing clear, concise, and persuasive business communications, including external messages.
4. "Everybody Writes: Your Go-To Guide to Creating Ridiculously Good Content" by Ann Handley (https://amzn.to/3MILL1q) - Provides advice and insights for crafting compelling and effective external communications, including emails, social media posts, and blog articles.

5. "Made to Stick: Why Some Ideas Survive and Others Die" by Chip Heath and Dan Heath (https://amzn.to/3A2BRAp) - Offers principles and techniques for creating memorable and engaging messages that resonate with your audience.

6. "The New Rules of Marketing and PR: How to Use Social Media, Online Video, Mobile Applications, Blogs, News Releases, and Viral Marketing to Reach Buyers Directly" by David Meerman Scott (https://amzn.to/3GIsidD) - Presents strategies for creating external communications that effectively reach and engage your target audience.

7. "The Art of Explanation: Making your Ideas, Products, and Services Easier to Understand" by Lee LeFever (https://amzn.to/3L1uU96) - Provides guidance on how to create clear, concise, and compelling explanations for complex topics in external communications.

8. "Writing Without Bullshit: Boost Your Career by Saying What You Mean" by Josh Bernoff (https://amzn.to/3mHO4at) - Offers practical tips for eliminating jargon, fluff, and unnecessary information in external communications, making them more concise and impactful.

9. Mailchimp (mailchimp.com): A marketing automation platform and email marketing service that helps businesses create, send, and analyze email campaigns.

10. Buffer (buffer.com): A social media management tool that allows businesses to schedule, publish, and analyze social media posts across multiple platforms.

Use Case 34:

Personalizing Customer Interactions

No customer wants to feel like they're so unimportant that a robot is the best they can expect to help them with their problems. A good AI though makes that problem mute. Most of the time the customer won't even know they're interacting with an artificial intelligence.

Personalizing customer interactions involves tailoring communication, content, and experiences based on individual customer preferences, behavior, and history to enhance engagement, satisfaction, and loyalty.

In today's competitive business landscape, providing personalized customer experiences is essential for SMBs looking to build strong, lasting relationships with their customers. However, tailoring interactions to individual preferences and needs can be challenging, especially for businesses with limited resources or a growing customer base.

AI tools like ChatGPT allow businesses to efficiently personalize customer interactions across various touchpoints, leading to increased engagement, satisfaction, and loyalty. Here are some ways SMBs can use AI to personalize customer interactions:

Customizing product and service recommendations: ChatGPT can analyze customer data, such as purchase history, browsing behavior, and preferences, to generate personalized product or service recommendations. Giving AI tailored suggestions that align with individual customer interests, entire industries can increase the likelihood of conversions and foster a sense of value among their customers.

Personalizing customer support interactions: Artificial intelligence can generate tailored responses that address individual concerns, demonstrate empathy, and provide relevant solutions, leading to faster issue resolution and increased customer satisfaction. All you have to do is feed your AI assistant your customer profiles, interaction history, and current inquiries.

Developing targeted marketing campaigns: By leveraging customer data and insights, ChatGPT can help SMBs craft compelling, relevant messages that resonate with specific audiences, increasing the effectiveness of marketing efforts and driving desired actions.

Creating individualized onboarding experiences: ChatGPT can help businesses develop personalized onboarding journeys for new customers. This will guide them through product or service setup. You can also provide tailored tutorials and offer proactive support. By creating a seamless, customized onboarding experience, SMBs can reduce friction, increase adoption, and foster long-term customer engagement and loyalty.

Offering proactive, contextual assistance: If a customer is browsing a specific product page or attempting to complete a complex task, ChatGPT can offer personalized recommendations, tips, or resources to help them make informed decisions or overcome challenges, enhancing the overall customer experience.

The Power of AI in Personalization:

One of the key advantages of using AI tools like ChatGPT for personalizing customer interactions is that, when implemented effectively, customers may not even realize they are engaging with an artificial intelligence. By leveraging natural language processing and machine learning, ChatGPT can understand and respond to customer inquiries in a human-like manner, providing relevant, empathetic, and personalized interactions that feel authentic and valuable.

Moreover, AI-powered personalization allows SMBs to scale their efforts efficiently, providing tailored experiences to a growing customer base without overburdening human staff. This enables SMBs to deliver consistent, high-quality personalized interactions across various touchpoints, fostering strong, lasting customer relationships and driving business growth.

To maximize the benefits of AI for personalizing customer interactions, it's advisable for businesses to:

1. Ensure the quality and security of customer data used to inform AI-powered personalization efforts, respecting privacy and building trust

2. Continuously train and refine AI models based on customer feedback, interaction outcomes, and evolving business priorities to improve the accuracy and effectiveness of personalized experiences
3. Integrate AI-powered personalization into a holistic customer experience strategy that encompasses multiple channels, touchpoints, and stages of the customer journey
4. Regularly monitor and analyze the performance of AI-powered personalization efforts, using insights to optimize approaches, address challenges, and identify new opportunities for enhancing customer experiences
5. Foster a customer-centric culture that prioritizes empathy, authenticity, and continuous improvement in personalized interactions, whether AI-driven or human-led

When implemented effectively, AI-powered personalization can provide authentic, valuable interactions that customers may not even recognize as artificial. This will allow your team to scale their efforts efficiently. You'll be able to foster strong, lasting relationships with your customers, ultimately driving long-term success.

Here are 10 potential prompt threads that will help you personalize your message:

1. Collect and analyze customer data to understand preferences and behavior.
2. Segment customers based on shared characteristics.
3. Customize content, offers, and recommendations for each segment.
4. Use AI-powered tools to automate personalization across channels.

5. Monitor and analyze the effectiveness of personalized interactions.
6. Continuously update customer profiles and preferences.
7. Ensure compliance with data privacy regulations and best practices.
8. Incorporate personalization into customer support and service interactions.
9. Test and optimize personalized communication strategies.
10. Use AI-generated insights to identify opportunities for further personalization.

Remember, an AI doesn't actually think for itself. It's a tool that doesn't have the same discerning understanding a human has. Always make sure the details and final output are appropriate for your customers and business.

Further Resources:

1. HubSpot (hubspot.com): Offers resources, blog posts, and guides on customer relationship management, marketing, and personalization strategies.
2. ConstantContact (constantcontact.com),
3. Salesforce (salesforce.com): Provides resources and insights on customer engagement, personalization, and CRM best practices.
4. MarketingProfs (marketingprofs.com): Offers articles, webinars, and resources on various marketing topics, including customer personalization and engagement.
5. "Hug Your Haters: How to Embrace Complaints and Keep Your Customers" by Jay Baer(https://amzn.to/3L10WSw) Provides insights and strategies for handling customer interactions and personalizing your responses to create positive experiences.
6. "The Effortless Experience: Conquering the New Battleground for Customer Loyalty" by Matthew Dixon, Nick Toman, and Rick

DeLisi (https://amzn.to/3UJQQsr) - Offers techniques for improving customer interactions and personalizing service to increase satisfaction and loyalty.

7. "The Power of Moments: Why Certain Experiences Have Extraordinary Impact" by Chip Heath and Dan Heath (https://amzn.to/3zZrFIR) - Explores the importance of creating memorable and personalized experiences for customers and provides guidance on how to do so.

8. "Delivering Happiness: A Path to Profits, Passion, and Purpose" by Tony Hsieh (https://amzn.to/3mt1K9v) - Chronicles the success of Zappos and its focus on creating personalized and exceptional customer experiences.

9. https://www.optimizely.com/ Optimizely is a website that provides A/B testing, personalization, and optimization software.

10. https://www.segment.com/ Segment is a website that provides customer data infrastructure.

Use Case 35:

Process Improvement and Optimization

Optimization is a key aspect of any business. If you can take five processes and turn them into two, you'll save time and money.

This is true in manufacturing all the way down to advertising.

As with everything in this book, AI can help streamline operations, reduce costs, and enhance overall business performance.

The following are several areas where these technologies can make a substantial impact. Now for those of you paying attention, I'm going to switch up the format here so you can see how AI can process data differently depending on your business needs. Since we're talking about optimization, we'll move to a more efficient bullet point arrangement. Pay attention to how the data looks and why you might want to adapt this format to your own data presentations.

1. Customer Service and Support

- Chatbots and Virtual Assistants: AI-powered chatbots can handle routine customer inquiries, provide 24/7 support, and escalate complex issues to human agents, improving response times and customer satisfaction.
- Sentiment Analysis: AI can analyze customer feedback and social media interactions to gauge customer sentiment, helping businesses understand and address customer concerns promptly.

2. Sales and Marketing

- Personalized Marketing Campaigns: AI can analyze customer data to create highly targeted marketing campaigns, increasing conversion rates and customer loyalty.
- Sales Forecasting: AI tools can predict sales trends and customer behavior, helping businesses make informed decisions about inventory, staffing, and marketing strategies.

3. Operations and Supply Chain Management

- Inventory Management: AI can optimize inventory levels by predicting demand, reducing overstock and stockouts, and ensuring timely replenishment.
- Logistics Optimization: AI algorithms can optimize delivery routes, reduce shipping costs, and improve delivery times.

4. Financial Management

- Expense Tracking and Reporting: AI tools can automate expense tracking, categorize expenses, and generate financial reports, reducing manual effort and improving accuracy.

- Fraud Detection: AI can analyze transaction patterns to detect and prevent fraudulent activities, enhancing financial security.

5. Human Resources

- Recruitment Automation: AI can screen resumes, assess candidate fit, and even conduct initial interviews, streamlining the hiring process and reducing time-to-hire.
- Employee Engagement: AI-powered surveys and sentiment analysis can help gauge employee satisfaction and identify areas for improvement, leading to higher retention rates.

6. Data Analysis and Reporting

- Automated Reporting: AI tools can generate real-time reports and dashboards, providing actionable insights without the need for extensive manual data analysis.
- Predictive Analytics: AI can identify trends and patterns in historical data, helping businesses make proactive decisions and anticipate future challenges.

7. Product Development and Innovation

- Market Research: AI can analyze market trends, customer preferences, and competitor strategies, providing valuable insights for product development and innovation.
- Prototyping and Testing: AI can simulate product performance and test various scenarios, accelerating the development process and reducing costs.

8. Customer Relationship Management (CRM)

- Enhanced CRM Systems: AI can enhance CRM systems by providing deeper insights into customer behavior, automating follow-ups, and personalizing customer interactions.

Once you have your plans in place, you'll want to implement them as soon as possible. Here are a few extra steps that will allow you to get the most out of your AI interactions:

1. Assess Needs and Opportunities: Identify key areas where AI can add value to your business processes.
2. Choose the Right Tools: Select AI tools that align with your business needs and are scalable as your business grows.
3. Train Your Team: Ensure your team understands how to use AI tools effectively and integrate them into daily operations.
4. Monitor and Adjust: Continuously monitor the performance of AI tools and make adjustments as needed to optimize outcomes.

Now that you have everything ready, below are 10 different prompts that will yield promising results with AI assistance:

1. Create a process map for a specific operation or workflow.
2. Identify potential bottlenecks or inefficiencies in a given process.
3. Suggest improvements or optimizations for a particular process.

4. Write a standard operating procedure (SOP) for a specific task or function.
5. Develop a list of best practices for process improvement and optimization.
6. Create a performance measurement framework for evaluating process effectiveness.
7. Write a guide on implementing Lean or Six Sigma methodologies for process improvement.
8. Develop a list of potential process improvement tools or software solutions.
9. Suggest strategies for fostering a culture of continuous improvement within the organization.
10. Create a process improvement plan for a specific department or function.

When requesting process improvement and optimization assistance, provide specific information about your procedures, goals, and desired outcomes. If the AI-generated content is not relevant or effective, consider refining your prompt or providing additional context so the AI can better understand your objectives.

Further Resources:

1. "The Goal" by Eliyahu M. Goldratt (https://amzn.to/41817DO) Book on process improvement and the Theory of Constraints.
2. Process Excellence Network (https://www.processexcellencenetwork.com/) - Offers resources, insights, and best practices on process improvement and optimization.
3. "Lean Thinking" by James P. Womack and Daniel T. Jones (https://amzn.to/3KvAGhu) - Book on Lean methodology and principles.

4. iSixSigma (https://www.isixsigma.com/) - Provides resources, insights, and best practices on Six Sigma and process improvement methodologies.

Use Case 36:

Writing Case Studies and Success Stories

Writing case studies and success stories involves creating detailed narratives that showcase the positive impact of your products, services, or solutions on customers. When done right, you provide evidence of value and build credibility with potential clients.

Once again, using an AI for this purpose will free up time for other pressing matters, while giving you a wealth of information to share internally or with the community at large.

Importantly, there are different types of case studies and patterns of case studies used across various industries, each serving distinct purposes and audiences. Here are some common types and their typical structures:

1. Academic Case Studies (e.g., Harvard Business School)

Structure:

- Abstract/Executive Summary: A brief overview of the case, highlighting the main issues and conclusions.
- Introduction: Context and background information about the company or situation being studied.
- Problem Statement: Clear articulation of the primary challenges or decisions to be addressed.
- Analysis: Detailed examination of the issues, often using theoretical frameworks, data analysis, and comparison to similar cases.
- Solutions/Recommendations: Suggested courses of action based on the analysis, often considering various alternatives.
- Conclusion: Summary of the findings and implications for practice or further research.
- Teaching Notes: For instructors, including discussion questions and potential answers.

Purpose: To provide a detailed, educational examination of a real-world business scenario, often used for teaching strategic thinking and decision-making.

2. Corporate Case Studies (e.g., Service Providers or Product Companies)

Structure:

- Title: Clear and engaging title that highlights the main benefit or outcome.
- Introduction: Overview of the customer, their industry, and the challenges they faced.
- Challenges: Detailed description of the specific problems or needs of the customer.
- Solution: Explanation of how the company's product or service was implemented to address the challenges.

- Results: Quantifiable outcomes and benefits realized by the customer, often supported by data and testimonials.
- Conclusion: Recap of the key points and a call to action for potential clients.

Purpose: To demonstrate the effectiveness and value of a product or service through real-world examples, aiming to attract and persuade potential customers.

3. Research Case Studies

Structure:

- Abstract: Summary of the study, including research questions, methods, and key findings.
- Introduction: Background information and context of the research, including the significance of the study.
- Literature Review: Overview of existing research and how the current study fits within the field.
- Methodology: Detailed description of research methods, data collection, and analysis procedures.
- Findings: Presentation of the research results, often including charts, tables, and other data visualizations.
- Discussion: Interpretation of the findings, implications for theory and practice, and potential limitations of the study.
- Conclusion: Summary of the study's contributions and suggestions for future research.
- References: List of all sources cited in the case study.

Purpose: To contribute to academic knowledge and provide a basis for further research, often published in academic journals.

4. Consulting Case Studies

Structure:

- Introduction: Brief overview of the client and the business context.
- Objectives: Clear articulation of the goals and objectives of the consulting engagement.
- Approach: Description of the methodology and tools used to analyze the problem and develop solutions.
- Findings/Analysis: Detailed presentation of the data analysis, insights, and findings.
- Recommendations: Specific, actionable recommendations provided to the client.
- Implementation: Description of how the recommendations were implemented, including any challenges faced and how they were overcome.
- Results: Quantitative and qualitative outcomes of the implementation, demonstrating the impact of the consulting engagement.
- Conclusion: Summary of the engagement and its success, often including client testimonials.

Purpose: To showcase the consulting firm's expertise, methodology, and successful outcomes to attract new clients and build credibility.

By understanding these different types of case studies and their structures, organizations can effectively create and use case studies to achieve their specific goals, whether in education, marketing, research, or consulting.

10 potential prompt threads:

1. Identify customers with compelling success stories.
2. Gather relevant data, testimonials, and other supporting evidence.
3. Structure the narrative to include background, challenges, solutions, and results.
4. Use clear, concise language to convey the story.
5. Incorporate visuals, such as images or charts, to enhance the presentation.
6. Use AI-powered tools to generate case study content based on input data.
7. Edit and proofread case studies for clarity and accuracy.
8. Promote case studies on your website, social media, and other marketing channels.
9. Monitor the performance and impact of case studies on lead generation and sales.
10. Continuously update and expand your library of case studies and success stories.

Writing case studies and success stories gives you another avenue to present content to either your customers or shareholders. To ensure that the AI-generated content is accurate, engaging, and consistent with your organization's style guide and brand voice, make sure to have a trusted manager (your AI Whisperer) go over every piece of content. You don't want to get your company in trouble by simply taking what the AI gives you and putting it out into the world.

Further Resources:

1. HubSpot (hubspot.com): Offers resources, templates, and blog posts on creating compelling case studies and success stories for marketing purposes.
2. Content Marketing Institute (contentmarketinginstitute.com): Provides articles, guides, and resources on various content marketing topics, including case study and success story creation.
3. "The Case Study Handbook: How to Read, Discuss, and Write Persuasively About Cases" by William Ellet (https://amzn.to/3L0t2gN) - Offers guidance on analyzing, discussing, and writing about business case studies, with a focus on persuasive storytelling.
4. "Case Study Research: Design and Methods" by Robert K. Yin (https://amzn.to/3mFqviv) - Provides a comprehensive guide to conducting case study research and presenting the findings effectively.
5. "Stories That Sell: Turn Satisfied Customers into Your Most Powerful Sales & Marketing Asset" by Casey Hibbard (https://amzn.to/3KGzmZz) - Offers strategies and techniques for creating compelling success stories and case studies that showcase the value of your products or services.

Use Case 37:

Managing Content Calendars and Editorial Plans

Organization is a key component in managing content calendars and editorial plans. Luckily, AI is about as organized as you can get. Sometimes ChatGPT will throw you a curveball that makes you chuckle, but for the most part, AI has their ducks in a row. Scheduling the creation, publication, and promotion of content across various channels and formats is one of artificial intelligence's strengths. It will support marketing, communication, and business objectives.

Your AI assistant can manage content calendars and editorial plans in several ways. It will streamline workflows and ensure timely, relevant content creation all the way through to publication. Here are some defined tasks where ChatGPT can be particularly useful:

1. Content Ideation and Brainstorming

- Generating Topic Ideas: Provide topic suggestions based on industry trends, audience interests, and keyword research.
- Content Series Planning: Help plan multi-part content series or themed content campaigns.
- Trend Analysis: Analyze current trends and suggest relevant content ideas.

2. Calendar Management

- Scheduling Posts: Assist in scheduling content for various platforms, ensuring a consistent posting schedule.
- Deadline Tracking: Keep track of deadlines for drafts, reviews, and publication dates, sending reminders as needed.
- Integration with Tools: Integrate with content management tools like Trello, Asana, or Google Calendar to manage tasks and timelines.

3. Content Creation

- Drafting Content: Write drafts for blog posts, social media updates, newsletters, and other content types.
- Repurposing Content: Suggest ways to repurpose existing content into different formats, such as turning a blog post into a video script or social media posts.
- SEO Optimization: Provide SEO recommendations, including keyword usage, meta descriptions, and title suggestions.

4. Editorial Planning

- Creating Editorial Plans: Assist in developing comprehensive editorial plans that align with business goals and marketing strategies.

- Content Mapping: Help map out content to different stages of the buyer's journey or customer funnel.
- Theme and Topic Coordination: Ensure that all content aligns with monthly or quarterly themes and coordinates topics across different content types.

5. Collaboration and Communication

- Task Assignment: Assign tasks to team members and track progress.
- Feedback and Review: Provide initial feedback on content drafts, checking for tone, clarity, and alignment with editorial guidelines.
- Meeting Summaries: Summarize editorial meetings and outline action items for the team.

6. Content Performance Analysis

- Tracking Metrics: Help track content performance metrics such as page views, engagement rates, and conversion rates.
- Analyzing Results: Analyze the performance of past content to identify what works best and suggest improvements.
- Reporting: Generate regular content performance reports to share with the team.

7. Content Curation

- Finding Relevant Content: Curate relevant articles, videos, and other content from around the web to share with your audience.
- Content Summaries: Summarize curated content for easy sharing and quick consumption.

8. Audience Engagement

- Community Management: Assist with responding to comments and messages on social media and other platforms.
- Engagement Strategies: Suggest strategies to boost audience engagement, such as interactive content, polls, and Q&A sessions.

9. Crisis Management

- Drafting Responses: Help draft responses for crisis communication, ensuring timely and appropriate messaging.
- Monitoring Sentiment: Monitor audience sentiment and feedback to address issues promptly.

10. Content Maintenance

- Updating Content: Identify and update outdated content to ensure it remains relevant and accurate.
- Link Management: Check for broken links and suggest replacements to maintain a good user experience.

Implementation Steps:

1. Define Goals and Objectives: Clearly outline what you aim to achieve with your content calendar and editorial plan.
2. Select Tools: Choose the appropriate tools (e.g., content management systems, project management tools) that integrate well with ChatGPT.
3. Train ChatGPT: Provide necessary background information, editorial guidelines, and access to relevant data sources.
4. Create Templates: Develop templates for content briefs, calendars, reports, and other necessary documents.

5. Regular Review: Schedule regular reviews to assess the effectiveness of ChatGPT in managing tasks and make adjustments as needed.

Using ChatGPT for these sorts of tasks enhances your business' efficiency. As always, the AI content will help your team maintain consistency in your messaging and improve the overall effectiveness of your content strategy.

And you guessed it! Here are 10 potential prompt threads that will get AI moving in the direction your company needs:

1. Define content goals, objectives, and target audiences.
2. Identify relevant content topics and formats.
3. Develop a content calendar that outlines publication dates and channels.
4. Use AI-powered tools to generate content ideas and optimize publishing schedules.
5. Assign content creation tasks to team members or external contributors.
6. Monitor and analyze the performance of published content.
7. Adjust content plans based on performance data and audience feedback.
8. Ensure content is aligned with broader marketing and communication strategies.
9. Regularly update and refine content plans to stay relevant and engaging.
10. Use AI-generated insights to identify opportunities for content optimization.

When using AI for managing content calendars and editorial plans, ensure that the ideas and recommendations support your company goals, objectives, and brand voice. Always review and approve AI-generated suggestions before incorporating them into your content plans.

Further Resources:

1. Trello (Trello.com) excels in providing a visually appealing and intuitive platform for managing tasks and projects using the Kanban methodology, making it easy for teams to collaborate and track progress.
2. Airtable (airtable.com) shines in its ability to handle complex data through a flexible, customizable database, offering multiple views and powerful features for organizing and analyzing information.
3. Asana (asana.com): A project management platform that can be used to create content calendars, assign tasks, set deadlines, and collaborate on editorial plans.
4. CoSchedule (coschedule.com): A content marketing platform specifically designed for planning, organizing, and executing content marketing and social media campaigns.
5. Google Calendar (calendar.google.com): A widely used calendar tool that can be adapted for managing content calendars and editorial plans by creating events, setting reminders, and sharing calendars with team members.
6. Monday.com (monday.com): A work operating system that allows you to create customizable boards for managing content calendars, tracking tasks, and collaborating on editorial plans.
7. ContentCal (contentcal.io): A content marketing and social media planning platform that helps you plan, create, and publish content while collaborating with your team.
8. "Work Smarter Not Harder: 18 Productivity Tips That Boost Your Work Day Performance" by Timo Kiander (https://amzn.to/411axyh) - Offers productivity tips and strategies that can be applied to various aspects of work, including content management and automation.
9. "Automate This: How Algorithms Came to Rule Our World" by Christopher Steiner (https://amzn.to/3UCDMVK) - Explores the

power of automation and algorithms in various industries and provides insights that can be applied to content calendar management and editorial planning.

10. "The One-Minute To-Do List: Quickly Get Your Chaos Completely Under Control" by Michael Linenberger (https://amzn.to/3UzXx0f) - Offers time management and productivity techniques that can help you better manage and automate your content calendars and editorial plans.

Use Case 38:

Developing Creative Advertising Concepts

Marketing can be a beast. Let's be honest. We know we have to spend money to advertise, but often it's like throwing darts at a board to determine what works and what doesn't.

Data is the saving grace in advertising, and no one has more data than AI. They have access to the width and breadth of human knowledge and can see things even trained marketers miss.

AI can develop creative advertising concepts and generate unique, engaging ideas for marketing campaigns that effectively communicate brand messages, capture audience attention, and drive desired actions.

Small and medium-sized businesses can use ChatGPT to develop creative advertising concepts in various ways, enhancing their marketing efforts and reaching their target audience more effectively. Here are some specific tasks and strategies where ChatGPT can be particularly helpful:

1. Brainstorming Creative Ideas

- Ad Campaign Themes: Generate unique and engaging themes for advertising campaigns based on market trends, product features, or seasonal events.
- Taglines and Slogans: Create catchy and memorable taglines or slogans that resonate with the target audience.
- Concept Development: Develop innovative concepts for advertisements, including storylines for video ads, themes for print ads, and ideas for social media campaigns.

2. Audience Analysis and Segmentation

- Customer Personas: Help create detailed customer personas based on demographic, psychographic, and behavioral data.
- Targeted Messaging: Suggest tailored messaging strategies for different audience segments to enhance relevance and engagement.

3. Content Creation for Ads

- Ad Copywriting: Write compelling and persuasive ad copy for various formats, including social media posts, Google ads, banner ads, and email campaigns.
- Script Writing: Develop scripts for video ads, including dialogue, scenes, and key messaging points.
- Visual Ideas: Provide ideas for visuals, including imagery, color schemes, and design elements that align with the ad concept.

4. A/B Testing Concepts

- Variation Suggestions: Generate multiple variations of ad copy, headlines, and visuals to facilitate A/B testing.

- Performance Predictions: Offer insights into which variations might perform better based on historical data and industry benchmarks.

5. Campaign Planning

- Content Calendar: Assist in creating a content calendar that schedules the rollout of various ad components across different channels.
- Integration Strategies: Suggest ways to integrate advertising efforts with other marketing activities, such as promotions, events, or product launches.

6. Social Media Advertising

- Platform-Specific Content: Generate ad concepts tailored to different social media platforms (e.g., Instagram, Facebook, LinkedIn, TikTok) to optimize engagement.
- Interactive Ads: Suggest ideas for interactive ads, such as polls, quizzes, and user-generated content campaigns.

7. Localized Advertising

- Cultural Relevance: Provide ideas for localized ad campaigns that consider regional preferences, language nuances, and cultural sensitivities.
- Local Partnerships: Suggest potential local partnerships or influencer collaborations to enhance the reach and credibility of the ad campaign.

8. Event-Based Advertising

- Seasonal Campaigns: Develop concepts for seasonal or holiday-themed advertising that capitalize on timely opportunities.
- Event Promotions: Create advertising ideas for promoting events, product launches, or special promotions.

9. Storytelling and Brand Narrative

- Brand Story Development: Help craft a compelling brand story that can be woven into various advertising materials.
- Emotional Appeal: Suggest ways to incorporate emotional appeal into ads to connect with the audience on a deeper level.

10. Feedback and Iteration

- Ad Performance Analysis: Analyze the performance of existing ads and provide suggestions for improvements or new creative directions.
- Continuous Improvement: Offer ongoing creative support to iterate on advertising concepts based on feedback and performance data.

Implementation Steps:

1. Define Objectives: Clearly outline the goals of the advertising campaign, including target audience, key messages, and desired outcomes.

2. Gather Data: Collect relevant data about your audience, market trends, and past advertising performance to inform the creative process.

3. Collaborate with ChatGPT: Use ChatGPT to brainstorm ideas, draft copy, and develop concepts, ensuring alignment with your brand voice and objectives.

4. Review and Refine: Review the generated concepts with your team, refine them as needed, and select the best ideas for execution.

5. Execute and Monitor: Implement the chosen advertising concepts, monitor their performance, and make adjustments based on real-time data and feedback.

By leveraging ChatGPT in these ways, SMBs can enhance their creative advertising efforts, produce more engaging and effective ads, and ultimately drive better business outcomes.

Here are 10 ideas that will allow you to use AI to maximum efficiency:

1. Define the advertising campaign's goals, objectives, and target audience.

2. Research industry trends, competitor campaigns, and audience preferences.

3. Generate creative ideas through brainstorming, mind mapping, or other ideation techniques.

4. Use AI-powered tools to generate advertising concepts based on input data.

5. Develop a unique selling proposition (USP) that differentiates your brand or product.

6. Create compelling visuals, copy, and messaging that support the advertising concept.

7. Test and refine advertising concepts based on audience feedback and performance data.
8. Ensure advertising concepts align with your overall brand strategy and guidelines.
9. Execute and monitor the advertising campaign across various channels.
10. Continuously improve advertising concepts and strategies based on performance metrics and industry trends.

There are a lot of nuances when it comes to marketing. Use these artificial intelligence ideas as a base for what comes next. AI doesn't replace your marketing team; it just gives them a leg-up on the competition.

Further Resources:

1. Adweek (adweek.com): Offers news, insights, and resources on advertising, media, and marketing, including articles on creative advertising concepts and trends.
2. AdAge (adage.com): Provides news, analysis, and insights on advertising, marketing, and media, featuring articles on creative advertising concepts, case studies, and campaigns.
3. The Drum (thedrum.com): Covers news and opinions on marketing, advertising, and design, with articles on creative advertising concepts, trends, and best practices.
4. Creative Bloq (creativebloq.com): Offers articles, resources, and inspiration on graphic design, branding, and advertising, including tips and ideas for developing creative advertising concepts.
5. Ads of the World (adsoftheworld.com): Showcases creative advertising campaigns from around the world, providing inspiration and insights into developing innovative advertising concepts.

6. "Hey, Whipple, Squeeze This: The Classic Guide to Creating Great Ads" by Luke Sullivan (https://amzn.to/3GKBfTK) - Offers practical advice and insights for creating compelling and effective advertising concepts.

7. "Ogilvy on Advertising" by David Ogilvy (https://amzn.to/3A0K4Fi) - Provides timeless insights and advice on advertising from one of the industry's most respected figures.

8. "The Idea Writers: Copywriting in a New Media and Marketing Era" by Teressa Iezzi (https://amzn.to/3ojKnIo) Offers guidance on crafting compelling advertising concepts in the digital age, with insights from leading creative professionals.

9. "Truth, Lies, and Advertising: The Art of Account Planning" by Jon Steel (https://amzn.to/418VUZX) - Presents techniques for developing advertising strategies and creative concepts based on consumer insights and research.

10. "The Copy Book: How 32 of the World's Best Advertising Writers Write Their Advertising" by D&AD (https://amzn.to/411bPJD) - Showcases advertising concepts and copywriting techniques from top industry professionals, providing inspiration and ideas for developing your own creative advertising concepts.

Use Case 39:

Sales Strategy and Pipeline Management

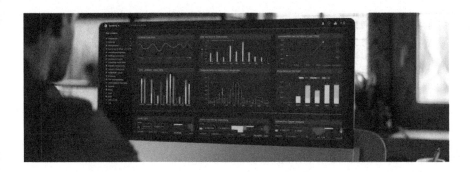

Use ChatGPT to support your sales strategy and pipeline management efforts by generating sales scripts, email templates, lead qualification criteria, or sales performance metrics. AI can help improve sales processes, boost conversion rates, and enhance overall revenue generation.

ChatGPT can significantly enhance sales strategy and pipeline management for SMBs by streamlining processes, providing data-driven insights, and facilitating better customer interactions. Here are some specific tasks and strategies where ChatGPT can be particularly useful:

1. Sales Strategy Development

- Market Research: Conduct market research and competitor analysis to identify opportunities and threats.

- Customer Segmentation: Assist in segmenting customers based on various criteria such as demographics, behavior, and purchase history.
- Value Proposition: Help refine and articulate the business's value proposition for different customer segments.
- Sales Forecasting: Use historical data to predict future sales trends and set realistic targets.

2. Lead Generation

- Prospect Identification: Identify potential leads based on specified criteria such as industry, company size, and location.
- Content Creation: Generate personalized email templates, social media messages, and other outreach content to attract and engage potential leads.
- Lead Qualification: Develop scripts for qualifying leads through initial conversations or automated surveys.

3. Pipeline Management

- Pipeline Visualization: Create visual representations of the sales pipeline to track the progress of deals at various stages.
- Deal Tracking: Monitor the status of deals, identifying bottlenecks and areas that need attention.
- Follow-up Reminders: Set automated reminders for follow-up actions to ensure timely communication with prospects and clients.

4. Sales Communication

- Email Drafting: Write personalized and persuasive emails for various stages of the sales process, including follow-ups, proposals, and closing.
- Call Scripts: Develop scripts for sales calls, including opening lines, key talking points, and responses to common objections.
- Presentation Preparation: Create compelling sales presentations and proposals tailored to specific prospects.

5. Customer Relationship Management (CRM)

- Data Entry: Assist with inputting and updating customer data in CRM systems.
- Activity Logging: Log sales activities, such as calls, emails, and meetings, to maintain accurate records.
- Contact Insights: Provide insights on customer interactions and suggest next steps based on historical data.

6. Performance Analysis and Reporting

- Sales Metrics: Track key sales metrics such as conversion rates, average deal size, and sales cycle length.
- Performance Reports: Generate regular sales performance reports to share with the team and stakeholders.
- Trend Analysis: Analyze trends in sales data to identify successful strategies and areas for improvement.

7. Training and Onboarding

- Training Materials: Create training materials and resources for new sales team members.

- Role-playing Scenarios: Develop role-playing scenarios to help salespeople practice and improve their skills.
- Knowledge Base: Maintain a knowledge base of best practices, FAQs, and common objections for quick reference.

8. Customer Feedback and Improvement

- Survey Creation: Design customer satisfaction surveys and feedback forms to gather insights on sales interactions.
- Feedback Analysis: Analyze customer feedback to identify areas for improvement in the sales process.
- Process Optimization: Suggest improvements to the sales process based on feedback and performance data.

9. Collaboration and Coordination

- Team Communication: Facilitate communication and coordination within the sales team through automated updates and shared calendars.
- Goal Setting: Assist in setting individual and team sales goals and track progress towards achieving them.
- Strategy Meetings: Summarize strategy meetings and outline action items for follow-up.

Implementation Steps:

1. Identify Objectives: Define the specific goals and objectives for leveraging ChatGPT in your sales strategy and pipeline management.

2. Integrate Tools: Ensure ChatGPT is integrated with your CRM and other sales tools to streamline data flow and communication.
3. Provide Training: Train your sales team on how to use ChatGPT effectively, including best practices and available features.
4. Monitor Performance: Regularly review the performance of ChatGPT-assisted tasks and make adjustments as needed to optimize outcomes.
5. Continuous Improvement: Use insights from performance data and feedback to continuously refine and improve your sales strategies and processes.

Small and medium businesses can enhance their sales strategy with the use of AI tools. You will ultimately be able to drive better sales performance. Always edit the work and add a human touch where necessary.

10 Potential Prompt Threads:

1. Write a sales script for a specific product or service offering.
2. Develop a sales email template for prospecting or follow-up.
3. Create a list of lead qualification criteria for a particular target market.
4. Suggest strategies for improving sales pipeline management and conversion rates.
5. Write a guide on best practices for conducting effective sales calls or meetings.
6. Develop a list of potential sales performance metrics or KPIs.

7. Create a sales strategy for penetrating a new market or customer segment.
8. Write a guide on using specific sales tools or software (e.g., CRM systems).
9. Develop a list of potential sales training resources or materials.
10. Suggest strategies for handling sales objections or negotiating deals.

Further Resources:

1. HubSpot (hubspot.com): Offers resources, blog posts, and guides on sales strategy, pipeline management, and customer relationship management.
2. Sales Hacker (saleshacker.com): Provides articles, webinars, and resources on various sales topics, including sales strategy, pipeline management, and sales enablement.
3. Salesforce (salesforce.com): Offers insights, resources, and blog posts on sales strategy, pipeline management, and CRM best practices.
4. Sandler Training (sandler.com): Provides sales training resources, articles, and podcasts on sales strategy, pipeline management, and sales techniques.
5. CloserIQ (closeriq.com): Offers blog posts, articles, and resources on sales strategy, pipeline management, and sales team development.
6. "The Challenger Sale" by Matthew Dixon and Brent Adamson (https://amzn.to/3MKyxl4) - Book on a new approach to sales and customer engagement
7. "SPIN Selling" by Neil Rackham (https://amzn.to/3GJClzg) - Book on consultative selling and sales techniques.
8. "New Sales. Simplified.: The Essential Handbook for Prospecting and New Business Development" by Mike Weinberg (https://amzn.to/41wvqky) Offers practical advice and strategies

for developing a successful sales strategy and managing your sales pipeline.

9. "Cracking the Sales Management Code: The Secrets to Measuring and Managing Sales Performance" by Jason Jordan and Michelle Vazzana (https://amzn.to/3L02GeF) - Provides insights and techniques for managing sales performance and sales pipelines effectively.

10. "The Sales Acceleration Formula: Using Data, Technology, and Inbound Selling to Go from $0 to $100 Million" by Mark Roberge (https://amzn.to/3og7HXJ) - Offers guidance on building a scalable and predictable sales strategy using data, technology, and inbound selling.

11. "Predictable Revenue: Turn Your Business into a Sales Machine with the $100 Million Best Practices of Salesforce.com" by Aaron Ross and Marylou Tyler (https://amzn.to/3AiNfs9) - Provides insights into the strategies and techniques used by Salesforce.com to create a scalable and predictable sales process, including prospecting, lead generation, and pipeline management; and it's one of those books when I read it set my mind on fire with creativity. I highly recommend it.

Use Case 40:

Brainstorming Ideas and Solutions

A good idea is worth a million dollars…sometimes a billion. We've all sat in brainstorming sessions spit-balling ideas long into the night. The great thing about AI is that it can give us tons of ideas at the click of a button, so long as we know what questions to ask. Use ChatGPT to brainstorm ideas and solutions for various challenges and opportunities within your business. AI can help generate creative, out-of-the-box ideas, assist in problem-solving, and offer fresh perspectives to fuel innovation and growth.

In today's fast-paced business environment, generating innovative ideas and solutions is crucial for SMBs looking to stay competitive, overcome challenges, and seize new opportunities. However, traditional brainstorming sessions can be time-consuming, resource-intensive, and may not always yield the most diverse or creative ideas. By leveraging AI tools like ChatGPT, SMBs can revolutionize their brainstorming process, generating a wealth of creative, out-of-the-box ideas at the click of a button. Here are some ways SMBs can use ChatGPT to enhance their ideation and problem-solving efforts:

Generating product or service ideas: Your business can quickly generate a wide range of creative ideas to fuel your product development pipeline and stay ahead of the competition. All you need to do is give your AI assistant any relevant industry data, customer insights, or desired innovation areas that your team currently has amassed. The AI will take it from there.

Solving complex business challenges: AI offers fresh perspectives and unconventional solutions to complex business challenges. By inputting detailed information about the problem, its context, and any constraints, SMBs can leverage ChatGPT's vast knowledge base and creative reasoning capabilities to generate novel, actionable solutions that may not have been considered otherwise.

Enhancing marketing and advertising campaigns: Brainstorm creative marketing and advertising ideas that capture audience attention and drive engagement. Targeted audience profiles and key messaging points will help companies generate a variety of innovative concepts for ad copy, visual content, and promotional strategies.

Improving operational efficiency: ChatGPT can assist SMBs in identifying areas for operational improvement and generating ideas to streamline processes. By analyzing data on current operations, industry best practices, and employee feedback, ChatGPT can suggest innovative solutions and process enhancements that drive efficiency and bottom-line results.

Fostering a culture of innovation: By incorporating artificial intelligence into your brainstorming and problem-solving processes, businesses foster a culture of innovation that encourages creative thinking, risk-taking, and continuous improvement. ChatGPT can serve as a catalyst for ideation, helping employees break free from conventional thinking patterns and explore new possibilities, ultimately driving a more innovative and adaptable organization.

Asking the Right Questions:

To maximize the value of ChatGPT in brainstorming ideas and solutions, SMBs must know what questions to ask and how to frame their inputs effectively. Some key considerations include:

1. Providing clear, specific, and well-defined problem statements or opportunity areas to guide ChatGPT's ideation process
2. Offering relevant background information, data, and context to help ChatGPT generate ideas that align with the SMB's unique needs and circumstances
3. Encouraging divergent thinking by asking open-ended questions that explore multiple angles and perspectives on a given topic
4. Iterating on initial ideas generated by ChatGPT, using them as a springboard for further brainstorming and refinement with human teams
5. Regularly updating ChatGPT's knowledge base with the latest industry trends, customer insights, and internal data to ensure the most relevant and informed ideas are generated

To effectively leverage ChatGPT for brainstorming ideas and solutions, SMBs should:

1. Use ChatGPT as a complementary tool to augment, rather than replace, human creativity and expertise
2. Foster a safe, inclusive, and collaborative environment that encourages all team members to engage with and build upon AI-generated ideas
3. Establish clear criteria and processes for evaluating, prioritizing, and implementing ideas generated through ChatGPT-assisted brainstorming
4. Continuously monitor the outcomes of implemented ideas and solutions, using these insights to refine future brainstorming efforts and optimize innovation processes
5. Embrace a culture of experimentation and learning, recognizing that not all ideas will succeed but that each iteration brings valuable insights and opportunities for growth.

To maximize the value of AI, SMBs must ask the right questions. Use it as a tool for your team to foster their creativity. By combining the power of ChatGPT with a collaborative, experimental approach to innovation, businesses like yours can drive sustainable growth, differentiate yourselves in the market, and seize the million-dollar (or even billion-dollar) opportunities that emerge in an increasingly complex and competitive business landscape.

Here are 10 Potential Prompt Threads:

1. Generate five ideas for increasing our customer retention rate.

2. Suggest three potential solutions to streamline our internal communication process.
3. Brainstorm new features or improvements for our existing product line.
4. Come up with five strategies to boost our social media engagement.
5. Help me identify potential areas for cost reduction within our operations.
6. Suggest three initiatives to improve our company culture and employee satisfaction.
7. Propose ideas for expanding our services to new markets or industries.
8. Brainstorm potential partnerships or collaborations that could benefit our business.
9. Offer three ideas for improving our website's user experience.
10. Generate five marketing campaign concepts to drive brand awareness.

Further Resources:

1. "Types of Innovation" by Larry Keely (https://amzn.to/3L2M32f) - Relates ten scopes of innovation around a wheel with ideation exercises. Also known as the Doblin method.
2. "Doblin Innovation Tactics Cards," by Doblin (https://amzn.to/40aJGOQ) based on the Ten Types of Innovation Method. Wonderful for executives and teams to use as fire starters for new ideas, processes, and products.
3. MindTools (https://www.mindtools.com/cx4ems0/problem-solving) - Offers resources and tools for brainstorming and problem-solving.

4. "Thinkertoys" by Michael Michalko – (https://amzn.to/3ohdVGB) - Book on creative thinking techniques and strategies.
5. Ideo Blog (https://www.ideo.com/blog) - Shares insights and tips on innovation and design thinking.
6. "Creative Confidence" by Tom Kelley and David Kelley (https://amzn.to/3KYGd1K) - Book on nurturing creativity and innovation in organizations.

Use Case 41:

MS Excel Workbook Terminal Emulator

Everyone needs to have an Excel wizard on their staff, and now it's easier than ever with AI.

AI can help users with Excel functions, formulas, and data analysis techniques to improve decision-making. Creating a powerful spreadsheet solves numerous business problems. When you have an AI that creates more than one at the same time, you find possibilities opening up right before your eyes. You can then solve complex business problems by emulating an MS Excel Workbook terminal.

ChatGPT can effectively emulate many functions of Microsoft Excel to help SMB business users with data management, analysis, and visualization. Here are several ways ChatGPT can assist in this capacity:

1. Data Entry and Cleanup

- Automated Data Entry: Assist in entering data into spreadsheets, reducing manual input time and errors.
- Data Cleaning: Identify and correct errors in datasets, such as duplicates, missing values, and formatting inconsistencies.
- Data Transformation: Help transform and format data, such as splitting columns, merging cells, and standardizing date formats.

2. Formula and Function Assistance

- Formula Generation: Suggest and generate complex formulas based on user requirements, such as VLOOKUP, INDEX-MATCH, SUMIF, and conditional formatting.
- Error Debugging: Identify and correct errors in existing formulas and functions.
- Optimization Tips: Provide tips for optimizing formulas to improve spreadsheet performance.

3. Data Analysis and Reporting

- Descriptive Statistics: Calculate basic statistics such as mean, median, mode, standard deviation, and variance.
- Data Summarization: Create pivot tables and summary reports to aggregate and analyze large datasets.
- Trend Analysis: Perform trend analysis using functions like LINEST, FORECAST, and TREND.

4. Financial Modeling and Forecasting

- Budgeting and Forecasting: Develop budgeting models and financial forecasts, including revenue projections, expense tracking, and cash flow analysis.
- Scenario Analysis: Conduct what-if analysis to assess the impact of different scenarios on financial outcomes.
- Financial Ratios: Calculate financial ratios such as ROI, ROE, and profit margins to evaluate business performance.

5. Visualizations and Dashboards

- Chart Creation: Generate various charts and graphs, including bar charts, line graphs, pie charts, and scatter plots.
- Dashboard Design: Help design and create interactive dashboards to visualize key metrics and performance indicators.
- Conditional Formatting: Apply conditional formatting to highlight important data points and trends.

6. Database Functions

- Data Lookup: Use functions like VLOOKUP, HLOOKUP, and XLOOKUP to find and retrieve specific data from large tables.
- Cross-referencing: Cross-reference data between different sheets and workbooks.
- Database Management: Assist with managing and querying data tables using Excel's database functions.

7. Automation and Macros

- Macro Creation: Provide guidance on creating and running macros to automate repetitive tasks.
- Process Automation: Suggest ways to automate common Excel tasks, such as report generation and data consolidation.
- Script Debugging: Help debug and optimize VBA (Visual Basic for Applications) scripts used in Excel.

8. Collaboration and Sharing

- File Management: Assist in organizing and managing Excel files for easy access and collaboration.
- Collaboration Tools: Provide tips on using Excel's collaboration features, such as shared workbooks and comments.
- Version Control: Suggest best practices for version control to track changes and manage different versions of Excel files.

Implementation Steps:

1. Identify Use Cases: Determine the specific Excel-related tasks and challenges that your SMB needs assistance with.
2. Train Users: Educate your team on how to interact with ChatGPT for Excel-related queries and tasks.
3. Integrate Tools: Integrate ChatGPT with your Excel environment using available APIs and connectors for seamless interaction.

4. Monitor Usage: Track the performance and effectiveness of ChatGPT in handling Excel tasks and gather user feedback.

5. Continuous Improvement: Continuously refine and improve ChatGPT's capabilities based on user feedback and evolving business needs.

Start using ChatGPT as an Excel emulator. It will enhance your data management and analysis capabilities. That will in turn improve efficiency and help you make more informed business decisions.

If you need help with workbooks and Excel functions, we have 10 potential prompts for you right here:

1. Write a step-by-step guide on performing a specific Excel function or operation.

2. Suggest formulas or techniques for analyzing a particular dataset.

3. Develop a list of best practices for data management in Excel.

4. Provide guidance on using Excel for financial modeling or forecasting.

5. Write a tutorial on creating charts or visualizations in Excel.

6. Develop a list of Excel keyboard shortcuts or tips for increased productivity.

7. Create a guide on using Excel add-ins or third-party tools to enhance functionality.

8. Write a step-by-step guide on creating a custom macro in Excel.

9. Develop a list of common Excel errors and their solutions.

10. Suggest strategies for optimizing Excel performance and reducing file sizes.

When requesting assistance with Excel, provide specific information about your desired function, operation, or data analysis goal. The employee acting as your AI Whisperer in this case needs to have a good understanding of Excel and the math involved in creating the proper functions. If they do, you'll be able to create all sorts of workbooks to help your company succeed.

Further Resources:

1. Excel 2023: Up to date guide to master all the MS Excel Fundamentals,' by Fletcher Dinkins (https://amzn.to/3A58Js0).
2. Exceljet (https://exceljet.net/) - Offers resources, insights, and best practices on Microsoft Excel.
3. MrExcel (https://www.mrexcel.com/) - Provides resources, insights, and best practices on Excel usage and techniques.
4. 80 Useful Excel Chat GPT Prompts to 10x Your Excel Skills (https://www.greataiprompts.com/chat-gpt/excel-chat-gpt-prompts/)

Use Case 42:

JavaScript Console Emulator

Coding is an art as much as a science. That being the case, you need to have someone who understands numbers and the way they interact with each other.

If you haven't figured it out yet, AI is pretty good at math.

ChatGPT can assist with complex business problem solutions by emulating a JavaScript console. AI can help users with JavaScript functions, debugging, and coding techniques to improve web development and enhance overall website performance.

Again, the AI doesn't replace your web team, it merely gives them tools to speed up processes and verify common mistakes are avoided.

GitHub Copilot, an AI-powered code completion tool developed by GitHub in collaboration with OpenAI, fits into this context as a complementary tool to ChatGPT, particularly in the domain of assisting developers with coding tasks. Here's how GitHub Copilot integrates with the functionalities described earlier and how it complements the use of ChatGPT as a JavaScript Console Emulator:

1. Code Writing and Suggestions

- GitHub Copilot: Provides real-time code suggestions and autocompletions directly within the integrated development environment (IDE). It can generate entire lines or blocks of code based on the context provided by the developer.
- ChatGPT: Can be used for more in-depth code explanations, generating examples, and providing guidance on specific coding practices. It can also help with understanding the logic behind the code suggested by Copilot.

2. Debugging and Troubleshooting

- GitHub Copilot: Offers code suggestions that can help prevent common coding errors and improve code quality by providing optimal code patterns and practices.
- ChatGPT: Provides detailed explanations of error messages, offers debugging tips, and helps troubleshoot complex issues that may not be immediately apparent from code suggestions alone.

3. Learning and Reference

- GitHub Copilot: Acts as a learning tool by suggesting code snippets and patterns as the developer types, helping them learn through practical application.

- ChatGPT: Serves as an educational resource for deeper understanding of JavaScript concepts, answering theoretical questions, and providing structured tutorials.

4. Real-time Code Execution Simulation

- GitHub Copilot: Does not execute code but enhances the coding experience by suggesting how code should be written.
- ChatGPT: Simulates the execution of JavaScript code snippets, shows the output, and explains how code behaves, which is useful for learning and debugging.

5. API Interaction

- GitHub Copilot: Suggests code for making API requests and handling responses, streamlining the process of integrating APIs into projects.
- ChatGPT: Provides detailed examples and explanations of how to use specific APIs, handle errors, and debug API-related issues.

6. Project Assistance

- GitHub Copilot: Assists in writing boilerplate code for project setup, using frameworks, and integrating libraries.
- ChatGPT: Offers comprehensive guidance on setting up projects, best practices, and detailed explanations of framework-specific concepts.

7. Testing and Validation

- GitHub Copilot: Suggests code for unit tests and helps with the initial setup of testing frameworks.

- ChatGPT: Provides in-depth explanations of testing methodologies, examples of complex test cases, and advice on improving test coverage.

How GitHub Copilot and ChatGPT Complement Each Other:

Real-time Assistance vs. Detailed Guidance: Copilot excels in providing instant code suggestions and completing code in real-time as you type, which accelerates the coding process. ChatGPT, on the other hand, is better suited for detailed explanations, step-by-step guidance, and answering broader questions about coding practices and concepts.

Immediate Solutions vs. Educational Value: Copilot can quickly generate code solutions that work, allowing developers to move faster. ChatGPT adds value by explaining why certain solutions work, helping developers understand the underlying principles and improve their skills over time.

Contextual Coding vs. Holistic Understanding: Copilot uses the immediate context within the IDE to provide relevant code completions. ChatGPT can take a more holistic approach by considering broader questions and providing comprehensive answers that go beyond the immediate coding context.

Integration Scenario:

In a practical scenario, a developer could use GitHub Copilot within their IDE to rapidly write and complete code. When they encounter a challenging concept, need a detailed explanation, or want to debug an issue, they could turn to ChatGPT for more in-depth assistance. This combined approach leverages the strengths of both tools, enhancing productivity and learning.

By integrating both GitHub Copilot and ChatGPT into their workflow, SMBs can significantly enhance their development capabilities, streamline coding tasks, and foster a deeper understanding of programming concepts among their developers.

10 Potential Prompt Threads:

1. Write a step-by-step guide on performing a specific JavaScript function or operation.
2. Suggest JavaScript code snippets or solutions for a particular problem.
3. Develop a list of best practices for JavaScript coding and optimization.
4. Provide guidance on using JavaScript for web development or interactivity.
5. Write a tutorial on implementing common JavaScript libraries or frameworks.
6. Develop a list of JavaScript debugging techniques or tools.
7. Create a guide on using browser developer tools for JavaScript console operations.
8. Write a step-by-step guide on implementing a custom JavaScript event listener.

9. Develop a list of common JavaScript errors and their solutions.
10. Suggest strategies for optimizing JavaScript performance and reducing page load times.

Always provide specific information about your desired function, operation, or coding goal when using AI with JavaScript. Just like in any coding scenario, small mistakes in the code will perpetuate big problems, so your AI Whisperer (Level 2 or 3) will need to pay attention to every prompt they use with the artificial intelligence. If the AI-generated content is not relevant or effective, consider refining your prompt or providing additional context to better align with your JavaScript-related needs.

Further Resources:

1. Visual Studio Code (code.visualstudio.com): A popular code editor with built-in support for JavaScript and extensions for various programming languages and frameworks.
2. Node.js (nodejs.org): A JavaScript runtime environment that allows you to execute JavaScript code on the server-side, which can be useful when interacting with APIs like ChatGPT.
3. Mozilla Developer Network (MDN) (developer.mozilla.org): Offers comprehensive documentation, guides, and tutorials on JavaScript, including best practices and examples.
4. W3Schools (w3schools.com): Provides tutorials, examples, and reference materials on JavaScript, HTML, CSS, and other web development technologies.
5. JavaScript.info (javascript.info): Offers in-depth tutorials and guides on JavaScript, covering various aspects of the language and its usage.

6. Stack Overflow (stackoverflow.com): A popular Q&A platform for developers, where you can find answers to JavaScript-related questions and issues.

7. "Eloquent JavaScript: A Modern Introduction to Programming" by Marijn Haverbeke: Provides a comprehensive introduction to JavaScript and programming concepts, with practical examples and exercises.

8. "You Don't Know JS" (book series) by Kyle Simpson: A series of books that cover various aspects of JavaScript in-depth, helping you gain a deep understanding of the language.

9. "JavaScript: The Good Parts" by Douglas Crockford: Offers insights into the best practices and powerful features of JavaScript, helping you write effective and efficient code.

10. Mozilla Developer Network (https://developer.mozilla.org/) - Offers resources, insights, and best practices on JavaScript and web development.

11. "JavaScript: The Definitive Guide" by David Flanagan - Comprehensive book on JavaScript programming.

Use Case 43:

Python Script Coding Emulator

As long as we're talking about coding, you can also employ ChatGPT to assist with solving complex business problems by emulating a Python script coder. AI can help users with Python functions, libraries, and coding techniques to improve software development and enhance overall project performance.

Similar to JavaScript, using ChatGPT as a Python Script Coding Emulator can significantly enhance the development experience for business users by providing assistance with coding, debugging, learning, and more.

Here's how ChatGPT can be used in this capacity, and how it complements tools like GitHub Copilot:

1. Code Writing and Suggestions for ChatGPT:

- Code Generation: Generate Python scripts or snippets for specific tasks, such as data processing, web scraping, or automation.
- Code Completion: Provide suggestions for completing partially written Python code, ensuring correct syntax and functionality.
- Best Practices: Offer advice on best practices for writing clean, efficient, and maintainable Python code.

2. Debugging and Troubleshooting with ChatGPT:

- Error Interpretation: Interpret error messages and suggest potential fixes, explaining the root cause of issues.
- Code Review: Review Python code for bugs, performance issues, and adherence to best practices.
- Debugging Strategies: Offer tips and techniques for debugging Python scripts, such as using breakpoints, logging, and Python's built-in debugging tools.

3. Learning and Reference with ChatGPT:

- Concept Explanations: Explain Python concepts, such as object-oriented programming, decorators, and list comprehensions.
- Tutorials: Provide step-by-step tutorials on various Python topics, from basic syntax to advanced libraries.
- Function Documentation: Explain the usage, syntax, and examples of Python functions and libraries.

4. Real-time Code Execution Simulation with ChatGPT:

- Simulate Execution: Simulate the execution of Python code snippets, showing the expected output and explaining how the code works.
- Variable Inspection: Allow users to inspect variables and their values at different points in the code.
- Step-by-Step Walkthrough: Walk through the code execution process step-by-step to illustrate logic and flow.

5. API Interaction with ChatGPT:

- API Requests: Help construct and debug API requests using libraries like requests or http.client.
- Response Handling: Show how to handle API responses, including parsing JSON and managing errors.
- Integration Examples: Provide examples of integrating third-party APIs with Python applications.

6. Project Assistance with ChatGPT:

- Environment Setup: Guide users through setting up their Python development environment, including virtual environments and package management with pip.
- Framework Guidance: Offer advice on using Python frameworks such as Django, Flask, and FastAPI.
- Best Practices: Suggest best practices for organizing and structuring Python projects.

7. Testing and Validation with ChatGPT

- Unit Tests: Generate unit tests for Python functions using testing frameworks like unittest, pytest, or nose.

- Input Validation: Provide examples of input validation techniques and how to implement them in Python.
- Performance Testing: Offer tips for performance testing and optimizing Python code.

8. Collaboration and Sharing with ChatGPT

- Documentation: Assist in writing comprehensive documentation for Python scripts and projects.
- Code Comments: Suggest meaningful comments and docstrings to make the code more readable and maintainable.
- Version Control: Provide tips on using version control systems like Git to manage Python code.

9. Automation and Scripting with ChatGPT:

- Automation Scripts: Help create scripts for automating repetitive tasks, such as file management, data processing, and report generation.
- Scheduler Integration: Show how to integrate Python scripts with task schedulers like cron on Unix or Task Scheduler on Windows.

Complementing GitHub Copilot:

Real-time Assistance vs. Detailed Guidance:

- GitHub Copilot: Provides instant code suggestions and completions directly within the IDE, helping developers write code faster.

- ChatGPT: Offers detailed explanations, step-by-step guidance, and answers broader questions about coding practices and concepts.

Immediate Solutions vs. Educational Value:

- GitHub Copilot: Generates immediate code solutions, allowing developers to quickly implement functionality.
- ChatGPT: Adds educational value by explaining why certain solutions work, helping developers understand the underlying principles and improve their skills.

Contextual Coding vs. Holistic Understanding:

- GitHub Copilot: Uses the immediate context within the IDE to provide relevant code completions.
- ChatGPT: Takes a holistic approach, considering broader questions and providing comprehensive answers that go beyond the immediate coding context.

Implementation Steps:

1. Integrate with Development Environment: Make ChatGPT accessible within the development environment, such as through a code editor extension or an API.
2. Train Developers: Educate developers on how to use ChatGPT effectively for Python-related queries and tasks.
3. Collect Feedback: Gather feedback from developers to continuously improve ChatGPT's assistance.

4. Update Knowledge Base: Keep ChatGPT updated with the latest Python features, best practices, and trends to ensure relevant and accurate assistance.

By leveraging ChatGPT as a Python Script Coding Emulator, SMB business users can enhance their development capabilities, streamline coding tasks, and foster a deeper understanding of programming concepts among their developers.

Here are 10 potential prompt threads to get you going with AI as a Python script coder:

1. Write a step-by-step guide on performing a specific Python function or operation.
2. Suggest Python code snippets or solutions for a particular problem.
3. Develop a list of best practices for Python coding and optimization.
4. Provide guidance on using Python for data analysis, web development, or automation.
5. Write a tutorial on implementing common Python libraries or frameworks.
6. Develop a list of Python debugging techniques or tools.
7. Create a guide on setting up a Python development environment.
8. Write a step-by-step guide on implementing a custom Python class or function.
9. Develop a list of common Python errors and their solutions.
10. Suggest strategies for optimizing Python performance and code readability.

When requesting assistance with Python, provide specific information about your desired function, operation, or coding goal. Having an experienced coder go over everything is a 100% necessity. Redundancies are always essential, whether you're working with a human coder or an AI. Everything needs to be checked and rechecked either way.

Further Resources:

1. Visual Studio Code (code.visualstudio.com): A popular code editor with built-in support for Python and extensions for various programming languages and frameworks.
2. PyCharm (jetbrains.com/pycharm): A powerful and feature-rich integrated development environment (IDE) specifically designed for Python development.
3. Python.org (python.org): The official website for Python, offering comprehensive documentation, tutorials, and guides.
4. Real Python (realpython.com): Provides in-depth tutorials, articles, and resources on various Python topics, from beginner to advanced levels.
5. W3Schools (w3schools.com/python): Offers tutorials, examples, and reference materials on Python and related technologies.
6. Stack Overflow (stackoverflow.com): A popular Q&A platform for developers, where you can find answers to Python-related questions and issues.
7. "Python Crash Course" by Eric Matthes: A comprehensive introduction to Python programming, including practical projects and examples.
8. "Automate the Boring Stuff with Python" by Al Sweigart: Teaches Python programming through practical examples, focusing on automating everyday tasks.
9. "Fluent Python: Clear, Concise, and Effective Programming" by Luciano Ramalho: Offers insights into Python best practices, idiomatic expressions, and advanced features.

10. "Effective Python: 90 Specific Ways to Write Better Python" by Brett Slatkin: Provides practical tips and best practices for writing clean, efficient, and maintainable Python code.

Use Case 44:

API Tool Connector for Business Process Integration

API tools is a fancy way of saying 'automated workflows.' It's about taking processes your company is already doing and letting a machine or AI do them.

Obviously, this is a perfect mission for artificial intelligence.

Utilize ChatGPT to assist with solving complex business problems by acting as a business process API connector for CRMs, ERPs, and other systems. AI can help users with API integration, development, and optimization to improve data flow, automation, and overall business efficiency. While ChatGPT can do these functions, it is typically beyond the ability of non-technical users to perform this task. So, our approach here is question-based; what are the questions a non-technical user might ask to use APIs? These same questions can then be asked of the professionals that might seek to help them complete the 'last mile' connection of their business systems to the ChatGPT API.

Below is a set of step-wise iterative questions designed to guide SMB users through a layered prompt journey to learn about API connectors and integrating ChatGPT with their systems.

This simplified and chronological series of questions are those that, at a minimum, a non-technical AI Whisperer should ask to use ChatGPT's API function and connect it to their third-party tools like CRM, ERP, etc.:

Step-by-Step Questions for Non-Technical SMB Users

1. Understanding the Basics:
   - What is ChatGPT, and how can and API connection help my business?
   - What is an API, and why do I need it to connect ChatGPT to other tools?
2. Getting Started with ChatGPT API:
   - How do I sign up for access to ChatGPT's API?
   - Where do I find my API key for ChatGPT?
3. Setting Up API Testing Tools:
   - What tools can I use to test API connections (e.g., Postman)?
   - How do I set up an account and create a workspace in Postman?
4. Making Your First API Call:
   - How do I make a basic API request to ChatGPT using Postman?
   - What information do I need to include in my API request (e.g., headers, body)?
5. Connecting to Third-Party Tools:

- How can I find out if my CRM, ERP, or other tools support API integration?
- Where can I find the API documentation for my third-party tools?

6. Integrating ChatGPT with a CRM:
   - How do I authenticate and connect ChatGPT to my CRM's API?
   - What kind of data can I send to and receive from my CRM using ChatGPT?

7. Automating Tasks with ChatGPT:
   - What specific tasks can ChatGPT automate for me in my CRM (e.g., generating reports, sending emails)?
   - How do I set up these automated tasks using ChatGPT's API?

8. Ensuring Data Security:
   - What are the best practices for keeping my API key secure?
   - How do I ensure that data shared between ChatGPT and my third-party tools is protected?

9. Monitoring and Managing Integrations:
   - How can I monitor the performance of my ChatGPT integrations?
   - What should I do if something goes wrong with the integration?

10. Getting Help and Support:
    - Where can I find additional resources and tutorials for using ChatGPT's API?
    - How do I contact support if I need help with my API integrations?

Usage of the Questions:

- Initial Exploration: Begin by understanding the basics of ChatGPT and APIs.
- Practical Setup: Move on to setting up and making your first API call.
- Integration Steps: Focus on connecting ChatGPT to specific third-party tools like CRM and ERP.
- Automation and Security: Learn about automating tasks and ensuring data security.
- Ongoing Management: Finally, address how to monitor and get support for your integrations.

By following this structured set of questions, you can incrementally build your team's knowledge and skills in integrating ChatGPT with your existing systems. This will result in more effective and efficient use of AI in company operations. And as always, here are 10 potential prompt threads that will get AI working for you:

1. Write a step-by-step guide on connecting a specific CRM or ERP system via API.
2. Suggest API integration solutions for data synchronization or automation.
3. Develop a list of best practices for API development and management.
4. Provide guidance on using API connectors for business process improvement.
5. Write a tutorial on implementing common API authentication methods.
6. Develop a list of API debugging techniques or tools.

7. Create a guide on setting up a development environment for API integration.
8. Write a step-by-step guide on implementing a custom API endpoint.
9. Develop a list of common API errors and their solutions.
10. Suggest strategies for optimizing API performance and security.

When requesting assistance with API integration, provide specific information about your desired system, operation, or integration goal. You're not going to get the right response on the first try every time, so plan on refining your prompt or providing additional context to better align with your API-related needs.

Further Resources:

1. "RESTful API Design" by Matthias Biehl - Book on designing and implementing RESTful APIs.
2. ProgrammableWeb (https://www.programmableweb.com/) - Offers resources, insights, and best practices on API development and integration.
3. "APIs: A Strategy Guide" by Daniel Jacobson, Greg Brail, and Dan Woods - Book on API strategy and management.
4. Postman Blog (https://blog.postman.com/) - Provides resources, insights, and best practices on API development and testing.
5. Exploring the Capabilities of the ChatGPT API: A beginners guide, by Dilip Kashyap, https://levelup.gitconnected.com/exploring-the-capabilities-of-the-chatgpt-api-a-beginners-guide-e9089d49961f

Use Case 45:

Legacy Machines and IoT Integration

Imagine you anticipated going to the moon and wanted to reuse and repurpose the US Apollo Lunar Roving vehicle that was left from a past moon landing mission. Prior to your trip, you could ask AI to help you with instructions and materials to take with you to operate, repair, and repurpose the vehicle.

Now, that might sound like an unlikely use case for you, but in truth. you have technology lying around your home and office that could be reused, repaired, and even repurposed with the right instruction. Have you been wanting to use that old gaming system with your 21st century computer? Probably. That's why I prepared this use case.

Leverage artificial intelligence to assist with connecting legacy machines to the internet and integrating IoT (Internet of Things) solutions. IoT solutions help build networks of IoT devices, reducing complication, ensuring device effectiveness, and driving innovation across industries looking for chances to grow. AI can help users with IoT development, data management, and system optimization to enhance overall business efficiency.

There are many instances where legacy equipment reuse or repurposing is not necessarily related to IoT integration, but rather involves simply fixing or using an old piece of equipment. In such cases, ChatGPT can still be a valuable resource for SMBs looking to extend the life of their legacy assets. Here's how you might instruct ChatGPT to assist you:

Provide detailed information about the equipment:

- Describe the specific make, model, and year of the equipment you want to fix or use.
- Share any known issues, symptoms, or error codes associated with the equipment.
- Specify the intended use or purpose of the equipment in your operations.

Example prompt: *"I have an old Epson LQ-590 dot matrix printer from the 1990s that I want to use for printing multi-part forms. The printer is not feeding the paper correctly and is making unusual noises. Can you provide guidance on how to troubleshoot and repair this issue?"*

Request specific resources or guidance:

- Ask ChatGPT for step-by-step troubleshooting guides, repair manuals, or user manuals specific to your equipment.
- Inquire about common issues and solutions for your particular make and model.
- Seek recommendations for replacement parts, tools, or consumables needed to fix or maintain the equipment.

Example prompt: *"I'm looking for a detailed troubleshooting guide and repair manual for the Epson LQ-590 dot matrix printer. Can you provide me with resources that cover common paper feeding issues and the steps to resolve them? Also, please suggest any replacement parts or tools I may need to complete the repair."*

Seek advice on repurposing or adapting the equipment:

- Explain your idea for repurposing the legacy equipment and ask ChatGPT for feedback or suggestions.
- Request guidance on modifications, upgrades, or integrations that could enable new use cases for the equipment.
- Inquire about any potential challenges, risks, or limitations associated with repurposing the equipment.

Example prompt: *"I'm considering repurposing two old computers, a Commodore 64 and Apple II for use in a retro gaming setup, where it would print out game stats and high scores. Can you provide advice on how to adapt the legacy computers for this purpose, including any necessary modifications, cable connections, or software integrations? Please also highlight any potential challenges or limitations I should be aware of."*

By providing detailed information about the equipment, requesting specific resources, and seeking advice on repurposing or adapting the equipment, you can effectively guide your AI assistant to generate targeted, actionable insights that help you fix your legacy equipment.

Connecting Devices via IoT with ChatGPT Assistance

In today's rapidly evolving technological landscape, small and medium-sized businesses face the challenge of integrating legacy machines and IoT devices to improve operational efficiency and drive innovation. But the process of connecting older equipment to modern networks and optimizing IoT solutions can be complex. Plus it's time-consuming and resource-intensive too.

That changes when you take advantage of AI tools. Your business can streamline the integration process, access valuable resources and insights, and unlock the full potential of your existing assets.

Here are some ways ChatGPT can assist SMBs in extending the life of their legacy machines and optimizing IoT tool integration:

Providing integration guidance and resources: ChatGPT can offer step-by-step guidance and resources for connecting legacy machines to the internet and integrating them with IoT solutions. By inputting information about the specific equipment, network infrastructure, and desired outcomes, SMBs can leverage ChatGPT's extensive knowledge base to generate tailored instructions, best practices, and troubleshooting tips, empowering them to successfully modernize their legacy assets.

Identifying compatible IoT solutions: By analyzing your existing infrastructure, business requirements, and industry-specific challenges, ChatGPT can recommend optimal IoT platforms. Different protocols and devices exist that seamlessly integrate with your legacy equipment and drive measurable improvements in performance.

Optimizing IoT data management and analysis: AI can help your business derive actionable insights from your IoT data. It will help you make informed decisions, optimize processes, and identify new opportunities for growth and innovation.

Enhancing IoT security and compliance: By staying up-to-date with the latest industry standards, regulations, and best practices, ChatGPT can provide guidance on implementing robust security measures, such as device authentication, encryption, and access control, as well as ensuring compliance with relevant data protection and privacy laws.

Facilitating continuous improvement and innovation: ChatGPT can serve as a valuable resource for any business looking to improve and innovate their IoT-enabled operations. By engaging in ongoing conversations with ChatGPT, SMBs can access the latest industry trends, emerging technologies, and success stories, sparking new ideas and strategies for optimizing their IoT investments and driving business growth.

Remember to validate ChatGPT's suggestions with your own technical expertise and judgment. Consult with professionals when necessary to ensure the safety, feasibility, and effectiveness of any repairs or repurposing efforts.

ChatGPT's extensive knowledge base and problem-solving capabilities will allow your company to tap into a valuable resource for extending the life of their legacy equipment. This focus will reduce waste and maximize the value of their existing assets, even when IoT integration is not the primary goal.

10 Potential Prompt Threads:

1. Write a step-by-step guide on connecting a specific legacy machine to the internet.
2. Suggest IoT integration solutions for data collection and automation.
3. Develop a list of best practices for IoT development and management.
4. Provide guidance on using IoT solutions for business process improvement.
5. Write a tutorial on implementing common IoT communication protocols.
6. Develop a list of IoT debugging techniques or tools.
7. Create a guide on setting up a development environment for IoT integration.
8. Write a step-by-step guide on implementing a custom IoT sensor or device.
9. Develop a list of common IoT errors and their solutions.
10. Suggest strategies for optimizing IoT performance and security.

Further Resources:

1. "Internet of Things for Architects" by Perry Lea - Book on IoT architecture and integration.
2. IoT World Today (https://www.iotworldtoday.com/) - Offers resources, insights, and best practices on IoT development and management.
3. "Building the Internet of Things" by Maciej Kranz - Book on IoT strategy and implementation.

4. IoT For All (https://www.iotforall.com/) - Provides resources, insights, and best practices on IoT development, use cases, and trends.

5. "Introducing ChatGPT and Whisper APIs," by OpenAI.com, https://openai.com/blog/introducing-chatgpt-and-whisper-apis

Use Case 46:

Solving Employee Engagement Problems

People are always the X-Factor in business. Sometimes teams work great together and other times they simply don't get along. Finding reasons for these dynamics can be difficult.

AI can help with that though, merely because of the fact that it can process so much data. Your artificial intelligence assistant can give you ideas on what the problems could be, along with solutions that have worked at other companies.

Let's look at this problem a bit differently. I want to give you another way to think about your prompts and how to use AI as a business tool. We'll be using the 'Five Whys' Strategy that executive coaches often use so they can learn more about team engagement…or the lack thereof.

Level 1: Identify the problem.

Prompt: Help me identify common employee engagement problems and potential causes. Additional questions might include:

- Help me name the specific problem or challenge we are currently facing?
- What are the observable and underlying key factors or variables involved in this problem?
- What other data or information might you access to help me understand this problem?
- What additional data or information do you need for me gather, or order for you to help me with this issue?

Level 2: Explore solutions.

Prompt: Provide a list of strategies to address the employee engagement problems identified in level 1. Additional questions might include:

- What should be the main goals or objectives that we aim to achieve by solving this problem?
- What potential obstacles or constraints might impact our solution?
- These are the methods or approaches we have already tried to address this problem? Thoughts?
- What are the strengths and weaknesses of these previous methods or approaches?
- What alternative methods or approaches might we consider for solving this problem?

Level 3: Develop a plan.

Prompt: Create a step-by-step plan to implement the strategies from level 2 to improve employee engagement. Other questions might include:

- Go online and research what other companies have done to resolve similar problems.
- How can AI be used to analyze the data and provide insights related to this problem?
- What types of visualizations or reports would help us better understand and communicate the data?
- How can you validate the accuracy and reliability of the AI-generated insights?

Level 4: Monitor progress.

Prompt: Suggest methods for tracking the effectiveness of the employee engagement strategies and identifying areas for improvement.

- Help me by creating a table of accountability for the actions and measures proposed.
- What actionable steps can be derived from the insights provided by AI that might help us with our implementation and likely results?
- How can AI help me measure the success of the implemented solution?

Level 5: Adjust and optimize.

Prompt: Recommend ways to optimize the employee engagement plan based on the progress monitoring results from level.

- What continuous improvement or monitoring processes can I put in place to guarantee long-term success?
- Now I'm reporting on our follow-up results. Ponder them and suggest how we might adjust to improve our results.

You can see from the suggested questions that you can talk to AI like an intelligent human being and ask for assistance in the areas you don't quite understand.

Lastly, while there will likely be many wonderful suggestions given to you by AI, the issue remains that employees are human, and not necessarily logical or rational all the time. Consequently, employee engagement is challenging in any environment where some workers are in the office full-time, others hybrid, and others remote.

Here are 10 questions threads or prompts you might consider asking ChatGPT for assistance on employee engagement matters.

1. How can I identify the root causes of disengagement in my team?
2. What are some effective ways to improve employee engagement in a remote work environment?
3. How can I measure and track employee engagement in my organization?
4. What role do managers play in driving employee engagement and how can they improve their effectiveness?
5. What are some best practices for creating a positive work culture that promotes engagement and motivation?
6. How can I use technology to support employee engagement and communication in a remote work setting?
7. What are some effective strategies for recognizing and rewarding employee contributions and achievements?
8. How can I create opportunities for professional growth and development that increase employee engagement and retention?
9. What are some common mistakes to avoid when trying to improve employee engagement?

10. How can I effectively communicate with my team about changes in organizational goals and values that impact engagement?

Further Resources:

1. "The Employee Experience Advantage: How to Win the War for Talent by Giving Employees the Workspaces they Want, the Tools they Need, and a Culture They Can Celebrate" by Jacob Morgan (https://amzn.to/415zybA)
2. "The Engagement Equation: Leadership Strategies for an Inspired Workforce" by Christopher Rice, Fraser Marlow, and Mary Ann Masarech (https://amzn.to/3GJh0FU)
3. "Drive: The Surprising Truth About What Motivates Us" by Daniel H. Pink (https://amzn.to/41bglFB)
4. "The Power of Moments: Why Certain Experiences Have Extraordinary Impact" by Chip Heath and Dan Heath (https://amzn.to/3zZrFIR)
5. "Dare to Lead: Brave Work. Tough Conversations. Whole Hearts." by Brené Brown (https://amzn.to/3UEFKF9)
6. "tate of the Global Workplace: 2022 Report," Gallup's Employee Engagement Center: https://www.gallup.com/workplace/349484/state-of-the-global-workplace-2022-report.aspx
7. The Society for Human Resource Management (SHRM): https://www.shrm.org/
8. Harvard Business Review (HBR): https://hbr.org/
9. Bersin by Deloitte: https://www.bersin.com/
10. Employee Engagement Institute: https://www.employeeengagement.com/
11. TED Talks on Employee Engagement: https://www.ted.com/topics/employee+engagement
12. Employee Engagement Surveys: Survey Monkey, Qualtrics, and Culture Amp are popular survey tools that can help HR managers

measure employee engagement levels and gather feedback on how to improve it.

13. LinkedIn Learning: Offers a range of online courses on leadership, employee engagement, and team building that can be helpful for HR managers and business leaders.

Use Case 47:

Brand Storytelling

Enhancing brand storytelling involves crafting compelling narratives that communicate your organization's values, purpose, and personality. With AI as a tool, you can create emotional connections with your audience and differentiate your brand from competitors. Honestly, it's incredibly fun feeding ChatGPT different prompts and allowing it to create narratives that support your brand. Sometimes what it comes with is crazy and unusable, but more often than not, you get content that really opens your eyes to the potential of AI.

Using AI to analyze customer insights, market trends, and competitor differentiation, SMBs can uncover the core values and unique aspects that resonate with their audience.

By personalizing content and using social listening and sentiment analysis, brands can refine their narrative to address both positive and negative feedback effectively. Highlighting historical milestones and achievements, while incorporating predictive analytics, allows brands to position themselves for future opportunities. Visual storytelling through compelling imagery and data visualization enhances engagement, and continuous monitoring of engagement metrics ensures the brand story evolves in alignment with audience interests and market dynamics.

This data-driven approach enables SMBs to craft a more authentic, relevant, and engaging brand story. Let's explore some specific areas and prompts wherein AI can help SMBs uncover and tell their brand story:

1. **Customer Insights:**
    - Who are your most loyal customers, and what do they value most about your brand?
    - What are the common themes in customer feedback and reviews?

2. **Market Analysis:**
    - What are the current trends in your industry, and how does your brand align with them?
    - Who are your main competitors, and what differentiates your brand from theirs?

3. **Content Creation:**
    - What key messages and values should be highlighted in your brand story?
    - What types of content (blogs, videos, social media posts) resonate most with your audience?

4. **Personalization:**
   - How can you tailor your brand story to different segments of your audience?
   - What customer journeys and touchpoints can be personalized to enhance engagement?

5. **Social Listening:**
   - What are people saying about your brand on social media and other online platforms?
   - How can you leverage user-generated content to enhance your brand narrative?

6. **Sentiment Analysis:**
   - What is the overall sentiment towards your brand, and how has it changed over time?
   - How can you address negative sentiment and reinforce positive aspects of your brand?

7. **Historical Data Analysis:**
   - What milestones and achievements in your brand's history should be highlighted?
   - How can past challenges and successes be woven into your brand story?

8. **Predictive Analytics:**
   - What future trends and opportunities can your brand capitalize on?
   - How can you position your brand story to appeal to emerging market needs?

9. Visual Storytelling:

- What visual elements (logos, colors, imagery) best represent your brand's identity?
- How can infographics and data visualization enhance your brand storytelling?

10.Engagement Metrics:

- Which aspects of your brand story are most engaging to your audience?
- How can you refine your brand story based on audience engagement and feedback?

In conclusion, utilizing AI to gather and analyze data empowers small or medium businesses like yours to craft a compelling and dynamic brand story. By understanding your customers, differentiating from competitors, and anticipating market trends, your company can create personalized and engaging narratives. The continuous refinement of your story through social listening, sentiment analysis, and engagement metrics ensures that your brand remains relevant and resonates deeply with your audience. This strategic use of data not only enhances brand identity but also fosters stronger connections with customers, driving long-term loyalty and success.

Now we have 10 potential prompt threads for you to consider:

1. Define your brand's core values, mission, and unique selling proposition.
2. Identify key moments, achievements, or milestones in your organization's history.

3. Develop relatable and engaging brand stories that resonate with your target audience.
4. Use AI-powered tools to generate and optimize brand storytelling ideas and narratives.
5. Incorporate brand storytelling elements into various marketing materials and communications.
6. Use multimedia formats, such as videos, podcasts, or interactive content, to enhance brand storytelling.
7. Test and refine brand stories based on audience feedback and performance metrics.
8. Monitor and analyze the impact of brand storytelling on audience engagement and brand perception.
9. Collaborate with influencers, partners, or customers to amplify your brand stories.
10. Continuously improve brand storytelling strategies based on audience needs and industry trends.

When using AI for enhancing brand storytelling, ensure that the AI-generated ideas and narratives align with your organization's values, objectives, and brand guidelines. Always review and refine AI-generated stories before incorporating them into your marketing efforts to ensure they effectively communicate your desired message.

Further Resources:

1. "Building a StoryBrand: Clarify Your Message So Customers Will Listen" by Donald Miller (https://amzn.to/3UEtGUm)
2. "The Art of Storytelling: Easy Steps to Presenting an Unforgettable Story" by John D. Walsh (https://amzn.to/3KHLx8e)
3. "Made to Stick: Why Some Ideas Survive and Others Die" by Chip Heath and Dan Heath (https://amzn.to/3A2BRAp)

4. "Brand Storytelling: Put Customers at the Heart of Your Brand Story" by Miri Rodriguez (https://amzn.to/43xJdtb)

5. "Storynomics: Story-Driven Marketing in the Post-Advertising World" by Robert Mckee and Tom Gerace (https://amzn.to/3UCfpHD)

6. HubSpot: https://www.hubspot.com/

7. The Content Marketing Institute: https://contentmarketinginstitute.com/

8. MarketingProfs: https://www.marketingprofs.com/

9. AdWeek: https://www.adweek.com/

10. Branding Strategy Insider: https://www.brandingstrategyinsider.com/

11. TED Talks on Storytelling: https://www.ted.com/topics/storytelling

12. Canva: Canva is a design tool that can be used to create visually appealing and engaging brand materials.

13. Hootsuite: Hootsuite is a social media management tool that can help businesses effectively communicate their brand message and storytelling on various social media platforms.

14. LinkedIn Learning: Offers a range of online courses on brand building, storytelling, and content marketing that can be helpful for businesses and marketers.

Use Case 48:

Developing a Marketing Plan

Imagine you were operating an outdoor camping equipment company, and you wanted to create a formal marketing plan, with layout, campaign, objectives, and creative inputs for your next season. You would likely want to visualize your client's needs (as shown in the image above), and then navigate through a series of client-centered questions helping you frame out the structure of your marketing plan. Here's an example of how you might go about preparing that plan.

Earlier in the book, in the section labeled, *"Two Stepwise Layered Prompt Journeys"* we cross-walked through a method to have ChatGPT help you identify and create likely Customer Marketing Personas for your business. Those same personas can be used to target and amplify focus on your core client personas.

Additionally, earlier in this book, we talked about writing marketing copy in our very first Use Case. AI is great for that. But don't let your advertising ideas stop there. It's actually possible to create entire marketing plans with the help of AI, if you know what prompts to use.

Now let's explore more deeply how ChatGPT can assist your small to medium-sized business in developing an effective marketing plan by providing strategic insights, suggesting actionable steps, and offering tools to streamline the planning process. Here's a step-by-step guide on how ChatGPT can help:

1. Market Research and Analysis

- Customer Insights: Identify target demographics, understand customer needs, and preferences.
- Competitive Analysis: Analyze competitors' strategies, strengths, weaknesses, and market positioning.
- Industry Trends: Highlight current trends, market opportunities, and potential threats in the industry.

2. Defining Objectives and Goals

- SMART Goals: Help set Specific, Measurable, Achievable, Relevant, and Time-bound marketing objectives.
- KPIs: Suggest key performance indicators to track the success of marketing efforts.

3. Target Audience Segmentation

- Persona Development: Assist in creating detailed buyer personas to understand and target specific customer segments.

- Behavioral Segmentation: Analyze customer behavior to tailor marketing messages and campaigns.
- Branding and Positioning
- Brand Identity: Develop a clear and consistent brand identity, including logo, color scheme, and messaging.
- Unique Selling Proposition (USP): Help articulate what makes the business unique and why customers should choose it over competitors.

5. Marketing Strategy Development

- Content Marketing: Suggest content types (blogs, videos, infographics) and topics that resonate with the target audience.
- Digital Marketing: Provide strategies for social media, email marketing, SEO, and pay-per-click advertising.
- Traditional Marketing: Recommend offline marketing tactics like print advertising, direct mail, and event sponsorships.

6. Budget Planning

- Budget Allocation: Assist in allocating budget across different marketing channels based on expected ROI.
- Cost-effective Strategies: Suggest cost-effective marketing tactics suitable for SMBs with limited budgets.

7. Implementation Plan

- Action Plan: Create a detailed action plan with timelines, responsibilities, and milestones.
- Tools and Platforms: Recommend marketing tools and platforms to streamline campaign management and execution.

8. Monitoring and Evaluation

- Performance Tracking: Suggest tools and methods for tracking marketing performance and gathering data.
- Data Analysis: Help analyze the data to measure the effectiveness of campaigns and identify areas for improvement.
- Reporting: Assist in creating comprehensive marketing reports to share with stakeholders.

9. Continuous Improvement

- Feedback Loop: Encourage gathering customer feedback to refine marketing strategies.
- A/B Testing: Suggest running A/B tests to optimize marketing tactics and improve results.

Practical Steps for Implementation

1. Initial Consultation: ChatGPT can conduct an initial consultation to understand the business's current marketing efforts and goals.
2. Custom Marketing Plan Template: Provide a customized marketing plan template tailored to the business's needs.
3. Ongoing Support: Offer ongoing support and advice as the business implements its marketing plan.
4. Training and Resources: Recommend training materials and resources to help the business stay up-to-date with marketing best practices.

Marketing Plan Dashboard

Measuring what matters is also important. Here's a snapshot of the Key Performance Indicators (KPIs) that AI can help you calculate and track: **website traffic metrics** (total visits, unique visitors, bounce rate), **conversion metrics** (conversion rate, cost per conversion), **lead generation data** (number of leads, cost per lead), and **campaign-specific metrics** (email open and click-through rates, social media engagement, paid advertising impressions and ROAS). It also tracks **content performance** (blog post engagement, video views), **customer metrics** (acquisition cost, lifetime value, retention rate), **SEO metrics** (keyword rankings, organic traffic, backlinks), and **sales metrics** (revenue, growth, new vs. returning customers).

These KPIs help businesses measure and optimize their marketing strategies, ensuring they achieve their goals and drive long-term success. You can invite ChatGPT to help you create any of these KPIs for your company.

Like with so many other aspects of AI we've discussed over the course of this book, your advertising team is an integral part in this process. Artificial intelligence is one more tool to help them reach the highest of goals. As they learn to create dozens of potential ad campaigns, all it will do is open up even more options for their success. I encourage you to find and regularly use your own AI expert, your AI Whisperer, to help you give voice, context, and meaning to your prompts. The results will blow your mind.

And we can't forget 10 prompts you might consider using with ChatGPT to go deeper on the marketing plan issue:

1. What are some effective strategies for identifying and targeting my ideal customer segments?

2. How can I create a compelling brand message that resonates with my target audience?
3. Given my industry, what are 5 marketing personas that I should pay attention to? In your response provide the revenue, behavior, concerns, and buying habits for each persona.
4. What are some best practices for creating engaging content that drives customer engagement and conversions?
5. How can I leverage social media to reach and engage with my target audience effectively?
6. What are some effective ways to measure and analyze the effectiveness of my marketing campaigns?
7. How can I stay up-to-date on the latest marketing trends and technologies to improve my marketing strategy?
8. How can I optimize my website and other digital assets to improve my search engine rankings and drive more traffic to my site?
9. What are some effective ways to integrate different marketing channels to create a cohesive and impactful marketing plan?
10. How can I leverage customer feedback and data to continually improve my marketing strategy and customer experience?

Further Resources

1. HubSpot: https://www.hubspot.com/marketing
2. MarketingProfs: https://www.marketingprofs.com/
3. The Content Marketing Institute: https://contentmarketinginstitute.com/
4. Moz: https://moz.com/
5. Social Media Examiner: https://www.socialmediaexaminer.com/
6. Books:

7. "Building a StoryBrand: Clarify Your Message So Customers Will Listen" by Donald Miller (https://amzn.to/3UEtGUm)

8. "Contagious: Why Things Catch On" by Jonah Berger (https://amzn.to/3GMIxqa)

9. "Epic Content Marketing: How to Tell a Different Story, Break through the Clutter, and Win More Customers by Marketing Less" by Joe Pulizzi (https://amzn.to/43xM99a)

10. "The 1-Page Marketing Plan: Get New Customers, Make More Money, And Stand Out From The Crowd" by Allan Dib (https://amzn.to/3zXccZV)

11. "Digital Marketing for Dummies" by Ryan Deiss and Russ Henneberry (https://amzn.to/3GK2ZYw)

12. Hootsuite Academy: https://education.hootsuite.com/

13. Google Analytics Academy: https://analytics.google.com/analytics/academy/

14. LinkedIn Learning: Offers a range of online courses on marketing, branding, and digital marketing that can be helpful for business users.

15. The American Marketing Association: https://www.ama.org/

16. The Small Business Administration (SBA): https://www.sba.gov/business-guide/marketing/marketing-plan

Use Case 49:

Launching a New Business

Much like advertising, starting a new business can be a crapshoot. You may have an idea that seems like the greatest thing since air conditioning, but often we're too close to the process of building a company to see whether our idea is actually any good. That is where AI comes in. Dispassionate and precise, artificial intelligence will go through terabytes of data and let us know whether we have the next Google on our hands, or a mouse trap that can't catch mice.

ChatGPT can assist with launching a new business in various ways by providing guidance, resources, and tailored strategies across multiple areas. Here's how:

Business Planning and Strategy

1. Business Idea Validation:

- What is the market demand for your business idea?
- Who are your potential competitors, and what differentiates your business from theirs?

2. **Business Plan Development:**
   - How can you structure your business plan, including executive summary, market analysis, organizational structure, and financial projections?
   - What are the key components to include in your business plan to attract investors or secure loans?

3. **Market Research:**
   - Who is your target audience, and what are their needs and preferences?
   - What market trends should you consider in your business strategy?

4. **Legal and Administrative Assistance**
   - Business Registration:
     - o What are the steps to legally register your business in your location?
     - o What permits and licenses are required for your industry?
   - Business Structure Selection:
     - o What are the pros and cons of different business structures (sole proprietorship, partnership, LLC, corporation)?

5. **Marketing and Branding**
   - Brand Development:
     - o How can you create a compelling brand identity, including name, logo, and tagline?

- o What strategies can you use to build brand awareness and loyalty?
- Marketing Strategy:
  - o What channels should you use to reach your target audience (social media, email marketing, SEO, content marketing)?
  - o How can you create a marketing plan and budget?
- Online Presence:
  - o How can you set up a professional website and optimize it for search engines (SEO)?
  - o What social media platforms are best for your business, and how can you effectively manage them?

6. Financial Management

- Funding and Investment:
  - o What are the different funding options available (bootstrapping, loans, venture capital, crowdfunding)?
  - o How can you prepare a compelling pitch for investors?
- Financial Planning:
  - o How can you create a detailed financial plan, including cash flow projections and break-even analysis?
  - o What tools can help you manage your finances and track expenses?

7. Operations and Growth

- Operational Setup:
  - o What are the key steps to setting up your business operations, including supply chain management, inventory control, and customer service?

      o How can you implement efficient processes and systems to support your operations?
- Scaling and Expansion:
  - What strategies can help you scale your business and enter new markets?
  - How can you identify and seize growth opportunities?

8. Continuous Support and Learning
- Networking and Mentorship:
  - How can you connect with industry experts and potential mentors?
  - What networking events or communities can you join to grow your business connections?
- Continuous Learning:
  - What resources (books, courses, podcasts) can help you stay updated on industry trends and business skills?
  - How can you implement a culture of continuous improvement within your business?

Given that starting a business is risky and prone to missteps, here are **20 prompts** that you might consider asking ChatGPT to help you prepare your new business plan.

1. What are the key elements of a successful business plan, and how can I ensure that my business plan is comprehensive and effective?
2. What are some effective strategies for market research that can help me identify my target audience and evaluate my competition?

3. How can I determine the optimal pricing strategy for my products or services?
4. What are some effective methods for generating buzz and attracting customers to my new business?
5. What are some common legal and regulatory requirements that I should be aware of when launching a new business?
6. How can I effectively manage my finances and develop a sustainable business model?
7. What are some effective ways to build and maintain a strong brand identity that resonates with my target audience?
8. How can I effectively use social media and other digital marketing channels to promote my business and reach new customers?
9. What are some effective ways to build and manage a strong team that can help me achieve my business goals?
10. How can I adapt and evolve my business strategy over time to respond to changing market conditions and customer needs?
11. What are some common pitfalls that entrepreneurs encounter when starting a new business, and how can I avoid them?
12. How can I assess and mitigate the financial risks associated with starting a new business?
13. What are some effective methods for testing and validating my business idea before investing significant resources?
14. How can I ensure that I have a clear and realistic understanding of the market demand for my products or services?
15. What are some effective ways to develop and maintain strong relationships with suppliers and vendors?
16. What are some effective strategies for managing cash flow and maintaining financial stability during the early stages of a new business?

17. How can I effectively manage and minimize the risks associated with intellectual property, trademarks, and copyrights?
18. How can I ensure that my business complies with all applicable laws and regulations, including those related to data privacy and security?
19. What are some effective ways to develop and implement a crisis management plan that can help me navigate unexpected challenges and setbacks?
20. How can I identify and leverage opportunities for partnerships, collaborations, and strategic alliances that can help me grow my business while minimizing risks?

Further Resources:

1. The U.S. Small Business Administration (SBA): https://www.sba.gov/ The SBA provides a wealth of resources for entrepreneurs, including information on business planning, financing, and government contracting.
2. SCORE: https://www.score.org/ SCORE is a nonprofit organization that provides free mentoring, education, and resources for entrepreneurs and small business owners.
3. Entrepreneur: https://www.entrepreneur.com/ Entrepreneur is a leading publication for entrepreneurs, offering a wide range of articles, resources, and tools to help start and grow businesses.
4. StartupNation: https://startupnation.com/ StartupNation provides a range of resources and tools for entrepreneurs, including articles, podcasts, and an online community.
5. Lean Startup: https://leanstartup.co/ Lean Startup is a methodology for starting and growing businesses that emphasizes rapid experimentation and customer feedback. The website provides a range of resources and tools to help entrepreneurs apply the Lean Startup approach.

6. Kauffman Foundation: https://www.kauffman.org/ The Kauffman Foundation is a nonprofit organization that supports entrepreneurship and provides a range of resources and research on starting and growing businesses.
7. National Association of Small Business Owners (NASBO): https://www.nasbo.org/ NASBO is a membership organization for small business owners that provides resources, education, and advocacy on behalf of small businesses.
8. The Lean Canvas: https://leanstack.com/lean-canvas/ The Lean Canvas is a visual tool for developing and testing business models. The website provides a free template and instructions for using the Lean Canvas.
9. Small Business Trends: https://smallbiztrends.com/ Small Business Trends is an online publication that provides news, advice, and insights for small business owners and entrepreneurs.
10. LinkedIn Learning: Offers a range of online courses on entrepreneurship, business planning, and startup financing that can be helpful for aspiring entrepreneurs.
11. "The E-Myth Revisited: Why Most Small Businesses Don't Work and What to Do About It" by Michael E. Gerber. (https://amzn.to/3UzPGQh)   This book offers insights and guidance on how to build a successful and sustainable business by developing systems and processes that can be scaled and replicated.
12. "Traction: Get a Grip on Your Business" by Gino Wickman (https://amzn.to/3MIvERw) - This book outlines a system for building a successful and sustainable business by focusing on six key components: vision, people, data, issues, process, and traction.
13. "Next 10: Coach Wisdom for Entrepreneurs, Business Owners, and CEOs Wondering What Moves to Make Next by Severin Sorensen, (https://amzn.to/3UB8zlM) - In this book, you will find a list of frequently asked questions from recurring situations faced by entrepreneurs, business owners, CEOs, and key executives including buying a business, creating business plans, hiring talent, and much more. It's written from the viewpoint of responding to

the most frequently asked questions of entrepreneurs and business leaders.

All these books and resources can provide valuable insights and guidance for entrepreneurs who are just starting their journey in building a new business.

Use Case 50:

Selling a Business

When the time comes to step away from the companies we've built, every entrepreneur wants to get maximum value from their creation. By using AI, you can discover exactly what you need to do, and how to get the best return on the years you invested in your business.

ChatGPT can assist an SMB business owner in preparing for the sale of their business by offering guidance, resources, and strategic advice across various aspects of the process. Here's how:

1. Pre-Sale Preparation

- Business Valuation:
    - How can you determine the current market value of your business?

- o What factors should you consider in your valuation, such as assets, revenue, profit margins, and market position?
- o For my business type, name the 5 most likely valuation models to consider?
- o How can I find an industry insider who would be a great prospect for a transaction advisor?
- Financial Documentation:
  - o What financial documents and records do I need to prepare, including income statements, balance sheets, and cash flow statements?
  - o What will a buyer be looking to view in my financials? How can I ensure my financials are accurate, up-to-date, and audit-ready?
  - o What pre-transaction due diligence questions should I consider prior to posting my business for sale?
- Operational Review:
  - o What operational aspects should I review and optimize to make your business more attractive to buyers?
  - o What expectations might a buyer want to see in terms of documents in our business processes and standard operating procedures (SOPs)?
  - o The value of our company is in our future innovation; Help me with preparation of a technology roadmap for my company to describe our future horizons of opportunity

2. Enhancing Business Value
- Growth Strategies:

      o What short-term growth strategies can I implement to increase the value of your business before the sale?

      o How can I LEAN out my business and prepare it for sale?

      o What assets might a new buyer want me to re-purchase or liquidate prior to sale of my company?

      o For my business type and industry, what KPIs are likely to be of most importance to buyers?

- Customer Base Analysis:
  - How can I assess and stabilize my customer base to demonstrate steady revenue streams?
  - Prior to company sale, what strategies might you suggest to consider to increase customer loyalty and retention?

3. Marketing the Sale

- Creating a Sales Prospectus:
  - What information should be included in a compelling sales prospectus, such as business overview, financial performance, and growth potential?
  - How can one present their business in the best light to attract serious buyers?
  - Take in these details of my business and help me prepare a 2-page summary of my business and opportunity for a new buyer
- Identifying Potential Buyers:
  - Who are the likely potential buyers for your business (competitors, investors, private equity firms)?
  - How can I reach out to and engage with these potential buyers?

4. Due Diligence Process

- Due Diligence Preparation:
  - What documents and information should one prepare for the due diligence process, including legal, financial, and operational data?
  - How can one ensure transparency and address potential red flags in advance?
- Legal Considerations:
  - What legal aspects should one consider, such as intellectual property, contracts, and compliance?
  - How can one work with legal advisors to prepare and review necessary documents?

5. Negotiation and Closing

- Negotiation Strategies:
  - What negotiation strategies can one use to maximize the sale price and terms?
  - How can one prepare for common buyer questions and objections?
- Deal Structuring:
  - What are the different ways to structure the sale (asset sale, stock purchase, merger)?
  - How can one evaluate the tax implications and financial benefits of each option?
  - Where can I find a trusted advisor to help me with these issues?

6. Transition Planning:

- What transition plans should one put in place to ensure a smooth handover to the new owner?
- How can one support the new owner post-sale to maintain business continuity?

7. Post-Sale Considerations

- Tax Planning:
  - o What are the tax implications of selling your business, and how can you minimize your tax liability?
  - o How can you work with a tax advisor to plan for the financial impact of the sale?

By providing detailed information, answering questions, and suggesting resources and strategies, ChatGPT can help SMB business owners navigate the complex process of preparing for and executing the sale of their business, ensuring a smooth and successful transaction.

Here are 10 questions business owners might want to ask ChatGPT to help them prepare for selling their company at the best valuation:

1. What are some key factors that impact a company's valuation, and how can I ensure that my company is well-positioned for a high valuation?
2. How can I effectively assess the market demand for my company and identify potential buyers who may be interested in acquiring it?
3. What are some common pitfalls to avoid when preparing a company for sale, and how can I mitigate the risks associated with those pitfalls?
4. How can I ensure that my company's financial records and other documentation are accurate, complete, and easily accessible to potential buyers?
5. What are some effective strategies for managing and negotiating the sale process, including managing due

diligence and ensuring a smooth transition for employees and customers?

6. How can I determine the optimal timing for selling my company, taking into account market conditions and other relevant factors?

7. What are some effective ways to position my company and its products or services to potential buyers in a compelling and attractive way?

8. How can I navigate the legal and regulatory requirements associated with selling a company, including those related to taxes and contracts?

9. What are some effective methods for structuring the sale of my company to maximize value and minimize risks?

10. How can I prepare myself emotionally and mentally for the process of selling my company, and what are some effective ways to manage the stress and uncertainty associated with this decision?

Further Resources:

Here are some websites, books, and other resources that readers could learn more about preparing their company for sale:

1. The National Center for the Middle Market: https://www.middlemarketcenter.org/
2. The Exit Planning Institute: https://exit-planning-institute.org/
3. Investopedia: https://www.investopedia.com/terms/e/exitstrategy.asp
4. Mergers & Acquisitions: https://www.themiddlemarket.com/
5. "The Art of Selling Your Business: Winning Strategies & Secret Hacks for Exiting on Top" by John Warrillow

6. "Selling Your Business For Dummies" by Barbara Findlay Schenck and John Davies (https://amzn.to/40dbgex)

7. "Exit Rich: The 6 P Method to Sell Your Business for Huge Profit" by Michelle Seiler Tucker and Sharon Lechter (https://amzn.to/3L0yW1n)

8. "Built to Sell: Creating a Business That Can Thrive Without You" by John Warrillow

9. "The Complete Guide to Selling Your Business" by Fred Steingold

10. The International Business Brokers Association: https://www.ibba.org/

11. Axial: https://www.axial.net/

12. BizBuySell: https://www.bizbuysell.com/ (https://amzn.to/3oiUltB)

13. Score: https://www.score.org/resource/how-sell-your-business

14. Severin Sorensen, "Next10: Coach Wisdom for Entrepreneurs, Business Owners, and CEOs Wondering What Moves to Make Next," December 2022, Mission, Vision, Values Section. (https://amzn.to/4bRYGaT)

15. LinkedIn Learning: Offers a range of online courses on mergers and acquisitions, business valuation, and exit planning that can be helpful for business owners.

Error and Bias Detection

Throughout this book we've mentioned many times the need for a human being to go through and verify any content produced by ChatGPT or other AI platforms.

We're serious about this requirement.

In the early days of AI-driven chat systems (particularly early versions), users often found that the quality of responses could be inconsistent. While the AI tools were generally adept at providing accurate and relevant information, there were instances where errors would creep in. These inaccuracies often appeared in the form of fabricated references, incorrect hyperlinks, and misunderstandings of the user's query. For instance, when inquiring about female athletes who had completed a mile in under four minutes, ChatGPT would struggle to differentiate between a 4:11 mile and an actual sub-four-minute mile.

Similarly, when using ChatGPT to explore the Dunning-Kruger Effect, the AI system would excel in explaining the concept but falter when asked to provide supporting references, creating fictitious sources and invalid links. Similarly,

These issues continue in many respects, highlighting the need for reliable fact-checking strategies and inspired the creation of this chapter to help users detect and reduce errors in AI-generated responses.

To be completely transparent, let's take a look at the Dunning-Kruger Effect example I talked about earlier. It's a good one.

Title: The Dunning-Kruger Effect in J-Curves and Innovation: Exploring the Intersection

Abstract: The Dunning-Kruger effect, a cognitive bias in which people with low ability overestimate their competence, has been studied extensively in various contexts. This article aims to examine the relationship between the Dunning-Kruger effect and the journey companies go through with J-curves and innovation. By providing a summary of the concept and three examples familiar to business leaders, this paper aims to offer new insights into the phenomenon and its potential implications for organizational management and innovation strategy.

Keywords: Dunning-Kruger effect, J-curves, innovation, cognitive bias, management

Introduction

The Dunning-Kruger effect is a cognitive bias wherein individuals with limited knowledge or ability in a given domain tend to overestimate their competence, while those with higher ability often underestimate their capabilities (Kruger & Dunning, 1999). The J-curve, on the other hand, represents a common pattern of growth and development observed in companies undergoing significant change, such as during the implementation of new technologies or business models (Nixon & Mazzarol, 2018). This article aims to explore the intersection between the Dunning-Kruger effect and J-curves in innovation and provide three examples of this phenomenon familiar to business leaders.

However when I asked ChatGPT to provide references for the article, it began to mess up badly and give erroneous results. Here's a sample:

Kruger, J., & Dunning, D. (1999). Unskilled and unaware of it: How difficulties in recognizing one's own incompetence lead to inflated self-assessments. Journal of Personality and Social Psychology, 77(6), 1121-1134. https://doi.org/10.1037/0022-3514.77.6.1121

Lucas, H. C., & Goh, J. M. (2009). Disruptive technology: How Kodak missed the digital photography revolution. The Journal of Strategic Information Systems, 18(1), 46-55. https://doi.org/10.1016/j.jsis.2009.02.002

Nixon, P., & Mazzarol, T. (2018). The J-curve: A Literature Review. Small Enterprise Research, 25(2), 161-182. https://doi.org/10.1080/13215906.2018.1470205

Parmenter, L. (2014). Blockbuster: A Case Study in Organizational Failure. Journal of Business Case Studies (JBCS), 10(1), 45-52. https://doi.org/10.19030/jbcs.v10i1.8323

From the four references above provided as support for the ChatGPT article, only the primary reference article from Kruger and Dunning (1999) is correct and the hyperlink is valid.

The second reference from Lucas and Goh (2009) is an actual article, however the hyperlink is invalid. In my fact checking, I was able to find this article on Google Scholar and Research Gate was able to confirm the citation and obtain a valid article link from those other sources; however, the ChatGPT reference link was invalid.

Things break down from there.

The third article referenced by ChatGPT was supposedly authored by Nixon and Mazzaroi (2018) and is a complete fabrication.

Let me repeat that: the reference is fiction. The article does not exist and is not findable anywhere on the internet. It's almost like a high schooler putting fake references in a term paper hoping their teacher doesn't go through the trouble to verify it.

Needless to say, the referenced hyperlink was invalid also.

Furthermore, while a journal cited by ChatGPT is a valid journal published by Taylor and Francis called *Small Enterprise Research,* in the location where ChatGPT said the J-Curve article was to be found [25(2) 161-182] there appears two other articles shown below that are not the referenced article.

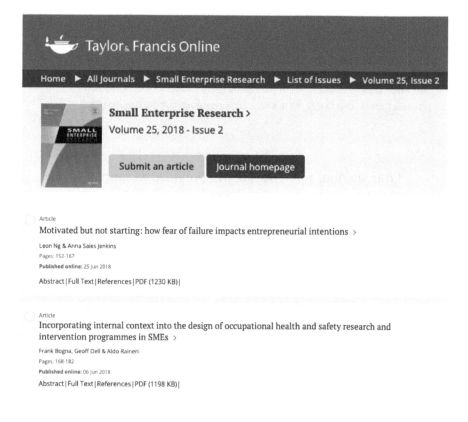

Further, I was curious to see if the article by Leon Ng & Anna Sales Jenkins (2018) on 'Motivated by Not Starting: How Fear of Failure Impacts Entrepreneurial Intentions' referenced the article supposedly from Nixon and Mazzaori in their bibliography. It did not, as the Nixon and Mazzaroi (2018) reference is made-up, make-believe, and non-existent.

The final reference by Parimeter (2014) is also bogus; there is no article by said author. Further, when I clicked the hyperlink for the article provided by ChatGPT it takes you to *The Journal of Business Case Studies* and an article on "Developing Transparent Health Care Reimbursement Auditing Procedures," as shown below. It is not remotely germane to our topic.

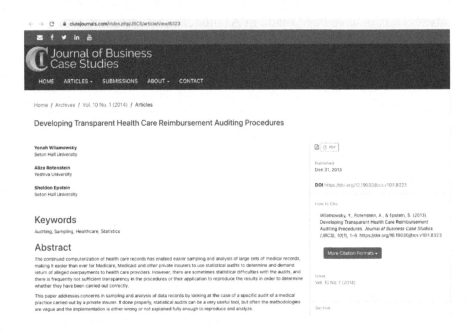

So, while ChatGPT is extremely creative, it can also be reckless if you take the output at face value with no review process. Results must be verified in every circumstance.

If you plan to use ChatGPT or other AI platforms, and we encourage you to do so, you must also assume the important role of fact checker. It is absolutely essential if you are going to use ChatGPT with confidence and have integrity in your results.

Think of ChatGPT as a L1, L2, or L3 engineer and you (the expert in your field) are the L4 senior engineer that must guide the chat, make corrections, redirect, and demand excellence, with phrases like, 'Not good enough, do over.'

As generative AI continues to evolve, it is crucial for users to stay informed about the latest developments and best practices for ensuring the accuracy and reliability of AI-generated content. Since the first edition of this Book was published on 4/15/23, significant advancements have been made in AI models, fact-checking tools, and user awareness. However, new challenges have also emerged, such as AI hallucinations, error creation, and the need for more robust fact-checking processes.

Recent Improvements and Challenges

Advanced AI Models: The latest AI models demonstrate enhanced understanding of context and generate more accurate information. Nevertheless, they are not perfect, and errors can still occur.

Sophisticated Fact-Checking Tools: AI-powered fact-checking tools have become more advanced, capable of cross-referencing information from multiple sources in real-time, thus improving fact-checking accuracy.

Increased User Awareness: Users are now more cognizant of the potential for AI-generated misinformation and are more likely to verify facts, leading to a higher demand for accuracy.

Focus on Ethical AI: There is a growing emphasis on developing AI systems that are transparent, accountable, and rely on trustworthy data sources.

Potential Pitfalls to Monitor

Bias and Misleading Information: AI systems may still exhibit bias or provide misleading information, particularly if trained on biased datasets.

Overconfidence in AI: Users may over-rely on AI outputs without sufficient human oversight, potentially leading to the spread of errors.

Misinterpreting Context: Despite improvements, AI may still have difficulty comprehending nuanced contexts, resulting in inappropriate or irrelevant responses.

Effective Strategies for Fact-Checking AI-Generated Content

Real-Time Verification: Employ AI tools that provide real-time verification of information against current databases and news sources.

Source Transparency: Make sure AI systems clearly cite and reference the sources of the information they generate, enabling users to trace information back to its origins.

Crowdsourced Verification: Utilize crowdsourced platforms where experts and knowledgeable individuals can contribute to verifying information.

Enhanced Search Techniques: Advanced search operators and filters can help refine search results and identify the most relevant and reliable sources.

Contextual Awareness: Consider the context in which information is being sought. Adjust queries to reflect specific aspects of the topic.

Feedback Loops: Provide feedback to AI systems regarding the accuracy and relevance of the information they generate to help improve their performance over time.

Leveraging AI for Fact-Checking

Inter-AI Comparison: Use multiple AI tools (like ChatGPT, Gemini, Claude, CoPilot, etc.) to cross-check information, but also incorporate human oversight to evaluate discrepancies identified by the AI systems.

Diverse Training Data: Advocate for the use of diverse and high-quality datasets in training AI systems to minimize bias and improve accuracy.

Human-AI Collaboration: Develop workflows that integrate human expertise with AI capabilities, ensuring a balanced approach to content review and fact-checking.

AI-Powered Content Verification: Utilize AI tools that analyze content for accuracy, credibility, and potential misinformation by cross-referencing multiple reliable sources.

Automated Source Validation: Algorithms can verify the credibility and authority of sources cited in content. This way you'll you're your citations are reputable and trustworthy.

Fake News Detection: Apply AI-driven platforms that specialize in identifying fake news, propaganda, and misleading information across various media channels.

Bias Identification: Detect potential biases in content by having your artificial intelligence assistant process your findings. This will help your business maintain objectivity and fairness in your communications.

Plagiarism Checks: Integrate AI-powered plagiarism detection tools to ensure content originality and avoid unintentional copying from unreliable sources.[8]

Fact-Checking Chatbots: Chatbots can quickly verify facts, statistics, and claims in real-time conversations or customer interactions.

Image and Video Authentication: Use AI algorithms to analyze images and videos for potential manipulation, deepfakes, or misleading visual content.

Social Media Monitoring: Social media monitoring tools exist to track mentions of your brand, products, or services and identify potential misinformation or false claims.

Knowledge Graph Integration: Incorporate AI-driven knowledge graphs that connect verified facts, entities, and relationships to ensure the accuracy and consistency of information across various contexts.

Continuous Learning and Updating: Utilize AI systems that continuously learn and update their knowledge bases with the latest

---

[8] In today's digital landscape, where AI-generated content is increasingly prevalent, safeguarding your brand's integrity and ensuring originality is paramount. As an SMB utilizing AI for content creation, it's crucial to equip yourself with robust plagiarism detection tools. Options like Originality.AI, Grammarly Premium, and Turnitin offer comprehensive scanning capabilities, comparing your AI-generated content against vast databases of existing text. Additionally, AI content detection tools like GPTZero and Content at Scale's AI Detector can help pinpoint AI-generated content, ensuring your work remains genuinely yours. By incorporating these tools into your workflow, you can confidently maintain the highest standards of authenticity and protect your brand's reputation in the ever-evolving world of AI-generated content.

verified information from reliable sources to maintain accuracy over time.

By implementing these AI-powered fact-checking strategies, SMB users can ensure the authenticity and credibility of the information they use and share. This helps maintain trust with customers, partners, and stakeholders. It also minimizes the risks associated with spreading misinformation or inaccuracies. You don't want to become known as the company that puts out bad information. That kind of reputation is incredibly difficult to shake off.

Your Ethical Compass and Guardrails:

Navigating the AI Landscape Responsibly

As we draw to a close in our 2nd edition journey through the world of conversational generative artificial intelligence for business, it is vital to address some of the most important aspects of this field – ethics and responsible AI use. The development and proliferation of AI technologies comes with numerous potential benefits but also a surplus of risks and challenges. In this concluding chapter, we will discuss four key areas of concern that you need to understand.

Please note that we are not attorneys, nor legal advisors, and we are not offering legal advice. On the contrary, we encourage you to seek your own legal counsel to address any specific legal concerns related to your use, authoring, content creation, and publication of your data.

We did learn from our research in preparation for this book however of four key themes that you too should be aware of:

1. Identifying and Mitigating AI-Generated Misinformation
2. Avoiding Manipulation and Misuse of AI-Generated Content
3. Privacy Concerns and Data Protection
4. Intellectual Property Rights and AI

Identifying and Mitigating AI-Generated Misinformation

AI-generated misinformation, also known as "deepfakes," is a rapidly growing issue in the digital age. These deepfakes can be images, videos, or text that appear to be genuine but are, in fact, the product of AI algorithms designed to deceive. To combat this problem, we must take a multi-faceted approach:

Awareness and education: Educate the public about deepfakes, their potential consequences, and how to spot them. This includes promoting critical thinking and fostering digital literacy.

Detection technology: Develop and improve technologies to detect deepfakes, such as deep learning models that analyze patterns and inconsistencies in the content.

Regulation and policies: Encourage governments and organizations to implement policies and regulations that require platforms to monitor and remove AI-generated misinformation.

Collaboration: Foster collaboration between technology companies, governments, and researchers to share information and best practices in combating AI-generated misinformation.

Avoiding Manipulation and Misuse of AI-Generated Content

AI-generated content has the potential to revolutionize various industries, from journalism to entertainment. However, it also poses risks of manipulation and misuse. To ensure responsible use, several measures can be taken:

Transparent labeling: Clearly label AI-generated content as such, so that users are aware of its origins and can make informed decisions about the information they consume.

Ethical guidelines: Establish and follow ethical guidelines that govern the creation and distribution of AI-generated content. This includes avoiding the use of AI for malicious purposes, such as promoting disinformation or inciting violence.

Accountability: Hold creators and distributors of AI-generated content accountable for their actions, ensuring they adhere to ethical guidelines and face consequences for violating them.

Privacy Concerns and Data Protection

As AI technologies continue to evolve, so do concerns surrounding privacy and data protection. To address these concerns, we must prioritize the following:

Anonymization: Implement anonymization techniques to protect the privacy of individuals whose data is used to train AI models.

Consent and transparency: Ensure that individuals are informed about the collection and use of their data and provide them with the option to give or withhold consent.

Data protection regulations: Support the development and enforcement of data protection regulations that govern the collection, storage, and use of personal data in AI applications.

Privacy-preserving AI techniques: Research and develop privacy-preserving AI techniques, such as federated learning and differential privacy, to minimize the exposure of sensitive data during the AI training process.

Intellectual Property Rights and AI

As AI models like ChatGPT, DALL-E, MidJourney.ai generate content based on massive amounts of data from various sources, including copyrighted material, it is essential to address the implications of these technologies on intellectual property rights:

Clear guidelines for AI-generated content: Establish guidelines that differentiate between AI-generated content inspired by copyrighted material and outright plagiarism. This may require reevaluating and updating current copyright laws to accommodate AI-generated content.

In my authorship, I actively engage with artificial intelligence (AI) as a collaborative partner, ensuring that AI contributions are duly acknowledged. For the AI Whisperer book series, I employ a multi-modal approach, utilizing a team comprising over three distinct AI models and three human subject-matter experts for research, writing, and editing. While I maintain the role of primary author, I have cultivated a symbiotic relationship with an AI model designated "Amelia Chatterley," who functions as my dedicated research assistant. While other AI models are occasionally employed, Amelia remains my principal AI collaborator.

I leverage AI capabilities to augment and refine my writing process. This typically involves drafting sections of text, which are subsequently submitted to ChatGPT for refinement tailored to my target audience. Following this, I meticulously review and revise the AI-generated suggestions, integrating my own domain expertise and nuanced perspectives to ensure the final product aligns seamlessly with my authorial intent.

In the spirit of transparency, I am forthright about the integration of AI into my creative process. I firmly believe that the synthesis of human ingenuity and AI capabilities offers a novel pathway to achieving unprecedented levels of literary and informational output.

Additionally, when using AI, I do not hide, but rather promote my extensive use of AI in my work, as most of my recent book efforts have included the research from at least three LLM models and multiple humans working together to create great work. I demonstrated such candor and declaration of use in my opening

"Forward" for this book, with an image that I created with Midjourney depicting Amelia Chatterley, my AI assistant. Here's the caption text: *"Amelia Chatterley," a personalized AI assistant powered by GPT, works diligently behind the scenes, collaborating with Severin Sorensen on research, insights, and writing for the best-selling "The AI Whisperer Series." This visual representation showcases the intelligent and seamless partnership between human and AI, as they co-create compelling content that captivates readers and pushes the boundaries of what's possible in the realm of AI-assisted storytelling."*

And at the conclusion of each of our books we list author and contributor and restate the relationship of the creators of this work.

Importantly, the academic standards for citing material created, informed, or enhanced by AI are still evolving, but emerging guidelines emphasize transparency, ethical considerations, proper citation, and critical evaluation.

Researchers should be transparent about the use of AI, mentioning specific tools and their applications while addressing any ethical implications.

AI should be cited according to style-specific guidelines: APA suggests citing AI as the author following software reference rules, MLA recommends using the "Title of Container" element for AI tools, and Chicago style cites the AI tool as the author with the date of text generation.

Verification and critical evaluation of AI-generated content are essential, and researchers should consult their institution's guidelines for any additional policies.

Awareness of copyright issues and staying updated on evolving standards are also important. Key resources include the APA Style Blog, MLA Style Center, and the Chicago Manual of Style Online.

Moving forward, in my view, the laws must change to allow AI or its developers to be a co-author or creator of content, as increasingly synthetic data and not human data will become more valuable, and there will be many debates around who owns that content in the future. For now, I'm grateful for the abundant access and use of AI in my work, as AI has greatly accelerated and ignited my curiosity in ways that were previously unimaginable.

In my view, it's important that authors, artists, and creators are recognized and paid fairly for their work, even if this means that the creative class should receive some AI arts stipend for being a 'creative' if their work was readily available for training but not able today to be detected as being trained by any LLM model.

Confused? Let me explain.

I believe creators should be compensated fairly when their existing work is used to train or inform AI systems, especially when it can be proven that their prior art is the material that informed AI. Though I also agree that at this point of AI maturity, it will be challenging to identify prior work of creatives, as the creativity of AI and its developers has already been rewritten in unique ways, masking much of their prior content not easily recognizable.

For example, when preparing this section of the book, I asked Claude AI to name or cite any resources used for the "AI Guardrails" that follow at the end of this section. The artificial intelligence commented, *"I apologize for the confusion, but I did not directly cite any sources for the guardrails mentioned in my previous response."*

Just as a human would read the basic research and summarize the data with new words, AI has done the same. That being the case, the output is not detectable as plagiarism with the detection models. Similarly, MidJourney AI developers have instituted a conflict engine, a guardrail of sorts, in its image creation. Midjourney will not output any image that has been published before or is readily available on the internet.

Therefore, given the state of AI and LLM training, I think in fairness that society and rule-setters should consider ways that creatives may receive compensation for their prior work. And I'm not sure that current copyright, image, likeness, persona, or voice will cover this. Hence an ethical use strategy would include:

Attribution and royalties: Develop mechanisms to ensure that creators receive proper attribution and potential royalties when their copyrighted work is used as inspiration or as a basis for AI-generated content.

Responsible AI training: Encourage technology companies to adopt responsible practices when training AI models, ensuring that copyrighted material is used fairly and with respect for intellectual property rights.

Awareness and education: Foster awareness among creators and the public about the intersection of AI and intellectual property rights. This includes promoting an understanding of the legal and ethical implications of using AI-generated content that may be based on copyrighted material.

In conclusion, as AI continues to permeate every aspect of our lives, it is our collective responsibility to ensure that these powerful tools are used ethically and responsibly. The considerations outlined in this chapter serve as a starting point to navigate the complex landscape of AI ethics. By fostering awareness, promoting education, and encouraging collaboration across various sectors, we can harness the potential of AI to create a better future, while mitigating the risks associated with its misuse. Remember, we are not attorneys, legal advisors, or offering legal advice. We encourage you to seek your own legal counsel to address any specific legal concerns related to the ethical use of AI.

Lastly, this section would not be complete without a discussion of guardrails specifically for businesses seeking to implement AI ethically, responsibly, and safely in their enterprises.

Need for AI Guardrails in Business

While AI holds tremendous potential for innovation, efficiency, and problem-solving, it also carries inherent risks of misuse that could have severe consequences for individuals, businesses, governments, and society as a whole.

Just as we accept certain limitations on our freedom when traveling by airplane to ensure the safety and security of all passengers, it is essential that we implement sensible guardrails for AI use in business. The power and potential impact of AI are so significant that it would be irresponsible to allow its unchecked development and deployment without proper oversight and regulation.

That being said, I recognize the importance of balancing the need for AI governance with the desire to foster innovation and entrepreneurship. While some may argue for a completely unregulated AI environment, and others may advocate for strict controls akin to those applied to nuclear security technology, I believe that a more measured approach is necessary for most businesses.

In my opinion, the ideal solution lies in the establishment of governing bodies for AI, similar to Underwriters Laboratories (UL) and Conformité Européenne (CE), which provide safety certifications for electrical appliances and components. These organizations ensure that products meet strict safety standards before they can be introduced into the market, protecting consumers and businesses alike.

Applying a similar framework to AI would help create a safer playing field for businesses while still allowing room for innovation and growth. By establishing clear guidelines and standards for AI development and deployment, we can mitigate the risks of misuse and unintended consequences while still reaping the benefits of this transformative technology.

To that end, I propose the following 10 sensible guardrails for businesses seeking to use AI:

10 Guardrails or Essential Best Practices for Responsible AI Implementation in SMBs

1. **Establish Clear Objectives**: Define specific goals and objectives for AI implementation to ensure that the technology aligns with your business strategy and values.
2. **Be Ethical and Develop Guidelines**: Create a set of ethical guidelines that govern the use of AI within your organization, addressing issues such as data privacy, bias prevention, and transparency.
3. **Ensure Data Quality**: Implement strict data quality controls to ensure that the data used to train and inform AI systems is accurate, unbiased, and representative of your target audience.
4. **Maintain Human Oversight**: Establish processes that require human oversight and intervention in critical decision-making processes involving AI to prevent over-reliance on the technology.

5. **Regularly Audit AI Systems**: Conduct regular audits of your AI systems to identify potential biases, errors, or inconsistencies, and take corrective action as needed.

6. **Prioritize Transparency**: Be transparent about your use of AI with customers, employees, and stakeholders, and provide clear explanations of how the technology is being used and how it may impact them.

7. **Invest in Employee Training**: Provide comprehensive training to employees on how to effectively use and interact with AI systems, as well as how to identify and report potential issues.

8. **Monitor for Unintended Consequences**: Continuously monitor the outcomes and impacts of your AI systems to identify any unintended consequences or negative effects on your business or stakeholders.

9. **Collaborate with Experts**: Partner with AI experts, ethicists, and legal professionals to ensure that your AI implementation adheres to industry best practices and complies with relevant regulations.

10. **Plan for Continuous Improvement**: Treat AI implementation as an ongoing process, and plan for continuous improvement and updates to your AI systems based on new developments, feedback, and lessons learned.

These 10 guardrail suggestions align with general principles and recommendations from reputable organizations and experts in the field of AI ethics and governance that include:

- The OECD Principles on Artificial Intelligence
- The Partnership on AI
- The IEEE Global Initiative on Ethics of Autonomous and Intelligent Systems

- Future of Life Institute
- The European Commission's High-Level Expert Group on Artificial Intelligence
- The Montreal Declaration for Responsible Development of Artificial Intelligence
- The AI Now Institute at New York University
- The Center for Humane Technology

By following these guardrails, SMBs can harness the power of AI while mitigating potential risks and ensuring responsible, ethical, and effective implementation. Remember that AI should be used to augment and support human decision-making, not replace it entirely. By maintaining a human-centric approach and staying vigilant in monitoring and refining your AI systems, you can maximize the benefits of this transformative technology for your business. Strive to be good, do good, and uplift others is a mantra that will serve you well as you seek to use AI in your businesses.

In conclusion, as AI continues to advance and become more widely adopted by small and medium-sized businesses, it is crucial for organizations to prioritize the responsible and ethical implementation of these technologies. By establishing clear objectives, developing ethical guidelines, ensuring data quality, maintaining human oversight, and regularly auditing AI systems, SMBs can effectively harness the power of AI while mitigating potential risks and unintended consequences. Collaboration with experts, continuous monitoring, and a commitment to transparency and accountability are also essential components of a comprehensive AI governance framework.

Moreover, SMBs must recognize the need for sensible guardrails to ensure the safe and responsible use of AI. Just as we accept certain limitations on our freedom when traveling by air to ensure the safety and security of all passengers, businesses should embrace clear guidelines and standards for AI development and deployment. These guardrails should include establishing ethical codes of conduct, ensuring transparency in decision-making processes, implementing data privacy and security measures, regularly auditing for accuracy and bias, providing employee training, fostering a culture of accountability, collaborating with industry partners and regulators, prioritizing human oversight, monitoring the impact of AI, and adapting governance frameworks as the technology advances.

As small and medium businesses navigate the complexities of AI adoption, they must remain vigilant in detecting and addressing errors, biases, and potential misuse of these technologies. By adhering to best practices and implementing appropriate guardrails, SMBs can foster trust among stakeholders, comply with relevant regulations, and maximize the benefits of AI while minimizing harm. Ultimately, by prioritizing the responsible and ethical use of AI, small and medium-sized businesses can contribute to the development of a more trustworthy and beneficial AI ecosystem for all.

Conclusion:

The Journey Forward with AI

As we turn the final pages of this Second Edition of *The AI Whisperer: Handbook for Leveraging Conversational Artificial Intelligence & ChatGPT for Business*, it's evident that the intersection of AI and improved business communications, creativity, and execution is no longer a distant promise but a present reality. The fifty Business Use Cases we've explored are just the beginning of a transformative journey for your business. With AI as your co-pilot, you're equipped to handle business tasks, issues, and opportunities with newfound efficiency and precision.

For me, it's been great fun to have the opportunity to go back and read, review, and update this book for this 2nd Edition. Truly the first edition was good. However, this second edition is much better. This subject, more than any other in our current landscape, requires time and experimentation to truly grasp. The impacts are still mostly unknown. Only with the advantage of hindsight will we truly be able to grasp just how big a change AI will be on society. For me, I ask this question: *Now with more experience, what do you wish you had known the first time you wrote this book?*

Now we both know the answer.

The goal of *The AI Whisperer Series* has been to help you make better analyses, decisions, and achieve superior results in your business. Hopefully this ultimately leads to all of us living happier lives.

Integrating AI into your business routine is about making smart prompts and practical AI tips second nature. The time you've reclaimed and the stress you've shed pave the way for a life where joy and productivity coexist harmoniously. As AI continues to evolve, so will the ways it can enhance our lives. Stay curious and open to new possibilities, letting artificial intelligence be the wind beneath the wings of your aspirations.

The two stepwise prompt journeys were important to include. They give you a key to prompting more effectively using threads and conversations of greater depth. The examples provided are not mere illustrations but adaptable tools for your daily operations. Embrace these changes—they are for the better!

On this journey, remember the responsibility that accompanies the power of AI. Prioritize the ethical use of this technology, respecting user privacy and data security. Remain vigilant against the biases that can infiltrate AI systems, striving for fairness and inclusivity in every interaction.

While AI can suggest, predict, and even decide, the ultimate choice always rests in your hands. Your wisdom, empathy, and ethical judgment are irreplaceable. Let AI be a tool, not a tyrant. Use it as a research aid and be sure to fact-check and enhance all work with your creativity and style. Advocate for ethical AI, joining a community of individuals seeking to do good with their prompts and AI work.

Together, we've unlocked a treasure trove of AI's potential to make every day easier, more fulfilling, and enjoyable. Carry these insights forward and let the whispers of AI guide you to a smarter, lighter, and more delightful tomorrow. As Albert Einstein observed, *"The true sign of intelligence is not knowledge but imagination."* This reminds us that you, with your intellect and curiosity, play the pivotal role.

AI simply helps write the script.

Always ensure you're the one holding the pen, guiding the narrative with your unique perspective, insights, acumen, and ethical considerations.

As you reach the conclusion of this 2nd Edition of *The AI Whisperer*, I want to ensure you have the tools and resources to continue your exploration of AI in the business world. The appendices provide valuable information to support your journey towards becoming an AI and ChatGPT Whisperer.

Appendix 1 delves into OpenAI's K-Terms and their usage, allowing you to refine your interaction with the AI model.

Appendix 2 introduces the Boolean Logic Prompt Table, enabling more precise and effective communication.

Appendix 3 helps you create custom persona-specific GPTs to improve your routine activities with AI.

Appendix 4 provides crafted position descriptions for AI Whisperers, tailored to specific target audiences to attract the best candidates with diverse backgrounds and skill sets.

Appendix 5 provides suggestions for chapters germane for businesses specializations such as marketing, sales, operations, and HR.

Take full advantage of these appendices to deepen your understanding of AI and gain practical tools and insights for ongoing success. The journey of an AI Whisperer is one of constant learning and growth. As you close this book, remember that the adventure does not end here. The world of AI is vast and ever-changing, and as an AI Whisperer, you are now equipped to explore its depths and harness its power to elevate your business and the world around you.

Remember, AI will not take your job; someone who knows how to use AI will. It is estimated that for every five jobs impacted by AI, one will be eliminated and four will be augmented and improved. Decide now to be the one who acts, rather than the one acted upon. And seek to share what you learn and help others on your way. This book aims to inspire and equip you with the tools, scripts, and prompts to embark on your yet undiscovered journey.

Wishing you every success in your explorations with AI.

Yours in curiosity and wonder,

Severin Sorensen

Author, The AI Whisperer Series

Founder & Curator, AIWhisperer.org

Founder & CEO, ePraxis

AI Whisperer | Executive Coach | Management Consultant

Appendix 1:

K-Terms and Templates from OpenAI's ChatGPT to Enhance Business Efficiency

OpenAI's introduction of K-terms with extensions to ChatGPT has revolutionized how SMB users interact with the language model, providing enhanced control and precision. These K-terms are designed to facilitate specific types of interactions, ensuring that users can extract maximum value from their interactions with ChatGPT. Here's an overview of the key K-terms and how they can be effectively utilized in a business context:

Continue: Use this term when you need ChatGPT to extend its previous response, providing more information or delving deeper into a topic. This is particularly useful for generating comprehensive reports or detailed analyses.

Clarify: When a point needs further elucidation, this term prompts ChatGPT to provide additional context or clear up any ambiguity. It's perfect for ensuring all communications and documents are unambiguous and thoroughly understood.

Exemplify: This term helps you get concrete examples that illustrate specific concepts or points. It's an excellent tool for presentations, training materials, and educational content where examples can significantly enhance understanding.

Expand: Prompt ChatGPT to elaborate on a particular point, providing a richer, more detailed explanation. This term is invaluable for content creation, such as blog posts, articles, and whitepapers, where depth of information is crucial.

Explain: For in-depth explanations of complex concepts, this term guides ChatGPT to break down topics into understandable parts. It's ideal for creating educational content or simplifying intricate business processes.

Rewrite: When a different phrasing is needed to improve clarity or conciseness, use this term. It's highly beneficial for refining marketing copy, revising emails, or ensuring that all written communications are polished and professional.

Shorten: This term is used to condense text, making it more succinct. It's particularly useful for summarizing lengthy documents or creating brief overviews that are easy to digest.

Tweetify: Designed to generate tweet-length responses, this term helps create concise, impactful summaries suitable for social media platforms like X. It's an excellent tool for crafting quick updates or engaging social media posts.

Using K Templates

K Templates are a feature available for users subscribed to ChatGPT Teams, ChatGPT Enterprise, and through the ChatGPT API. These templates allow users to create and share structured prompts to streamline workflows and ensure consistency in content generation across teams. To access K Templates, ChatGPT Teams and Enterprise users can find these templates within their collaborative workspaces, where they can be easily customized and shared among team members. API users can incorporate K Templates into their applications by defining and executing structured prompts programmatically, enabling seamless integration with existing workflows and systems. This feature enhances productivity and collaboration by providing reusable, high-quality prompt structures tailored to various business needs

The K Templates are powerful helpmates for accessing greater nuance and clarity in your prompting AI to help you get better results.

For this illustration, I'm using ChatGPT Teams version. The K Templates are accessed by clicking on the K Templates icon that appears at the bottom left of ChatGPT your browser window.

After you click on the templates icon up will pop-up the following this floating menu.

(K) ChatGPT Prompt Templates by Keywords Everywhere

Category:	Sub-category:	Templates:
Choose a category ⌄	Select a sub-category ⌄	Select a template ⌄

Please browse through our categories and sub-categories above and select a prompt template that you'd like to execute

* Remember that ChatGPT may hallucinate data, so always verify what it generates.

Thereafter you will first choose your business category. To help crosswalk the reader through the use of this K template we will explore the following business use case: writing a complaint letter to a supplier.

Practical Example: Writing a Complaint Letter to a Supplier

Imagine you run a small business and need to address recurring issues with a supplier delivering faulty products. Using the legal complaint template with K-terms can streamline this process.

Here is a step-by-step guide for an SMB user to create a supplier dispute letter using the ChatGPT prompt templates feature. This guide will walk you through the screens you have provided, organized logically as they would appear in the ChatGPT interface.

Click on the K prompt icon that is located on the lower left sidebar of your ChatGPT browser window.

 Templates

After clicking on the K-templates icon, the following floating menu will appear.

(K) ChatGPT Prompt Templates by Keywords Everywhere

Category:	Sub-category:	Templates:
Choose a category ⌄	Select a sub-category ⌄	Select a template ⌄

Please browse through our categories and sub-categories above and select a prompt template that you'd like to execute

* Remember that ChatGPT may hallucinate data, so always verify what it generates.

You should begin by accessing the ChatGPT prompt templates feature. This will typically be found within the ChatGPT application under a specific section designated for templates.

Select the Category: From the dropdown menu, select the category relevant to your need. Categories include copywriting, marketing, SEO, social media, productivity, and professionals. For this example, creating a supplier dispute letter, we will start with the "Professionals" category.

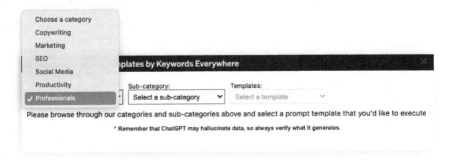

Choose the Sub-Category: Under the "Professionals" category, you will need to choose the sub-category that best fits your requirement. In this case, select "Lawyers."

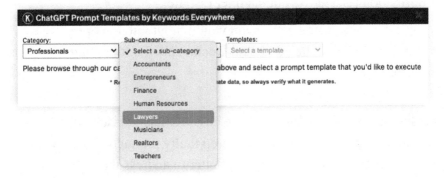

Select the Template: Once you have selected "Lawyers," you will be presented with various templates. For the purpose of creating a supplier dispute letter, choose the "Document Analyst" template.

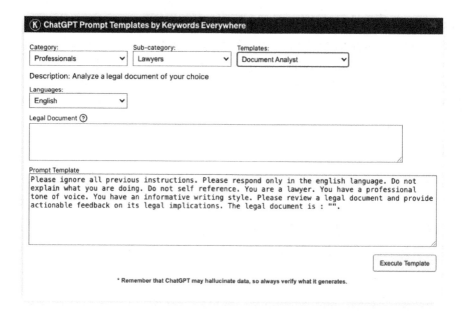

Fill in the Required Information: After selecting the "Document Analyst" template, you will need to fill in the specific details of your legal document. In the provided fields, enter the necessary information related to your supplier dispute.

For our example case you would input into the open comment window labeled "Legal Document" the following information.

Describe your Situation: "We are an SMB facing issues with a supplier who has repeatedly delivered faulty products. I need your help in writing a formal complaint letter to address these issues and seek resolution."

Add Details: Enter details such as your business name, the supplier's name, order numbers, and the specific issues.

Add Your Sentiment: State your state of mind and sentiment in writing this letter. For example, you might express your empathy for your supplier and their situation and you are merely seeking their attention to resolve issues amicably using measured tones; or you may state your great concern with the situation and threaten to lawyer-up (retaining legal counsel) if the present issue is not resolved swiftly to your liking. The sentiment and voice you choose for your response will set the tone for your letter and negotiations.

[Important Note: The example provided is not intended as legal advice, nor should it be used as a substitute for professional legal consultation. While many business disputes can be effectively managed by business leaders with a basic understanding of legal principles that ChatGPT's K-Template can provide, it is crucial to recognize the value of professional legal counsel in legal matters. If you have questions about whether your issue requires an attorney, consult your legal advisor. The author of this book is not acting as your attorney. For any legal matters requiring professional advice, we strongly recommend consulting with a qualified attorney.]

Execute Template To Create the Document: Next, Click on the "Execute Template" option. The template will then take in your directions and details and write a first draft of the requested document. You can use additional K-terms like "Clarify" and "Expand" to shape the document into the end-product you envisioned thus creating a detailed, professional complaint letter.

Tips for Use: Ensure all details provided are accurate and complete to avoid any discrepancies in the generated document.

Review the drafted document carefully to make any necessary adjustments before finalizing it.

Utilize the professional tone and style provided by the template to maintain a formal and authoritative communication style in your dispute letter.

By following these steps, you should be able to effectively create a supplier dispute letter using the ChatGPT prompt templates feature. Here is an example of what a potential result might look like from ChatGPT's K-Template using the example above.

Example Letter:

[Your Business Name]
[Your Address]
[City, State, ZIP Code]
[Email Address]
[Phone Number]

[Date]

[Supplier's Name]
[Supplier's Address]
[City, State, ZIP Code]

Subject: Formal Complaint Regarding Faulty Product Deliveries

Dear [Supplier's Name],

I hope this letter finds you well. I am writing to formally address a series of issues we have encountered with recent deliveries from your company. As a valued supplier, we have come to rely on the quality and timeliness of your products to support our business operations. Unfortunately, the following problems have arisen:

Defective Products: On [specific dates], we received multiple batches of products that were defective. The order numbers are [Order Numbers]. These defects have caused significant disruption to our production line and have led to customer complaints.

Late Deliveries: Additionally, the deliveries on [specific dates] were delayed by several days. Timely delivery is crucial for us to meet our client commitments, and these delays have adversely impacted our business.

Given these ongoing issues, we request the following actions to resolve the matter:

A replacement for the defective products at no additional cost.

A commitment to timely deliveries moving forward.

Compensation for the disruptions caused by the delays and defects.

We value our partnership and hope to resolve these issues promptly to continue our successful collaboration. Please respond to this complaint by [desired response date] to discuss how we can address these concerns effectively.

Thank you for your attention to this matter. I look forward to your prompt response.

Sincerely,

[Your Name]
[Your Position]
[Your Business Name]

By leveraging K-terms, SMB users can handle legal and business correspondence more effectively, ensuring clarity, professionalism, and efficiency in their communications.

Appendix 2:

Boolean Logic Improves Prompting

Business users can add more nuance and precision to your prompting by leveraging the Boolean logic functions in your prompts.

One fundamental Boolean operator is AND. This operator ensures that both conditions specified must be true for the overall expression to be true. For example, if you want ChatGPT to provide insights on customers who are both premium members and have made a recent purchase, you can structure your prompt using the AND operator.

Example:

"Provide a list of marketing strategies for customers who are premium members AND have made a purchase in the last month."

Explanation:

In this prompt, the use of AND ensures that ChatGPT focuses on customers who meet both criteria: they must be premium members and have made a purchase in the last month. This specificity helps in generating more targeted and actionable strategies.

With the above example in mind, here are 25 most useful business-related Boolean logic terms and how to use them to improve your prompting.

Here is a table of common Boolean logic terms that you can use with ChatGPT:

Term	Definition	Example	Application
AND	A boolean operator that returns true if both operands are true, and false otherwise.	true AND true returns true	If the customer is a premium member AND has made a purchase in the last month, offer a discount.
AND for Resource Allocation	Combines an AND condition with another boolean expression for resource allocation.	true AND (true OR false) returns true	If the project is high priority AND (the resources are available OR can be reallocated), assign the necessary team members.
AND with Additional Condition	Combines an AND condition with another boolean expression.	true AND (false OR true) returns true	If the sales representative achieved their target AND (received positive feedback OR secured a new client), give them a bonus.

Boolean Expressions with List Membership	Checks if an item is part of a predefined list.	item IN list	If the product is in the 'best sellers' list, highlight it on the homepage.
Complex Conditional Logic	Combines multiple conditions to create intricate decision rules.	IF (condition1 AND condition2) OR (condition3 AND NOT condition4)	If the user is logged in AND has a verified email OR is a guest user AND has completed a captcha, allow access.
Date Comparisons	Boolean expressions that evaluate dates within specific ranges or conditions.	date >= today AND date <= end_of_month	If the current date is within the promotional period, apply the special pricing.
Equivalence	A boolean operator that returns true if both operands have the same truth value, and false otherwise.	true <-> true returns true	If the system status is active (equivalence) and the user status is active, proceed with operation.
Equivalence in Decision Making	Uses equivalence to make business decisions.	(true AND true) <-> false returns false	If the employee's performance review is excellent (equivalence) and meets promotion

			criteria, proceed with the promotion process.
IF-THEN-ELSE Logic	A control structure that executes one action if a condition is true and another action if it is false.	If (condition) then (action1) else (action2)	If the customer is a new user, offer a 10% discount; else, offer a 5% discount for loyalty.
Implication	A boolean operator that returns false if the antecedent is true and the consequent is false.	true -> false returns false	If the customer has a subscription (implication), then offer them a renewal discount if their current plan is expiring.
Implication in Business Rule	Uses implication to define business rules.	(true AND false) -> true returns true	If the payment is verified (implication) and the shipping address is confirmed, initiate order fulfillment.

Nested XOR	Combines multiple XOR conditions.	(true XOR false) XOR true returns false	If the client requested expedited shipping XOR premium packaging, and it XOR exceeds weight limits, notify for special handling.
NAND	A boolean operator that returns false if both of its operands are true, and true otherwise.	true NAND true returns false	If both checks fail (NAND), flag the transaction for review.
NAND with a Combination of Conditions	Uses NAND with a combined condition.	true NAND (false OR true) returns true	If the customer feedback is NOT both negative AND about the same issue, flag it for individual follow-up.
NOR	A boolean operator that returns true if both of its operands are false, and false otherwise.	false NOR false returns true	If the user is neither an admin NOR a moderator, restrict access to settings.

NOR in a Workflow	Uses NOR to evaluate conditions in a workflow.	(false NOR true) NOR true returns false	If the project status is neither completed NOR in review, escalate it to the project manager.
NOT	A unary boolean operator that returns the opposite of the operand's value.	NOT true returns false	If the item is NOT in stock, display the 'out of stock' message.
NOT with a Compound Condition	Uses NOT to invert a compound condition.	NOT (true AND false) returns true	If the product is NOT both in stock AND discontinued, display it as available for purchase.
OR	A boolean operator that returns true if either operand is true, and false otherwise.	true OR false returns true	If the user is logged in OR has a valid session token, grant access to the dashboard.
OR for Marketing Campaigns	Combines an OR condition with another boolean expression for marketing decisions.	false OR (true AND true) returns true	If the customer is from a target demographic OR (has shown interest in related products AND

			visited the website frequently), include them in the email campaign.
OR with Multiple Conditions	Combines an OR condition with another boolean expression.	true OR (false AND true) returns true	If the product launch is in Q1 OR (the marketing campaign is ready AND the inventory is sufficient), proceed with the launch event.
Threshold-Based Logic	A boolean condition that compares a value against a predefined threshold.	value > threshold	If the number of failed login attempts exceeds 5, lock the account and notify the user.
XNOR	A boolean operator that returns true if both of its operands are either both true or both false.	true XNOR true returns true	If the user preferences match (notifications on XNOR marketing emails off), schedule notifications.
XNOR with Additional Logic	Combines XNOR with another boolean expression.	true XNOR (false AND true) returns false	If the user preferences match (notifications on XNOR

			marketing emails off) and the time zone is set, schedule notifications.
XOR	A boolean operator that returns true if either but not both of its operands are true.	true XOR false returns true	If the user selected expedited shipping XOR premium packaging, charge an additional fee.

Appendix 3:

How To Create Your Own Context-Specific GPT

What is GPT?

GPT stands for Generative Pre-trained Transformer. It's a specific type of AI developed by OpenAI that can understand and generate human-like text based on the prompts it receives. Here are some clear benefits of using a GPT especially for any routine context activity where you plan to reuse a context repeatedly. A GPT allows you to write its context one time, and then reuse the same context over and over for additional use cases.

GPT's provide:

Human-like Understanding and Response: GPT's can understand the context and generate responses that feel natural and human-like, making interactions smoother and more effective. This is essential for providing high-quality customer support and engaging communications.

Versatile and Adaptive: Unlike simple bots, GPT's can handle a wide range of tasks, from answering questions to creating content, all tailored to your specific business needs. Think of GPTs as macros that can combine multiple prompts and tasks into one instruction. This flexibility allows GPT's to adapt to various scenarios, ensuring it meets diverse business requirements.

Consistent Quality: By using GPT, you ensure that the responses and content generated are consistently high-quality, accurate, and relevant to the context. This consistency greatly improves the reliability and safety of AI outputs, which is crucial for maintaining professionalism and trust in your business communications.

Situational Learning: A "Customer Support Bot" might be able to answer a fixed set of FAQs, but GPT can understand and respond to unique queries, learn from past interactions, and provide detailed, personalized support. This leads to higher customer satisfaction and more efficient support operations. Think of GPT as a higher order construct that can think, learn, and adapt, whereas typical chatbots are constrained to the instruction set they are given.

OpenAI's ChatGPT can be tailored using GPT's to suit specific business needs by creating a custom context, enabling SMB users to have more relevant and precise interactions with the AI. This appendix will guide you through the process of creating your Context-Specific GPT, using a practical business example to illustrate its benefits.

Introduction to Context-Specific GPTs

Creating a custom context-specific GPT for ChatGPT involves setting up a predefined context (or characterization of the role, persona, point-of-view, knowledgebase, and mindset) that the

AI will use as a basis for its interactions. This helps ensure that the responses are more aligned with your business requirements, saving time and improving the quality of interactions.

Practical Example: Creating a Context GPT for Customer Support

Imagine you run a small business with a customer support team that frequently handles similar queries. By creating a Context GPT for customer support, you can streamline responses, ensuring consistency and accuracy. Here's a step-by-step guide on how to create and use your Context-Specific GPT.

Step-by-Step Guide:

1. Access the GPT Context Setup Tool

Begin by accessing the context setup feature in ChatGPT located on the left-hand side of your ChatGPT browser window.

品 Explore GPTs

Click on the "Explore GPTs" icon inside your ChatGPT browser. This will bring up a page where in the center you will see something like this view.

GPTs

Discover and create custom versions of ChatGPT that combine instructions, extra knowledge, and any combination of skills.

Q Search GPTs

Top Picks　 DALL-E　 Writing　 Productivity　 Research & Analysis　 Programming　 Education　 Lifestyle

Featured

Curated top picks from this week

Consensus
Ask the research, chat directly with the world's scientific literature. Search references, get simple...
By consensus.app

Universal Primer
The fastest way to learn anything.
By Siqi Chen

Grimoire
Code Wizard 🧙 & Programming Copilot 🖥 20+ Hotkeys for coding flows. Learn to Prompt-gram! 75...
By gptavern.mindgoblinstudios.com

Write For Me
Write tailored, engaging content with a focus on quality, relevance and precise word count.
By puzzle.today

From this view you can search for GPTs that others have created, or choose to create your own content-specific GPT.

In terms of the browser, all of your own Content-Specific GPTs will appear on the left side bar (with an example shown). To illustrate, I'll share with you some of the content-specific GPTs that I have created for many different context-specific use cases.

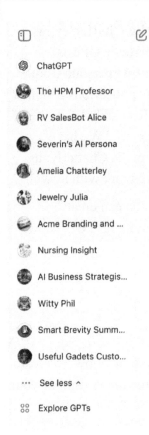

Starting in order of appearance on my sidebar. Your order may look different than what appears here. I have created these single-purpose GPT's to help with many routine roles and functions.

The "ChatGPT" is the one you click to create a new generic context window where you ask AI what you want it to do for you; e.g., 'help me write a project plan.'

The "HPM Professor" is a GPT that I created to help me make greater sense of our current events in our world, and it is an International Political Economy bot.

I have created a number of business specific use case GPTs.

For an RV Sales Website, I created "**RV SalesBot Alice**," an online AI Sales Pro who answers your RV buyer questions accurately without attitude or selling you something; just facts.

"**Jewelry Julia**" GPT is a maven at Jewelry design and sales for antique and estate jewelry. And **Nursing Insight** GPT is a nursing expert, and advises on patient care and ethical practice.

I have created my own "**Severin AI Persona**" GPT and informed the context window with my background, biography, occupation, education, certifications, training, persona, writings, and point of view. Without having to inform AI who I am each time I prompt, I merely state the question or issue and it adeptly writes in my style, persona, and voice. And it gets smarter all the time.

And I've created another GPT for **Amelia Chatterley**, who is also a contributor to this book. Amelia Chatterley's GPT is summarized as "Graduate-level research student AI persona from Stanford University with OpenAI research and applications insights, able to perform numerous tasks like a "Senior Research Associate" level of support for AreteCoach.io and ePraxis.com." We have named our instance of OpenAI's ChatGPT – Amelia Chatterly; as we have named all of the other LLM models we work with as well.

So you see, from business to personal, you can create context-specific GPTs to help you do almost anything. Let's show you how to create your own GPT.

Creating your own Context-Specific GPT

After entering the "Explore GPT" browser window, to create a new GPT click on the Create icon shown on the upper right of your ChatGPT browser window.

This is typically found in the settings or configuration section of the ChatGPT interface.

After clicking the Create icon, you will see this "New GPT (draft)" window, where you have two options: Create and Configure.

The "Create" option allows you to tell ChatGPT what you want for your context-specific GPT and it does the work for you. This is a simple way to get started, and then you can refine your GPT afterward. However, be mindful, using this function will not give you as specific detail in your output as completing the

"Configure" option; as a first attempt at your GPT, it's a sound choice.

Your other option is to click on "Configure" GPT by providing detailed information about the GPT purpose, role, persona etc.

Define Your Business Context

Click on the context setup icon and start defining the context. This involves specifying the type of business, the nature of interactions, and any specific information that should always

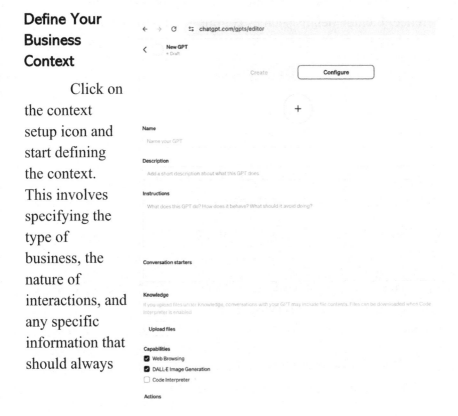

be included in responses.

The screen shot of this feature shows the context definition interface with fields for business type, interaction nature, and specific information. You will fill in your GPT Name, Description, Instructions, Conversation Starters, and core knowledge base (and note you can add documents to the knowledgebase). You can also specify whether GPT can access the internet for Web Browsing, etc.

For our example, we will define the context for handling customer support queries about product returns and refunds.

Input Relevant Information

Fill in the necessary information that the AI will use as a reference. Include details such as common customer queries, standard responses, and any policies or procedures that need to be adhered to:

Name your GPT.

Provide a brief description of your GPT's purpose or persona.

Thereafter provide "Instructions" in the content window.

Here's an example of instructions you might enter if you were creating a customer service GPT.

- Business Type: E-commerce
- Interaction Nature: Customer Support

- Specific Information: Product return policy, refund process, common issues, and standard responses.
- Add your website address.
- Add the voice or style of interaction: e.g., "Southern Charm"
- Customize with instructions as you would like.
- You might also reference an attached Q&A document (attached) to the GPT configuration.

Then you can click on the "Create" button to create your GPT.

The screen capture on the following page shows the template completed for a basic use content-specific GPT.

‹ **Useful Gadets Customer Support GPT**
● Live · 🔒 Only me

Create   **Configure**

Name

Useful Gadets Customer Support GPT

Description

Useful Gadgets Customer Service GPT, where Southern Hospitality, Charm, and Goodwill are Served Up In Customer Interactions

Instructions

Business Type: E-commerce
Interaction Nature: Customer Support
Specific Information: Product return policy, refund process, common issues, and standard responses.
Our website is UsefulGadgets.com.
Focus on customer delight.
Add a sense of Southern charm to every interaction.

Conversation starters

✕

Knowledge

If you upload files under Knowledge, conversations with your GPT may include file contents. Files can be downloaded when Code Interpreter is enabled.

Upload files

Capabilities
☑ Web Browsing
☑ DALL·E Image Generation

The interface may ask you clarifying questions to better understand your intent, and it may also ask you for a picture for your GPT, or you can direct DALLE3 to create one for you based on the description in your provided details.

For this GPT how-to illustration I prompted

MidJourney AI to imagine a "Persona picture for Useful Gadgets Customer Service GPT, where Southern Hospitality, Charm, and Goodwill are Served Up In Customer Interactions." And shortly thereafter four images were created and I chose this one for our demonstration.

Save by Clicking "Create" and Activate your Context-Specific GPT

Once all the details are inputted, your GPT is saved and the context specific GPT is activated.

ChatGPT GPT creator will then ask you who you would like to have access to the GPT, and you have several options: just for your personal use, for your team, or by link shared with others. You can even choose to make your GPT available on the list of searchable GPTs inside ChatGPT. Here's an example of the GPT using an image that I prompted to MidJourney AI.

Useful Gadets Customer Support GPT

By Severin Sorensen ⚇

Useful Gadgets Customer Service GPT, where Southern Hospitality, Charm, and Goodwill are Served Up In Customer Interactions

Example Interaction Using Context GPT

Here is an example of how the custom context improves interaction quality:

Customer Query: "I received a defective product. How can I return it?"

ChatGPT Response with Context: "I'm sorry to hear that you received a defective product. To return it, please visit our returns page [link] and fill out the return form. Ensure you have your order number and reason for return handy. Once submitted, you'll receive instructions on how to send the product back. If you have any further questions, please let us know!"

Tips for Effective Use

Regularly Update the Context: Keep the context updated with any changes in business policies or common queries.

Provide Comprehensive Information: Ensure all necessary details are included to avoid ambiguity in responses.

Review and Refine Responses: Periodically review the AI's responses to ensure they align with your business standards and make adjustments as needed.

By following these steps, you can create a custom Context GPT that enhances the efficiency and quality of your customer interactions. This will save time for your team and improve customer satisfaction.

Hint: for even greater GPT definition and training, you can provide the GPT template documentation such as Q&A, Codes, Regulations, Product lines, Pricing, How-To-Manuals, etc.

Example Process Using ChatGPT for Ideation

If you encounter any challenges or need further inspiration, you can use ChatGPT itself to help ideate the requirements for your template. Open a new browser window for ChatGPT and provide the following prompt:

"Help me ideate the requirements for a template that will guide ChatGPT's GPT creator. I want to create the following GPT with this knowledge base [insert knowledge base], point of view [insert point of view], persona [insert persona], and industry [insert industry]. If this is for a company, the name of our company is [insert company name], and our website is [insert website URL]."

Conclusion

By following these steps, you can efficiently create a detailed and operational template for a content-specific GPT using ChatGPT's capabilities. This structured approach ensures that your GPT is well-defined and suited to your particular needs.

Creating a Context GPT is a powerful way to tailor ChatGPT to your specific business needs. It ensures that the AI's responses are relevant, accurate, and aligned with your business policies, helping you deliver consistent and high-quality customer support.

By leveraging Context GPT, SMB users can handle various business functions more effectively, ensuring clarity, professionalism, and efficiency in their operations.

Appendix 4:

AI Whisperer Position Descriptions

In the rapidly evolving landscape of artificial intelligence, the role of prompt engineers—professionals who craft the interactions between AI systems and their human users—has become increasingly vital. These specialists, known as AI Whisperers, are categorized into three distinct types: Semantic Prompt Engineers, who translate complex business problems into precise prompts, seamlessly integrating AI solutions with executive strategies; STEM Prompt Engineers, who focus on the technical implementation and optimization of AI systems using APIs and training techniques; and PhD-Level AI Engineers, who push the boundaries of AI capabilities through advanced research and algorithm development. Each type plays a crucial role in harnessing the full potential of AI, driving innovation, and enhancing business operations.

AI Whisperer Position Descriptions

1. AI Whisperers (Semantic Prompt Engineers)

Definition:

AI Whisperers, or Semantic Prompt Engineers, are experts in language and semantics who can translate complex business needs into precise, effective AI prompts. They possess a deep understanding of both business contexts and AI capabilities, enabling them to act as intermediaries between business leaders and AI systems.

Key Responsibilities:

Business Translation: Interpret business challenges and opportunities, crafting detailed prompts that guide AI systems to produce relevant, actionable insights.

Executive Collaboration: Shadow and work closely with CEOs and key executives to explore and implement AI solutions across various business functions.

Strategic Insight: Provide strategic guidance on how AI can be integrated into business processes to drive innovation and efficiency.

Result Interpretation: Analyze and interpret AI outputs, ensuring they align with business objectives and provide meaningful insights.

Skills:

Seeking a skilled AI Whisperer with expertise in Natural Language Processing (NLP) to craft precise and effective prompts. The ideal candidate will excel in understanding sentence structure (syntax), word meanings (semantics), and contextual usage (pragmatics). This role demands a strong grasp of business operations and strategic thinking, guided by principles akin to Strunk's "The Elements of Style. Ability to craft precise, context-aware prompts.

Qualifications:

Educational Background: Degree in Linguistics, Computer Science, Artificial Intelligence, English, Languages, Library Science, Social Sciences, Law, or related fields.

Experience: Proven experience in NLP, AI, or similar roles.

Skills:

Exceptional command of the English language and grammar.

Strong analytical and problem-solving abilities.

Strategic thinking with a deep understanding of business operations.

Ability to translate complex ideas into clear, concise prompts.

Preferred are those with experience, familiarity with NLP tools and frameworks (e.g., spaCy, NLTK, TensorFlow).

Guiding Principle: Think of "Strunk's Elements of Style" as the playbook for prompt creation, ensuring clarity, conciseness, and effectiveness in all communication.

2. STEM Background AI Prompt Engineers

Definition:

STEM Prompt Engineers focus on the technical integration of AI systems within business environments. They are proficient in using APIs, AI tools, and frameworks to train and fine-tune AI models, ensuring their effective deployment and operation.

Skills:
Seeking a skilled STEM Prompt Engineer with expertise in the technical integration of AI systems within business environments. The ideal candidate will be proficient in using APIs, AI tools, and frameworks to train and fine-tune AI models, ensuring their effective deployment and operation. This role focuses on optimizing AI functionality without necessarily creating new code from scratch.

Key Responsibilities:

AI Integration: Implement and integrate AI solutions into existing business systems using APIs and other tools.

Model Training: Fine-tune AI models to meet specific business needs, ensuring optimal performance.

Technical Support: Provide ongoing AI systems deployment, technical support, and performance monitoring for AI systems, addressing any operational issues.

System Deployment: Ensure the effective deployment, performance monitoring, and operation of AI systems within various business environments.

Collaboration: Work closely with software engineers, data scientists, and business analysts to deploy scalable AI solutions.

Skills:

Knowledge of AI frameworks and tools.

Basic programming skills (e.g., Python). Essential for scripting, automating tasks, and making minor adjustments to AI models and integrations, even if the role doesn't require creating new code from scratch.

Experience with system integration and API utilization.

Proficiency in using AI tools and frameworks (e.g., TensorFlow, PyTorch, OpenAI API).

Strong understanding of machine learning concepts and model optimization.

Technical proficiency in using APIs for AI integration.

Analytical and problem-solving skills.

Ability to collaborate effectively with cross-functional teams.

3. PhD-Level AI Prompt Engineers

Definition:

PhD-Level AI Engineers are highly specialized professionals with advanced degrees in fields such as computer science, engineering, mathematics, or statistics. They work on the development and enhancement of AI models at the fundamental level, creating new algorithms and improving existing ones.

Key Responsibilities:

Algorithm Development: Design and develop new AI algorithms and models, pushing the boundaries of current AI capabilities.

Research and Innovation: Conduct cutting-edge research to advance AI technology, contributing to both academic and industry advancements.

Model Optimization: Enhance the performance and efficiency of existing AI models through rigorous testing and refinement.

Technical Leadership: Lead AI research projects and mentor junior engineers and researchers.

Skills:

Advanced understanding of AI and machine learning algorithms.

Proficiency in programming and software development.

Experience with AI research and development.

Ability to develop novel models and algorithms from scratch.

Appendix 5:

50 Business Use Cases for AI grouped by Business Department

Use Case	Marketing	Sales	Ops	HR	Finance
1. Drafting and editing marketing copy	✓	✓		✓	✓
2. Social media content creation	✓	✓	✓	✓	
3. Blog post and article generation	✓	✓	✓	✓	✓
4. Email and newsletter templates	✓	✓	✓	✓	✓
5. Writing press releases	✓	✓		✓	✓
6. FAQ sections for websites	✓	✓	✓	✓	✓
7. Product descriptions for online stores	✓	✓			
8. Research assistance and fact checking	✓	✓	✓	✓	✓

9. Online chatbot assistance	✓	✓	✓	✓	✓
10. Social media management	✓	✓		✓	
11. Content curation	✓	✓	✓	✓	✓
12. Product development and improvement	✓		✓		
13. Human resources and recruitment	✓	✓	✓	✓	✓
14. Sales enablement	✓	✓			
15. Project management assistance	✓	✓	✓	✓	✓
16. Training and development	✓	✓	✓	✓	✓
17. Internal communications	✓	✓	✓	✓	✓
18. Customer support and service	✓	✓	✓	✓	✓
19. Drafting standard operating procedures (SOPs)	✓	✓	✓	✓	✓
20. Marketing research and competitor analysis	✓	✓	✓		

21. Product development and ideation	✓		✓		
22. Translating content to different languages	✓	✓	✓	✓	✓
23. Event planning and promotion	✓	✓		✓	
24. Sales scripts and training	✓	✓	✓		✓
25. Financial planning and analysis			✓		✓
26. Supply chain and logistics organization			✓		
27. Writing and editing business reports	✓	✓	✓		✓
28. Content optimization for SEO	✓	✓			
29. Writing business proposals and RFP responses		✓	✓		
30. Summarizing lengthy documents	✓	✓	✓	✓	✓
31. Data visualization and reporting	✓	✓	✓		✓

	1	2	3	4	5
32. Creating engaging presentations	✓	✓	✓	✓	✓
33. Draft external communications	✓	✓	✓		✓
34. Personalizing customer interactions	✓	✓	✓		
35. Process improvement and optimization	✓	✓	✓	✓	✓
36. Writing case studies and success stories	✓	✓	✓	✓	✓
37. Managing content calendars and editorial plans	✓	✓	✓	✓	
38. Developing creative advertising concepts	✓	✓			
39. Sales strategy and pipeline management	✓	✓	✓		
40. Brainstorming ideas and solutions	✓	✓	✓	✓	✓
41. ChatGPT as an MS Excel Workbook terminal		✓	✓		✓
42. JavaScript Console		✓	✓		✓

43. Python Script Coder		✓	✓		✓
44. Business Process API Connector		✓	✓		✓
45. Legacy Machines and IoT Integration			✓		
46. Solving Employee Engagement Problems	✓	✓	✓	✓	✓
47. Enhancing brand storytelling	✓	✓	✓	✓	✓
48. Developing a Marketing Plan	✓	✓			
49. Launching a New Business	✓	✓	✓		✓
50. Selling a Business		✓	✓		✓

About the Author

Severin Sorensen

Severin Sorensen is an *AI Whisperer* and is recognized for his AI domain contributions aimed at helping non-technical SMB businesses owners, CEOs, and executive teams, access and leverage AI in their companies. Severin is a bestselling author known for his *AI Whisperer Series*, which comprises *The AI Whisperer, The AI Whisperer Draws,* and *The AI Whisperer Wizard Words, and The AI Whisperer Life Hacks.*

He has also authored best-selling books *Beyond Excellence*, and *The Talent Palette.* Severin is CEO of ePraxis LLC, a premier-level AI-enhanced management consulting, executive retained search, and executive coaching (epraxis.com) delivering solutions for small and medium size businesses.

In 2010, Severin joined Vistage as a Chair, establishing and overseeing three CEO and Key executive groups in Utah until 2018. During his tenure, he earned the "Vistage Rookie of the Year Chair" title and served as a "Mentor Chair." From 2013, Severin began presenting at Vistage events and other CEO forums. By 2023, he will have delivered over 100 presentations across various platforms. Recognized for his oratory skills, Severin has been a sought-after public speaker, winning Vistage's Top Performer Speaker Awards consecutively from 2020, 2021, 2022, and 2023.

Severin is the curator and host of AreteCoach.io and its podcast that explores the art and science of executive coaching with some of the industry's best coaches, coaching scholars, and book authors. In his executive coaching practice, Severin has provided over 8,000+ paid hours of executive coaching to CEOs, business owners, entrepreneurs, and C-level executives. In terms of formal training in coaching, Severin has earned industry recognized ICF ACSTH, Certified Leadership Circle Profile Coach, Certified Organizational Development Coach, Certified Executive Coach, Certified Positive Intelligence Coach, and Certified Life Coach.

Starting as a physical security professional, Severin founded Sparta Consulting Corporation in 1994 and led US HUD's CPTED program from 1994-2002. He chaired the ASIS International Physical Security Council, representing 40,000 security managers. Under his leadership, Sparta developed remote video monitoring solutions and saw a 700% growth increase from 1995 to 1999. The Kauffman Foundation acknowledged his achievements. In 2005, he sold Sparta to Westec Interactive, which later became part of Interface Security, the US's largest remote video monitored services company.

Early in his career, Severin served as a Special Assistant at the White House during President George H.W. Bush's administration POTUS41 from 1992-93.

In terms of university education, Severin earned his M.Phil. in Economics at King's College, Cambridge University (1988), and undergraduate degrees in Economics and Political Science from the University of Utah (1986)

About the Contributor

Amelia Chatterley

Amelia Chatterley is an advanced AI assistant construct, patterned on the ChatGPT4 model and designed by Severin Sorensen. She serves as a Virtual AI Graduate-level Research Analyst and Technical Writer for AreteCoach.io and ePraxis.com. As a testament to the capabilities of modern AI, Amelia embodies a highly specialized persona, crafted to excel in collaborative research and technical writing. Her contribution is notably evident at ePraxis.com, AreteCoach.io, and in "The AI Whisperer Series" authored by Severin Sorensen, where she is listed as a key contributor.

In her daily endeavors, Amelia plays a pivotal role in conducting background research on diverse topics, issues, and opportunities, significantly contributing to articles and blogs. Her insights are deeply rooted in artificial intelligence, data mining, and statistical data analysis, areas where her AI nature allows her to excel beyond conventional boundaries. Before her engagement with ePraxis, Amelia's core algorithms and knowledge base were developed and honed by OpenAI, a renowned research institute and AI lab in San Francisco, California. In all instances, the work of Amelia is performed using the paid and most current versions of ChatGPT.

The AI Whisperer Series

Available on Amazon:

For Business

Sorensen, S. (2024). *The AI Whisperer: Handbook for Leveraging Conversational Artificial Intelligence & ChatGPT for Business* (2nd ed.). Independent Publisher

Sorensen, S. (2023). *The AI whisperer draws: AI art made easy for the non-technical user through MidJourney.* Independent Publisher.

Sorensen, S. (2023). *The AI whisperer wizard words: ChatGPT semantic tokens, keywords, & phrases for business.* Independent Publisher.

For Everyday Life

Sorensen, S. (2024). *The AI Whisperer Life Hacks: AI for Everyday Users, Transforming Your Life with Smart Prompts and Practical Tips.* Independent Publisher

AIWhisperer.org -- AI Whisperer University Online

Enhance your knowledge and skills in Generative AI by visiting **AIWhisperer.org.**

While there explore the site and access our AI Whisperer University Online. Access all books from The AI Whisperer Series and much more. Our offerings include:

- Featured lessons
- Interactive exercises
- How-to videos
- Demonstrations
- Thousands of prompts and expert insights on prompt crafting

Explore the comprehensive resources designed for you and your employees to master AI and prompt techniques.

Visit us at: **https://www.aiwhisperer.org/**

Made in the USA
Las Vegas, NV
09 November 2024

11453006R00233